"If you're doing something *you've never done before, it's easier to feel more relaxed about it. When you're doing something you have done before, and you can't make it any better, then it starts the worry."* Ornette Coleman (1930–2015)

Endpapers The functional difference between a shovel and a pitchfork is the metal that is *missing*.

The Elements of Graphic Design, Third Edition

Space, Unity, Page Architecture & Type

Alex W. White

*"**Elegance** is not the abundance of simplicity. It is the absence of complexity."* Anonymous

ALLWORTH
PRESS
NEW YORK

This book is concerned with *what things look like*, but supposes that *what is being said* is worth the effort of clarity. In other words, design exists to substantiate communication.

Allworth Press books may be purchased in bulk at special discounts for sales promotion, corporate gifts, fund-raising, or educational purposes. Special editions can also be created to specifications. For details, contact the Special Sales Department, Allworth Press, 307 West 36th Street, 11th Floor, New York, NY 10018 or info@skyhorsepublishing.com

26 25 24 23 22   5 4 3 2 1

Published by Allworth Press, an imprint of Skyhorse Publishing, Inc., 307 West 36th Street, 11th Floor, New York, NY 10018. Allworth Press® is a registered trademark of Skyhorse Publishing, Inc.®, a Delaware corporation.

www.allworth.com

Book design, composition, and typography by Alex W. White

Library of Congress Cataloging in Publication Data is available on file.

Print ISBN: 978-1-62153-759-5
eBook ISBN: 978-1-62153-762-5

Printed in China

The Elements of Graphic Design, 3rd Edition

Space, Unity, Page Architecture, and Type

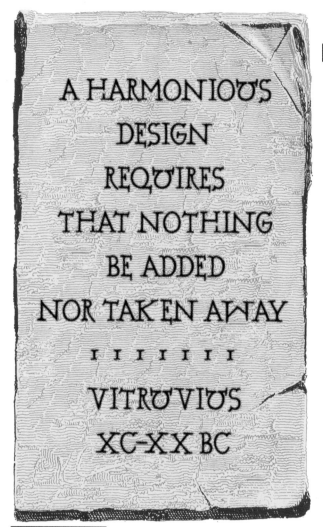

A HARMONIOUS
DESIGN
REQUIRES
THAT NOTHING
BE ADDED
NOR TAKEN AWAY

I I I I I I I

VITRUVIUS

XC–XX BC

The lettering used here is adapted by the author from lettering carved into the walls at Ephesus, Turkey, circa the first century AD.

Preface

Most design education is concerned with combining and inventing bits of content. It concerns relationships of forms and almost always overlooks the critically important part of the design that goes unnoticed: the background spaces and shapes. It is a reflection of believing what *is* is more important than what *isn't*. But emptiness, when treated as a full partner in design, becomes dynamic. It, along with an original visual idea, is what defines *great* design.

Dynamic white space plus abstraction, the process of removing unnecessary details, are essential to *sophisticated* design. Abstraction can be harmful, though, when it obscures the message by removing necessary markers. Finding a balance of implicit meaning and clarity is the goal. Judgment in abstraction's use is essential – and is improved with practice and experience.

Unlike mathematics, where there can only be a single "right" answer, design has many alternate solutions. It is up to the designer to find the best among these. Design is misused if it is merely an opportunity to self-indulgently show off one's latest visual experiments. Experimentation *in service to the message*, though, is always a welcome approach.

Vitruvius foretold Step 3 on the facing page. There is a huge difference between *nothing wrong* and *nothing right* about a design. Being able to identify what is right about one's work is crucial to organizing material for clarity. Merely *having nothing wrong* is no assurance that a design is successful in communicating. There must be something *identifiably right* in a design for it to achieve elegance.

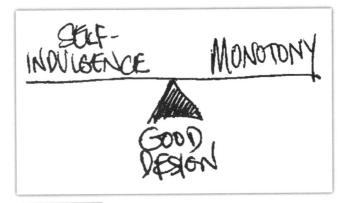

One definition of good design is the balance between the designer's self-indulgence and monotony.

On the other hand, monotony is not good design either, even if the basic structure of that monotony is pretty. Why? Because sameness doesn't catch or hold viewers. Good design balances deliberate consistency with flexibility so *some* of the goodies will stand out. Designers serve their readers by revealing value, accelerating learning, and making content stick.

Design – whether graphic, industrial, interior, or architecture – is the process of taking unrelated parts and putting them together into an organized unit. Each discipline works with solids and voids, and each must respond to three questions: What are the elements I have to work with? Where do these elements go? What structure is necessary so they go together? Design is simpler when you remember it is a *process*, not a *result*:

☞ Define the problem you have been given. This is usually a redefinition because what you have been given is an *apparent* problem. The redefinition must home in on the real issues. If in this redefinition process you don't become clearer about how to handle the material, you haven't redefined the problem accurately enough.

☞ Know the material. Discuss it. Digest it fully. At the very least, *read* it.

☞ Distill the essential from the mass of confusing muchness. Nothing may be missing, and nothing may be extraneous. This is the definition of *elegance*.

☞ Abstract the main point so its importance to the reader is clear and it is visually arresting. A message that doesn't first stop readers won't be read.

☞ Unify all elements so they don't outshout each other. Shouting at readers doesn't provide a solution or an explanation or an expression of importance to their interests and needs. Clear, predigested content does.

Thanks to:

☐ The seven wonderful professionals who contributed their expertise and passions to this edition: Ashley Schofield, Brian D. Miller, Fons Hickmann, Geray Gençer, Max Shangle, Niklaus Troxler, and Tad Crawford. ☐ Rocky and Enzo for making the office a much nicer place each day. ☐ This book is lovingly dedicated to Eponymous, who fills each day with cheerful happiness HDGL.

Alex W. White

Carinthia, Austria

1235. Dummies waiting to be unwrapped.
Photo by Herbert Migdoll.

Clarity and value to the reader are what designers add to a message. These wrapped dummies are like messages that have not yet been revealed.

"Perfect communication is person-to-person. You see me, hear me, smell me, touch me. Television is the second form of communication; you can see me and hear me. Radio is the next; you hear me, but you don't see me. And then comes print. You can't see or hear me, so you must be able to interpret the kind of person I am from what is on the printed page. That's where typographic design comes in." Aaron Burns (1922–1991)

Introduction

*N*othing puzzles me more than time and space; and yet nothing troubles me less, as I never think about them. Charles Lamb (1775–1834)

To design means to plan. The process of design is used to bring order from chaos and randomness. Order is good for readers, who can more easily make sense of an organized message. An *ordered message* is therefore considered good design. But looking through even a short stack of design annuals, you will see that what is judged "good" changes with time. It is apparent that style and fashion are aspects of design that cannot be ignored. Stephen A. Kliment, writing in an *Architectural Record* magazine editorial, advises, "Do not confuse style with fashion. Style is derived from the real needs of a client or of society. Fashion is a superficial condition adopted by those anxious to appear elegant or sophisticated." Leslie Segal, writing in the introduction to *Graphis Diagrams*, says, "Given two designs of equal simplicity, the one conveying

The design process reveals significance by sifting through all the information to find that which is essential. This is done in stages, first by removing the large chunks of less valuable content, then looking through increasingly fine grades of information, even to the granular level, often expressed in subtle typographic adjustments. Having at last identified the essential, designers enhance its significance for their readers, as in this magazine story's opening spread.

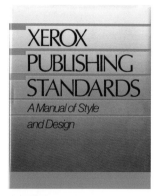

The Xerox *Publishing Standards* is a comprehensive 400-page reference on how to organize, edit, and manage content to make documents useful, read, and understood.

Visual simplicity eliminates unnecessary elements and structures those that remain in a logical, consistent system, as in this magazine cover.

Good design reduces navigational effort, thereby encouraging readership. This Web site keeps things very simple, which is an accurate representation of their brand experience.

more information is more elegant. Conversely, of two designs conveying the same information, the simpler is the more elegant. The lack of elegance is a frequent design failing."

A communicator's job

Having material on the page read and absorbed is a visual communicator's chief responsibility. The Xerox Corporation completed a landmark corporate design project by distributing their Xerox *Publishing Standards* (page 10). In it, they describe their design rationale: "The principal goals of page layout are visual recognition and legibility. These goals are accomplished through consistent typography, effective use of white space and graphics, and controlled use of [lines]... A repeated visual logic guides the eye and helps the reader scan."

It is important to make the page look inviting – a "reader magnet." Visual stimulation draws viewers into the page, arousing their curiosity and actively involving them in the process of absorbing information. Visual simplicity eliminates unnecessary elements and structures those that remain in a logical, consistent system. Good design reduces the effort of reading as much as possible, thereby encouraging readership and understanding.

BY MICHAEL FINKEL

When Christian Longo asked if I wanted to watch him die, I told him I did.

Visual stimulation draws viewers into the page, arousing their curiosity. I dare any reader not to turn the page and give at least the first paragraph of this story a chance.

"It is better to be *good than to be original."* Ludwig Mies van der Rohe (1886–1969)

Correction.

As most of you know, one of our proudest boasts is the fact (properly researched) that 3 out of 4 architects specify California redwood for their own homes. Now, along comes "Record Houses of 1967" with 4 out of 5 architects' own homes featuring redwood.

Our advertising people, unaccustomed as they are to understating, explain it this way: When you have a concentration of quality such as "Record Houses," the ratio of redwood inevitably increases.

Certified Kiln Dried Redwood

For any information at all about redwood, write: California Redwood Association, 617 Montgomery St., San Francisco, CA. 94111.

Everything the designer does should be calculated to help a reluctant reader become effortlessly involved with the text, which is where the story usually is. The visual simplicity, vast area of empty space, and an interesting if very short headline make us willing to read at least the first sentence of the copy of this 1967 ad.

What not to do with space: though fulfilling other societal needs, we have not improved the landscape by overfilling it with construction. There is no room left to enjoy solitude. Equivalently overfilling a design does not serve the need for a *balance* of content and quiet.

Too much of a good thing turns both coffee and information into a problem. Avoid this by leaving a little space at the top of the cup *and* on the page.

Readers respond to consistent page structure. The job is not to fill in all the space in order to impress the reader with sheer quantity of information. That will just overwhelm the reader with overfullness.

Imagine coffee being poured in a cup. If the cup is filled to the very top, it is difficult to avoid spilling it as you take the first sip. By having *too much* of a good thing, we have created a problem. This is the same reaction readers have to being given too much information at once. It is perceived as a problem and their response is to avoid it. Umberto Eco writes about too–muchness in his description of William Randolph Hearst's castle in San Simeon, "The striking aspect of the whole is not the quantity of antique pieces plundered from half of Europe... but rather the sense of fullness, the obsessive determination not to leave a single space (unfilled)... The insane abundance makes the place unlivable."

Again, *the designer's job is not to fill in all the space.* It is to make information accessible and appealing. The best use of the page's empty space is to help make information scannable, not to make the pages pretty. The point is to increase the page's *absorbability.*

This invitation is an example of intentional overfullness in which there is little room to breathe. Though handsome and an excellent expression of Alejandro Paul's letterform designs, its use of space is equivalent to the crowded housing development above.

"Art is not a mirror. *Art is a hammer."* SoHo graffito, NYC

What makes this image startling is the juxtaposition of the familiar with the unfamiliar. There are many definitions of art, but the one that makes more sense than most is *Art is making the familiar unfamiliar.* By that standard, this Volkswagen Beetle has been made into art. Further, the definition of *creative* is "Characterized by originality and expressiveness; imaginative."

Readers are looking for valuable bits among the muchness of information, like sea glass among the shells on the beach.

Physical form conveys meaning. Matching an element's form to its meaning helps reveal the message. And it is clearly a *purposeful* design decision, which is the wonderful and much-to-be-admired opposite of a random design decision.

The mind searches for meaning

As humans evolved, an important attribute we acquired was the ability to see potential dangers around us, to see *differences* in our surroundings. Anything that moved irregularly or was a different color or texture was worthy of our attention. After all, it might eat us. Noticing differences became an evolutionary advantage for humans. As a result, when we look at a screen or printed document, our eyes instinctively look for similarities and differences among the elements. We search for the unique, which is determined by *relative unusualness*.

Perception is like looking for sea glass on the beach. We look for clues that one spot or one sparkle is more valuable than the stones and shells we also see. Similarly, our brains sift images and words. We innately group similar elements. If we cannot easily make these connections, we perceive confusion. Most readers are disinclined to exert much effort in digging out the meaning or importance of a message. They may be too busy or they may be simply uninterested in the subject. In fact many readers subconsciously look for reasons to *stop* reading: it's demanding work, it takes concentration, and we're all a little lazy. Be quick: Victor O. Schwab,

Substituting form attracts attention because it results in unexpected contrast. A shirt made from bread? Makes sense if the "Breakfast Collection" shirts are "bread colored." Or if a fish is made out of the sports-specific sunglasses being advertised.

HARD TIMES FOR A

The West is a myth that is no longer a valued truth

LEGEND

Words **M. Batek**
Art **E. Weiss**

HARD
THE WEST IS A MYTH
TIMES
THAT IS NO LONGER A
FOR A
VALUED TRUTH WORDS
LEGEND
M. BATEK ART E. WEISS

Making the content a reader magnet: the top example is suboptimal because its three unrelated typefaces – and their placement – do not connect thoughts; there is a lack of alignment between elements; they are about equal in importance; and the empty space has been distributed evenly throughout the spread. The best thing one can say about this top example is that the colors are harmonious. The bottom example is a better design because its relationships are clearer. The type aligns and connectedness with the artwork has been created through shared colors and shading. The same primary typeface was used in both examples' display headings; the secondary type and the bylines have been unified into a single perception; and somewhat delicately, the spaces between the headlines echo in the horizontal spaces between the three drawings.

The stylized "Y" inside this logo for a Finnish life insurance provider is easily visible. But it takes a moment longer to recognize the "S" shape that represents the first half of the company's name, Suomi-Yhtiö, which means "Finland Group." The company's home page is shown here as a sample of the logo's application.

The places where type becomes image, image becomes space, and space becomes type are the most interesting and fruitful areas for the designer.

a great advertising copywriter said, "Tell me sweet, tell me true, or else my love, to hell with you."

Designing is the process of looking for and showing off the similarities and differences inherent in the content of a visual message. Though this can sometimes take a good deal of time if the similarities do not quickly present themselves, the search for similarities is at the heart of what a designer does.

In addition to searching for similarities and differences, we look for meaning in the physical form of the *individual* things we see. The form of a thing tells us certain things about itself. Designers reveal the meaning of their messages by using type, imagery, and space. If they are used well, the meaning is illuminated. If used poorly, the meaning is confused or is subsumed by the message's prettiness.

Successful designs describe the content fully and as simply as possible. This is the definition of *elegance.* Ideally, the reader should be unaware of the act of reading, for reading is then truly effortless. In design, more is *not* better. There must be an economy in using type and imagery. If it hasn't got a purpose that pushes the message forward, it shouldn't be used. The excellence of a design is in direct proportion to its simplicity and clarity.

Target, long known for playful design, uses the *absence* of the promoted item to make passersby notice their billboard. They recognize that emptiness has value.

"The usefulness of a water pitcher dwells in the emptiness where water might be put, not in the form of the pitcher."* Lao-tse (604–531 BC)

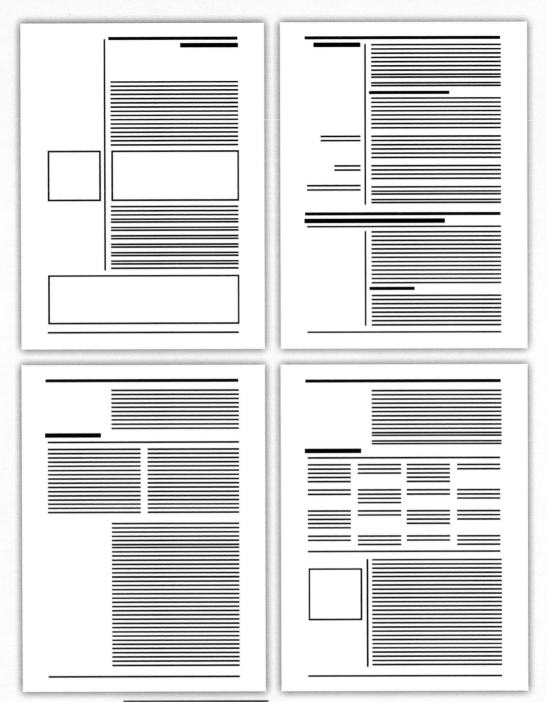

Publications need structure *and* flexibility. Structured white space makes headings stand out, helping readers quickly find what they need. These samples, from the Xerox *Publishing Standards*, show a wide main column that fits text economically. The narrower column creates headline visibility and a specific place for imagery. The basic page structure allows great flexibility in placing unusual combinations of materials while maintaining enough consistent proportions to engender its own look and feel as a publication.

Published for
Lukens Steel employees and retirees and their families

Volume 60
Number 3

LUKENS
LIFE 60 13

Overfilling a page is good only if it actually helps get the message across, as shown here. Otherwise, an overfilled page repels readers.

Each of the six pieces (plus two rules) in this magazine "flag," or logo for the cover, is carefully sized and positioned to have its own integrity and to fit into the overall design. Contrasts in addition to size include black and white color, roman and italic, baseline alignment, caps and lower case, and bold and light type weights.

Space attracts readers

Vinyl records have a narrow space of relatively empty vinyl between songs. The songs share similar texture because the spiral groove in which the needle tracks is tightly spaced. The space between songs, by comparison, is smooth vinyl interrupted by only a single groove for the needle to follow. The visual dividers make it possible to count the number of songs and estimate their relative length, serving as cues when finding a specific cut. Digital media makes far more accurate information available, but it can't be seen by the naked eye on the disk itself.

The spaces between songs on a record show content the way white space does. Space attracts readers by making the page look accessible, un-threatening, and manageable. Leaving too little white space makes a page look crowded – good only if that's the point you want to make. Leaving too much white space is almost impossible. I say "almost" because you will get groans of disapproval if you toss around chunks of *unused* white space, that is, emptiness purely for its own sake, rather than for the sake of the message. Readers are far less likely to notice or object to too much white space than to an unreadable, crowded page.

A vinyl record ordinarily has one long groove on each side of the disc. Monty Python, the British comedy troupe, released a record in the 1970s that was billed as a "Three-sided, two-sided record." Python put two con-centric grooves on one side, making it a matter of chance before a listener would happen to put the needle down on the alternate groove. Their gag worked because *they reinvented the rules* of vinyl recordings.

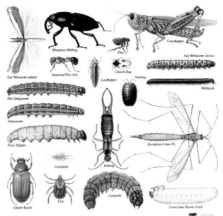

Buy Sevin® SL for this. Get these free.

White Grub

Your reasons for choosing a turf insecticide could be summed up in two words:
Kills grubs.
Which, frankly, is reason enough to choose SEVIN® brand SL carbaryl insecti-

cide. Because, when it comes to grubs, no other turf insecticide is more effective.
We have the efficacy data to prove it.
But if that still isn't enough to make you a con-

firmed SEVIN® brand SL user, consider this:
With SEVIN® brand SL carbaryl insecticide, you also get effective control of 27 other turf pests.
Including tough ones,

like chinch bugs, billbugs, armyworms, cutworms, and sod webworms.
And SEVIN® brand SL carries a Toxicity Category III Caution label. Which makes it ideal for use on golf

courses, parks, lawns, or any turf area frequently used by people and animals.
So ask your turf chemicals supplier for SEVIN® brand SL carbaryl insecticide. It may be the best

example yet of getting more than what you pay for.

From the turf care group at Union Carbide.

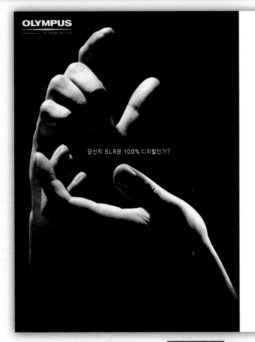

Use the paper's whiteness to attract readers. Does this much "emptiness" justify its cost to the client? Yes, if the emptiness communicates the message, which it does in these two examples.

The space *where a camera would be held* is more arresting than a mundane shot of a camera being held. The camera (albeit not in proportional size) is then placed horizontally across the spread from the space, creating a visual link between the two images.

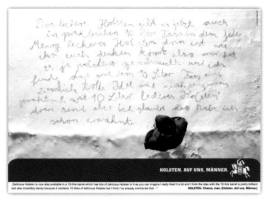

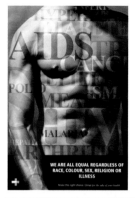

Illegibility results when an image is put behind text. This hurts the value of the image (it is being covered up!) and the varied background makes the text hard to read.

Lack of color contrast adds to illegibility, with yellow on white the weakest contrast of all. This German ad for a 10-liter barrel of beer nevertheless uses yellow lettering on white quite appropriately.

Overlapping display type over type and over an image makes each individual element harder to read but increases their overall impact as a unified visual.

Readability is a term that refers to the adequacy of an object to attract readers. It should not be confused with *legibility*, which describes the adequacy of an object to be deciphered. Good readability makes the page look comfortable to read. Poor readability makes pages look dull or busy. Richard Lewis, an annual reports expert, says, "Make exciting design. Dullness and mediocrity are curses of the annual report. For every overdesigned, unreadable report there are a hundred undistinguished ones that just plod along." Regarding legibility, Lewis says, "Designers who play with type until they have rendered it unreadable are engaged in a destructive act. Hard-to-read [design] is useless." Make unnecessary demands on your readers only when you are sure the extra effort they are being asked to make will quickly become payoff for them.

Considered use of white space shows off the subject. Go through the pages of any newspaper and you will find wall-to-wall ads of even grayness, occasionally punctuated by a darker area of bold type. Few ads utilize the whiteness of the paper to attract attention. Using the whiteness of the paper is an additionally good approach if the paper's whiteness expresses *the idea of the ad.* `EoGD3`

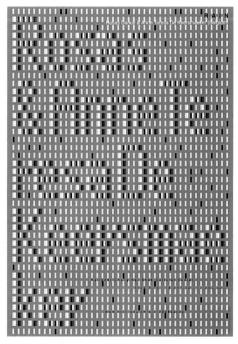

Flirting with illegibility is a powerful way to get attention, but knowing when the elaborate presentation overwhelms the content is essential.

"What you see depends to a great extent on what you expect to see, what you are used to seeing."
Sir Jonathan Miller (1934–2019)

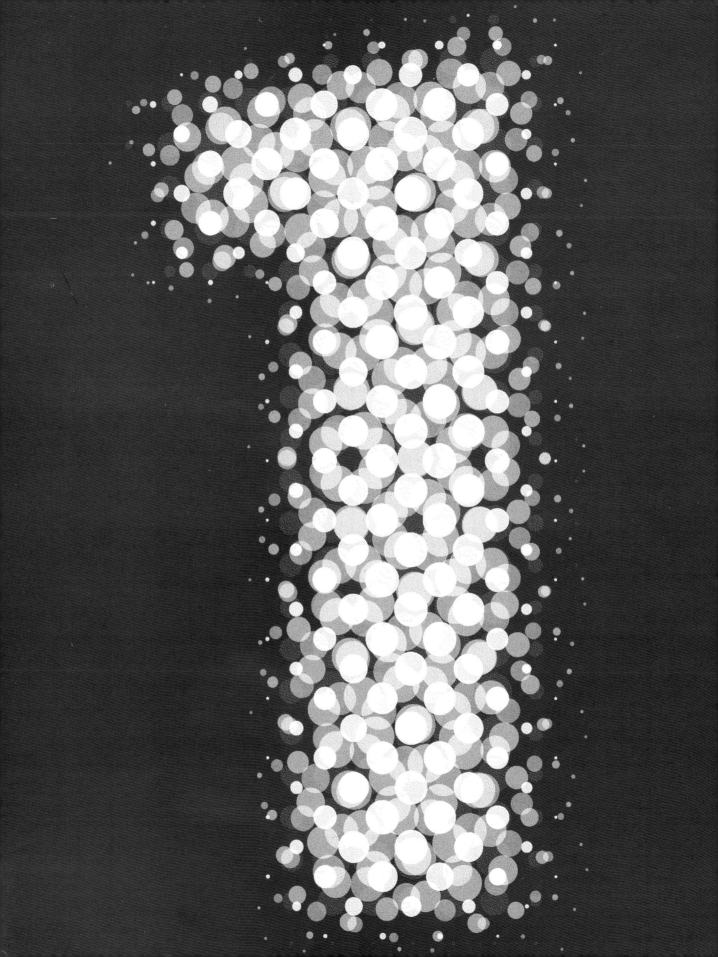

"The question is,
'What's the mill?'
Not, 'What's the grist?'"
Phillip Glass (1937–)

A little bit of entertainment, please!

Niklaus Troxler
troxlerart.ch

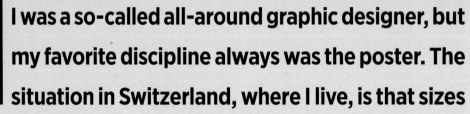

I was a so-called all-around graphic designer, but my favorite discipline always was the poster. The situation in Switzerland, where I live, is that sizes are tightly regulated in all the cities and communes, with designers restricted to two possible formats: the so-called „Weltformat" (*world format*) in 90 x 128cm (35½" x 50¼") and the „triple oft hat" in 270 x 128cm (109½" x 50¼"). Despite this restrictive size uniformity, I think it is important in my messages to bring some entertainment value to people. When I am on the receiving end, I like the idea that an entertaining poster gives me something, even if I have no interest in what is being announced. I see the same thing in reverse when I design posters for jazz events. People call me up: they are not interested in jazz at all, but are keen to have a copy of the poster.

When I really start to work on a design, it mostly happens fast. I might be walking down the street and suddenly – „ah" – I make a connection. You cannot go out and find exactly the right trigger, so you have to have time to feel free. Sometimes I start working on paper without an idea. I might do a simple brainstorm, using words and exploring objects. I try combinations of different elements. I sometimes make lists. There is not one recipe in my process. I rely a great deal on my instinct. Afterwards, I don't backtrack on my thinking, I can only describe why I settled on the final idea. To me it's all important that the result looks fresh, like it was just done – even after it has been printed. And, of course, I hope it entertains people! EoGD3

All posters shown are in „Weltformat": 90 x 128cm, silkscreen print

Internationally-honored designer and professor Niklaus Troxler's work is in the collections of museums worldwide.

2003 **Simon Nabatov Solo Piano** Jazz concert with piano player Simon Nabatov *Jazz in Willisau*

Jazz in Willisau
Sa 26. Nov. 05 20.30 h Foroom

Bob Stewart tuba
Arthur Blythe alto sax

2005 **Bob Stewart-Arthur Blythe** Jazz concert with tuba player Bob Stewart and alto sax player Arthur Blythe *Jazz in Willisau*

Jazz in Willisau / Fr 22. Oktober 2010 / 20.00 Stadtmühle
Joe McPhee ts, tp / Fred Lonberg-Holm cello / Michael Zerang perc

Joe McPhee Survival Unit III

2010 **Joe McPhee Survival Unit III** Jazz concert with Joe McPhee (saxophone) and his group „Survival Unit" *Jazz in Willisau*

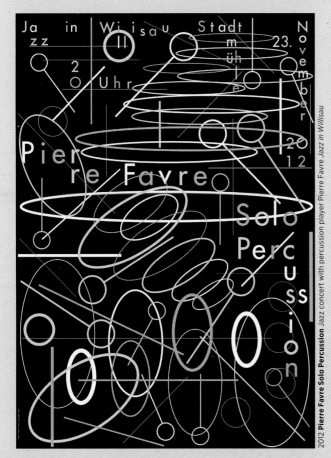

Ja zz in Wi lisau Stadt m üh le 23. Nov em b er 20 12
2 O Uhr

Pierre Favre Solo Percussion

2012 **Pierre Favre Solo Percussion** Jazz concert with percussion player Pierre Favre *Jazz in Willisau*

Urs Leimgruber, sax
THE
Omri Ziegele, sax, voice
WOR
Christian Weber, bass
KER
Alex Huber, drums
S Jazz im bau 4 Altbüron
Fr 18. Okt. 2019, 20 Uhr

2019 „**The Workers"** Jazz concert with the group Bau 4 *Altbüron*

Geray Gençer

geraygencer.com

My design practice does not focus on problem solving or storytelling. I basically define myself as an interpreter. I try to transform ideas into visual language through art and design. My approach towards design and life are almost the same: for me good design has the power to enhance the meaning of life. I try to create powerful and persuasive images in order to convey the message. Being a versatile designer, I love to explore diverse artistic expressions and emotions through illustrations, typography, and photography.

In my way as a designer I always feel free to explore new dimensions of my profession and don't want to restrict myself. It is really crucial to have a wide vision and range of interests, which, as a result, not only makes my work fresh and exciting, but it keeps me young as well.

My priority is constructing trustworthy relationships with my clients. When it is possible to create such a bond, the outcome is very strong. I'm a part-time lecturer at a university and a part-time designer in my studio. This combination makes my designs well rounded. Most of my clients are cultural institutions and publishing houses. This intellectual environment provides me wide space to create abstract and experimental works. EoGD3

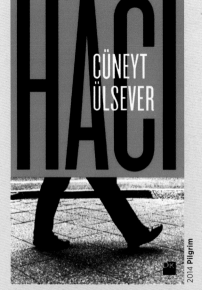

2014 Pilgrim

Designer and professor Geray Gençer lives and works in Istanbul.

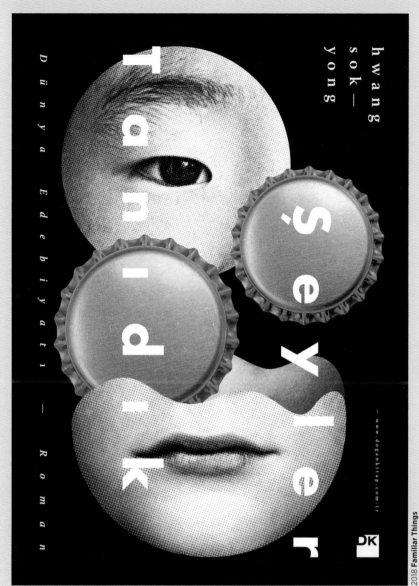

2018 **Familiar Things**

2013 **Why Nations Fail**

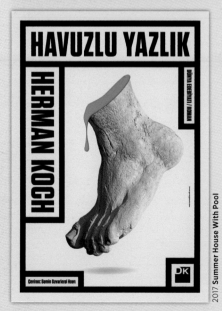

2017 **Summer House With Pool**

2020 **Istanbul Music Festival**

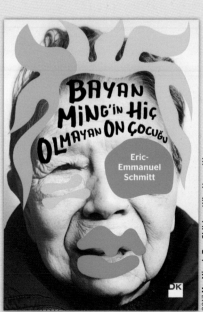

2017 **Ms. Ming's Ten Children Who Never Were**

Iceland

We asked some local crevasse jumpers for their advice. They told us to get out now, immediately.

ADVENTURE

Donuil
Neidpath
Text
C.W.
Wilson
Photos

Architecture and graphic design have much in common. Architecture is defined as, "The art and science of designing and erecting buildings," whereas the definition of design is simply "to plan."

Symmetry is the distinct similarity – if not necessarily the exact reflection – of both sides of an object. It is expressed in both an early nineteenth century New England home and a magazine spread.

The power of nature's emptiness creates drama as in the granite rock that is *absent* in this Swiss valley.

The Grand Canyon's drama is also caused by what is *missing*. Had the Colorado River not carved out the land, the surface that has become the Grand Canyon would be just another area of relatively flat, uninterrupted plains.

1

Space is emptiness

fill up a place, which may be better... when I have made it empty. William Shakespeare (1564–1616), *As You Like It*

Emptiness is an essential aspect of life. It is the unavoidable opposite of fullness, of busyness, of activity. It is the natural and universally present background to everything we see. Emptiness is silence, an open field, a barren room, a blank canvas, an empty page. Emptiness is often taken for granted and thought best used by filling in. It is generally ignored by all but the few who consciously manipulate it to establish contrast, to create drama, or to provide a place of actual or visual rest. It is best used as counterpoint to filled-in space. Composers and architects use it. Painters, photographers, and sculptors use it. And designers use it.

The most important step toward sensitizing yourself to using space is first seeing it. Gregg Berryman writes in his *Notes on Graphic Design and Visual Communication*, "Everyone 'looks' at things but very few people 'see' effectively. Designers must be able to see. Seeing means a trained super-aware-

White space is a raw ingredient. Here it is, just as the paper manufacturer made it. But don't think of it as emptiness waiting to be filled in. Filling in emptiness is not what designers do: *using* emptiness is. This space has been used by pushing this caption and the aggressively horizontal image into it.

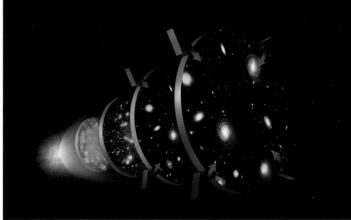

"Space is a human need." Ken Hiebert (1930-). New York City's Central Park, shown before the surrounding countryside was developed, c1870, and as it appears today, a vital sanctuary surrounded by an intense city.

The universe was *entirely* empty before the Big Bang. Its size is now measured by the area occupied by galaxies, and what has been thought of as "empty space" is being given very careful consideration: it may be equally filled with matter that we can't yet measure.

ness of visual codes like shape, color, texture, pattern, and contrast. These codes make a language of vision, much as words are building blocks for verbal language." Being trained to see more critically is best guided by a teacher, but such training relies on exposure to excellent art and design samples.

The figure/ground relationship

The single most overlooked element in visual design is emptiness. The lack of attention it receives explains the abundance of ugly and unread design. (*Ugly* and *unread* describe two separate functions of design which occasionally occur at the same time. *Ugly* refers to an object's aesthetic qualities, an evaluation of whether we *like* the object. *Unread* is infinitely more important, because an unread design is an utter failure. A printed document, regardless of its purpose or attributes, is never intended to be ignored.)

Design elements are *always* viewed in relation to their surroundings. Emptiness in two-dimensional design is called white space and lies behind the type and imagery. But it is more than just the background of a design, for if a design's background alone were properly constructed, the overall design would immediately double in clarity and usefulness. Thus,

Even ordinary objects in space can draw attention when the relationship is imbalanced. Here, the object is severely cropped and placed in a disproportionate amount of emptiness. The central axis is enhanced by a flush left placement of a narrow type column.

ra gamma
cattivanti. I
ono intensit

Lack of controlled white space produces visual noise. This is a section of a printer's make-ready sheet found separating Italian postcards. Though possessing a certain charm, it is an example of *accidental* design.

Space is defined when something is placed in it. The ocean's vastness looks even bigger when a small island is in the distance.

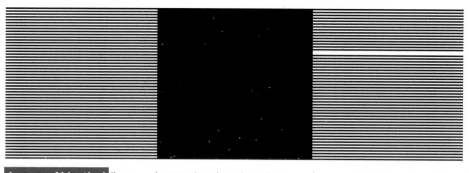

An area of identical lines and spaces produces a gray value. Neither figure nor ground demands more attention than the other. Removing the white spaces by jamming the black lines together creates an area of solid black. By eliminating a single black line, the white space becomes dominant and is *activated*.

American prisoners were once dressed in black and white striped clothes so they would be easily identified in case of a breakout: only prisoners wore such stripes.

when it is used intriguingly, white space becomes foreground. The emptiness becomes a positive shape and the positive and negative areas become intricately linked.

In an area of identical lines (above), we see a field of gray because the lines and their background are in harmony. In order to create a gray field, the white and black areas are equally essential. If we eliminate a single black line, the white space becomes *activated*. This white line is an *anomaly* and appears to be in front of the gray field.

White space (named for white paper, the typical background material of its day, but white space needn't be white: it is the *background*, regardless of color) has various other names. Among them are "negative space," which is a fully interchangeable term; "trapped space," which refers to space surrounded by other elements; "counterform," referring to spaces within letters; "working white," emptiness that serves a purpose and forms an integral part of a design; and "leftover space," which is emptiness that still has unrealized potential.

Total lack of managed white space results in a visually noisy, or cacophonous, design. This can be a desirable solution under a few certain

The direction and thickness are the most important characteristics of a line. Here, direction is contrasted while thickness is kept constant in this poster titled *Pedestrians in the City* by Gérard Paris-Clavel.

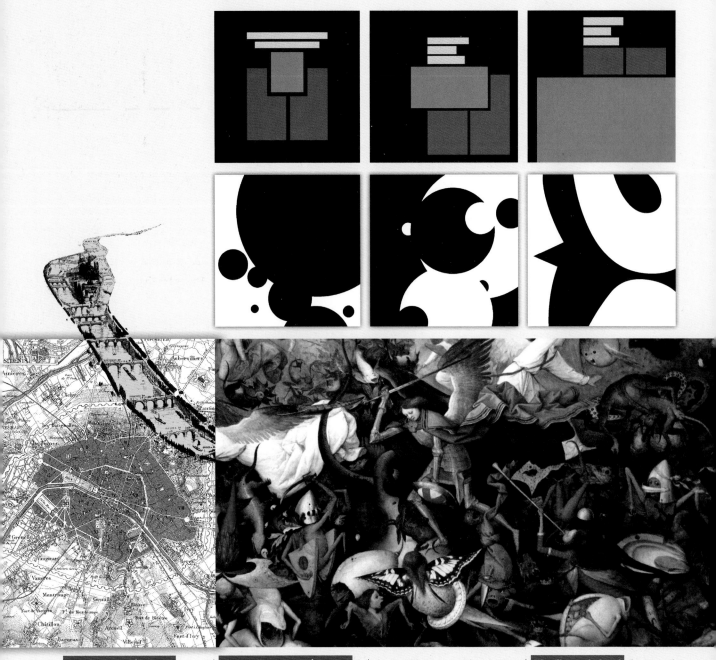

Stable figure/ground relationship (top row, l-r): Centering a figure *neutralizes* space; placing the figure off-center *activates* space; and bleeding the figure makes a composition *dynamic*.

Reversible figure/ground relationship (second row, l-r): a figure in space is seen to be "in front"; figure and ground are reversible when the figure and ground are in equilibrium, neither is "in front"; *ambiguous figure/ground* requires cropping both the black and white shapes so both are equally interesting. This requires abstraction.

The figure is land (bottom row) outlined in a Paris map; the figure is the river in the diagram of Parisian bridges; Breugel the Elder painted ambiguous, overfull ground, as in this detail from his 1562 *The Fall of Rebel Angels*.

Figure/ground relationship studies explore the fundamental design relationship of black and white shapes. Each of these freshman

studies uses a single letterform. Glyph abstraction is one of the goals of this exercise and success is dependent on activating the negative space as a full

partner in each design. We must be drawn to the white shapes as much as to the black shapes.

The unity of opposites is expressed in the Chinese symbol of yin/yang in which white and black *mutually depend on each other.* This is by Shigeo Fukuda.

circumstances, if for example, the subject being discussed is audio or video interference, or a visual translation of anxiety, or reading conditions on a jolting train, or eidetic (vivid or total recall) imagery. Some designers use computer-inspired cacophonous styling in what they think is fashionable experimentation, regardless of content and appropriateness. The results have been unreadable, confusing, and ugly.

Space is undefined until it is articulated by the placement of an object within it. Until a design element – a small square ■, for example – is placed in a framal reference ◆ , little about the space can be determined.

Graphic emptiness can be made to look vast and unending or it can be manipulated to look finite and segmented. Placing an object in space creates a figure/ground relationship. When a single element is placed in a space, it may be difficult to tell whether the element is big or small, high or low, or near or far. It is merely floating in space. The perimeter of the space, whether defined by a box or by the edge of the page, helps describe the element's position in it.

There are three types of figure/ground relationships:

"The reality of a room is to be found in the vacant space enclosed by the roof and walls, not in the ceiling and walls [themselves]." Lao-tse (604–531 BC), Book of Tea

HOUSE & GARDEN.

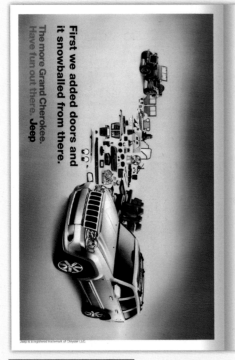

First we added doors and it snowballed from there.

The more Grand Cherokee. Have fun out there. Jeep

Jeep is a registered trademark of Chrysler LLC.

byINNO™

byINNO™는 이노디자인이 제안하는 디자인 기프트 컬렉션입니다.

Ambiguous white space can be seen in the *House & Garden* poster (top). Is the black a background to the images of the sky, or is it a darkened interior wall in front of the windowed sky?

Indeed, which matters more, the reality of how this image came to be, or the reader's perception of the photo's emptiness?

Space can be "turned on its ear" by using a magazine's binding as a reference point.

Space that exists behind the horizontal band of this full-page ad "leaks" into the two shopping bags in the lower right. The front bag covers half the letters, defining its edge while still leaving the back letters legible.

Full-bleed photos, images that touch the edge of the page on all four sides, are examples of intentional lack of context. A full-bleed photo's strength is its ability to overwhelm the reader with a sense of actuality: the image is so big that it can't be contained by the page.

Think of a photo on a page as a window into another space. In a way, the reader looks through the page at the scene beyond. A full-bleed wall of photos is equivalent to a peek into a gallery of images whose number and scale elicits emotional connection.

■ **Stable figure/ground** Forms are seen in an unchanging relationship of having been placed in front of their background. Ordinarily, either the figure or the ground dominates a design. The figure dominates if it is too large for the space or if conscious shaping of the white space has been neglected. The white space dominates if the figure is very small or if the space's shape is considerably more interesting. Balancing the sizes and shapes of the figure and ground activates both and makes it difficult to tell which is "in front" of the other, creating a unified design.

■ **Reversible figure/ground** Figure and ground can be seen equally. The figure and ground interpenetrate. A balanced figure/ground relationship creates tension where one threatens to overwhelm the other. This describes a dynamic design. It is even possible to create an element that so extremely dominates its space that it propels itself into the background.

■ **Ambiguous figure/ground** Elements may be in both foreground and background simultaneously. White space doesn't literally have to be white. It can be black or any other color. It just has to take the role of emptiness; we see it subconsciously as background.

Another way of programming the context of a design is to fill the space with a full-bleed typographic treatment. A headline sized large enough to fill a page will certainly have immediacy. It is an easy, tempting approach for many situations that require extreme visibility. However, unless *the meaning* of the headline is best expressed by wall-to-wall type, this approach is only graphic exploitation and should be resisted.

Is this "wasted space" (top)? Siena's magnificent piazza is the city's gathering place. Four hundred years after its construction, it remains the city's focal point.

Or is this vital space? This aerial photo shows Siena's narrow streets spreading out from the piazza. The high-lighted area shows the site from the perspective in which the top photo was taken.

BigTen B1G

Negative space is positive in this redesign for a league that admitted an eleventh member. It changed its logo when it later expanded to fourteen teams.

Very dark space blends into and merges into the figure in this *Self Portrait at the Age of 63* (1669), one of the last paintings by Rembrandt van Rijn.

The positive and negative have been equally attended to (the white shapes are as interesting as the black) in Armin Hofmann's 1962 poster for Herman Miller.

The headline reads "Keep chopping." Negative space is exploited conceptually in an ironic public service ad for a nature conservancy organization.

Framing and framal reference

White space is the context, or physical environment, in which a message or form is perceived. As we have already seen, two–dimensional space is an environment that can be manipulated. In design, spatial context is bounded by the *framal reference*, the physical perimeter of the page or a drawn border. The terms can be confusing because a perimeter can suggest what inside the box is in front of what is outside the box. Spatial context and figure/ground exist at the same time. They are not exclusive of one another.

Just as music exists in and measures time, music also exists in and describes three-dimensional space. Music played in a vast cathedral sounds quite different when played in a cozy night club. Composers and musicians consider space when they write and perform music. Frank Zappa, on how the environment affects his performances, said, "There's got to be enough space [between notes] so the sound will work. ... Music doesn't happen on paper: it works in air. You hear it because air molecules are doing something to your eardrums. You're talking about sculptured air. Patterns are formed in the airwaves and your ear is detecting those patterns."

Leo Lionni's 1960 *Fortune* magazine cover makes the background visible by deleting "missing" letters. The shifting colors and empty spaces add vibrancy. Lionni (1910–1999), art director, author, and illustrator, said,

"I rarely ever put type or image on angles unless there was a good reason to do it. My ultimate design influence is the Bauhaus, although I've never been directly connected with them."

1 31

Designate elements that will break into emptiness at least once to avoid the emptiness looking like "wasted space" (top row). The first example is chock-a-block full and looks like a chore to read. The second has cut text to make room for the center empty column. It *has* empty space, which, though unused, is still better for the reader than filling the page with text. The third example *uses* the space to show off elements that are different in meaning and emphasis. Elements put into emptiness become visible and attract attention. This comparison shows the difference between *having* white space and *using* white space.

The same amount of white space is used in these two examples. The first layout disperses its emptiness. The second has grouped emptiness into significant chunks, joining its facing pages into a single horizontal spread.

Deliberate use of white space creates negative and positive shapes that are equally embracing. This artwork is in the floor at the Cathedral of Siena.

An abundance of white space, visible in overwhelming disproportion to the size and amount of type, is used to express vastness.

Little white space remains, shoved to the perimeters and beyond, outside the framal reference, as an expression of silence-filling volume.

"White space is the lungs *of the layout. It's not there for aesthetic reasons. It's there for physical reasons."* Derek Birdsall (1934–)

Space must look deliberately used

"One of the highest delights of the human mind," wrote architect Le Corbusier (Charles-Édouard Jeanneret: 1887–1965), "is to perceive the order of nature and to measure its own participation in the scheme of things; the work of art seems to be a labor of putting into order, a masterpiece of human order." Le Corbusier collaborated on essays and books between 1917 and 1928 exploring Le Purisme – Purism – in which logic and order, universal truths, and hierarchy of sensation were the main tenets.

It must be evident to the viewer that a design's material has been predigested and presented in an organized way. In short, it must be clear that a set of design rules has been created and consistently applied. The use of too little white space results in an over-full page. The use of too much white space makes a page or spread look incomplete.

It is possible to dress up a page with white space, to inappropriately spread it around to look like it is judiciously used. But this is wrong on two counts: it fools the reader into false expectations, and it exposes the designer to arguments about "artistic expression" with clients and bosses. Visual communication relies on creating a connection

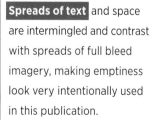

Spreads of text and space are intermingled and contrast with spreads of full bleed imagery, making emptiness look very intentionally used in this publication.

Giovanni Battista Piranesi (1720-1778) was an Italian artist and printmaker. Trained as an architect, his works depicted views of Rome and grand buildings and, famously, "Carceri d'invenzione," a series of imaginary prisons. In the series of sixteen works, Piranesi distorted space, treating foreground and background whimsically in studies of gigantic vaulted spaces that lead to and from nowhere.

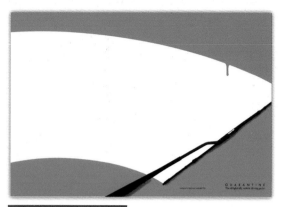

A bloodied windshield describes a "delightfully violent driving game," but the wiped area is actually a brilliantly utilized area of blank paper. This "non-

existent" raw material is available to be exploited in every design, whether paper or screen based.

The horn that appears to be in front of the bull's side is actually *and simultaneously* the deep red background. This is an example of activated white space.

"The closer you look at something, the more complex it seems to be." Vint Cerf (1943-), co-creator of the Internet

with *the reader*. The connection starts weakly because the reader has no commitment to the message. Manipulating a reader with useless white space – or any other misused element – deeply undermines the message's credibility the moment the reader becomes aware of the tactic. On the second point, designers wish to avoid confrontational discussions about artistic expression whenever possible. As service providers hired to solve others' problems, the designer usually loses these disagreements. The solution? To make design decisions that are defendable and logically explainable as solutions to real problems. Using emptiness is part of a valid and logical solution to design problems. Unlike images and words, which come with their own obvious reasons for being included in a design, emptiness is more subtle. It is within the designer's responsibility to look for and take advantage of emptiness on each design assignment and be able to explain and justify it.

Expressive use of white space requires an asymmetrical design. Centering elements kills white space because the figures' position, their centeredness, has eclipsed the need for interestingly shaped negative space. Placing the figure off to one side –

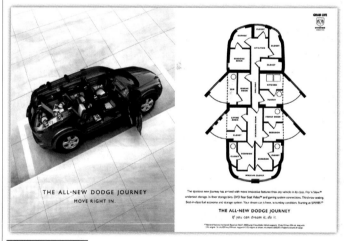

Expressive use of space describes the roominess inside a vehicle, exaggerating it by likening it to a house.

Stores that want to nurture an image of quality have an open floor plan and an uncrowded look. Stores that project a bargain image overwhelm with "muchness."

Ronald Searle, the British cartoonist, reveals a distorted sense of three-dimensional space to illustrate the futility of at least some moments of life.

Franz Kline's 1961 *Slate Cross* relies equally on white and black areas. Kline's many preliminary studies ensured spontaneous craft with pre-planned composition.

Edward Wadsworth's *In Drydock* is a 1918 example of figure/ground in magnificent harmony. His contrasts of line weight make this a particularly attractive example.

You first see the "at" sign at the center of this spiral. After half a moment, you see the serpent and its egg in this detail of a poster by Ken-Tsai Lee.

even bleeding off an edge – activates the white space. A truism in design is that if you arrange the white space well, the elements on the page will look great, but if you only arrange the positive elements on the page, the white space will almost inevitably be ineffective and the design will lack power.

Peter Stark wrote an excellent description of an equivalent way of seeing in an extreme-skier profile in *Outside* magazine: "I looked down at a very steep snowfield dotted with jagged rock piles. As I tried to figure out whether my trajectory, if I fell, would take me into the rocks, Coombs took off skiing down the pitch. 'Don't rocks bother him?' I asked Gladstone. 'That's the difference with Doug,' she replied. 'Where you and I see rocks, he sees patches of snow and the chance to turn.'"

Have you noticed how expensive, quality-oriented stores have an open floor plan and an uncrowded look, while cost-oriented stores are stuffed wall-to-wall with merchandise? In the former, you rarely see more than three of anything because it signals rarity. In the latter, there are stacks of every item because sales volume is the store's goal.

Applied to two-dimensional space, this disparity is expressed by Ken Hiebert, a design professor

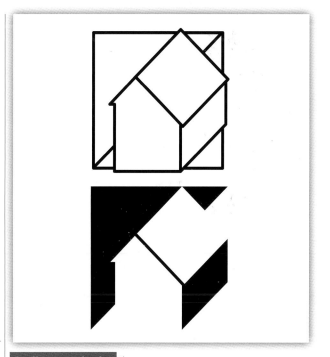

Outlines emphasize the perimeter of shapes and force space into the background. The same artwork can be described using figure and ground, abstracting the content and making it look more "filtered" and refined.

Some artwork is recognizable for its extraordinary fullness in which every millimeter is used. Australian aboriginal works can certainly be described this way, especially in works since the 1970s, when a dotting motif emerged in the Papunya Central Desert region. Dotting was developed as a way to disguise cultural symbolism and hiding sacred messages in plain view. This example, *Possum Dreaming*, is by Tim Leura Tjapaltjarri from the Madjura/Walbri Tribe.

Mail-order catalogues' design reveals the character and nature of the products being sold: jam-packed versus carefully spaced communicates "bargain" versus "quality."

Typefaces also contribute to the message: pseudo hand-lettered type says "rough" and "great bargain" while

sophisticated typographic contrasts complement the imagery with quiet organization.

Organized fullness uses space arranged into a quadrant, with each area containing material in a two-axis chart describing sophistication and taste.

with whom I studied one summer in the 1970s: "It is common to use space as a kind of luxury, projecting generosity or classic simplicity – a formula for 'class.' But if space is used only as a formula or device, it is also readily suspect as being either wasteful, arrogant, or elitist. Yet space is a human need, and the experience of space is typically an exhilarating one."

Catalogues each have their own identity. Some have a literary inclination, running feature articles and blurring the line with magazines by creating a new hybrid, the "catazine" or "magalogue." Some create an artistic appearance, leaving a lot of space unoccupied, speaking intelligently, suggesting to the reader that the merchandise is of high quality. Some shove as many products and descriptions as possible onto each page, filling in every inch, and know there is an audience for such slow-speed junk wading. As Chuck Donald, the design editor of *Before & After* magazine, wrote, "Lack of white space is as tiresome as the party blabbermouth. [On the other hand,] margins and white space beckon the reader in."

Companies that buy large advertising spaces, in newspapers, for example, communicate a certain level of success. Buying a large space and then

"White space is like the calm just before an ice skater begins a routine: it sets into perfect contrast the graceful animation that follows."
Anonymous

graphisches kabinett münchen

buchdruckerei franz eggert, heßstr. 60

briennerstrasse 10   leitung guenther franke

ausstellung der sammlung jan tschichold

plakate der avantgarde

arp	molzahn
baumeister	schawinsky
bayer	schlemmer
burchartz	schuitema
cassandre	sutnar
cyliax	trump
dexel	tschichold
lissitzky	zwart
moholy-nagy	und andere

tsch   24. januar bis 10. februar 1930   geöffnet 9–6, sonntags 10–1

buchdruckerei franz eggert, heßstr. 60

graphisches kabinett münchen

briennerstrasse 10   leitung guenther franke

ausstellung der sammlung jan tschichold

plakate der avantgarde

arp baumeister bayer burchartz cassandre cyliax dexel lissitzky moholy-nagy

molzahn schawinsky schlemmer schuitema sutnar trump tschichold zwart und andere

24. januar bis 10. februar 1930   geöffnet 9–6, sonntags 10–1
tsch

These are before and after examples: the top illustration is a 23½" x 16½" poster designed by Jan Tschichold in 1930. Tschichold was one of the earliest practitioners of the then-revolutionary asymmetrical style that he described in his 1928 book, *Die Neue Typographie*. I have reorganized the identical content into a symmetrical format to show how white space in the original design added quality. Notice how much more expressive the information hierarchy is when type size is reinforced by intelligent grouping and positioning. This idea was the heart of Tschichold's philosophy.

These figure/ground reversals show the arrangement of the spaces in Tschichold's original poster and the centered iteration. The only thing that differs is the way the negative space has been distributed.

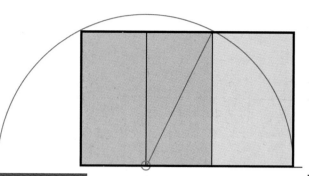

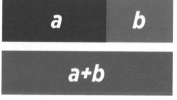

Traditional book margin proportions are two units on the inside; three units at the head; four units on the outside; and five units at the foot.

How to construct a Golden Rectangle: draw a square; divide the square in half; use the midpoint as the base of a radius that extends to the baseline; extend the square's horizontal lines and draw a vertical where the arc intersects the baseline. The area of the square *plus the added rectangle* is a Golden Rectangle.

The Golden Section is a line segment divided according to the Golden Ratio: *a* is to the shorter segment of *b* as the total line length *a+b* is to the longer segment *a*.

leaving much of it empty speaks even more highly of the company's success.

One of the oldest examples of exploitation of emptiness for utilitarian use is the *scholar's margin*, a wider outside margin reserved for note taking. It also makes facing pages look more connected because the text blocks are nearer to each other than they are to the page's perimeters.

Organizing two-dimensional space has been a concern of scribes and bookmakers since AD 500 – the fall of Rome and the beginning of the early Middle Ages, when monks elevated their work with ornamental initials. Scribes of the late Middle Ages realized the proportional perfection of the page by following Phidias' design of the Parthenon in a mathematically harmonious ratio. Called by Euclid (c325-365 BC) the "extreme and mean ratio," and by Luca Pacioli, in 1509, the "Divine Proportion," the Golden Section is the finest proportion ever developed. According to Jan Tschichold, "Many books produced between 1550 and 1770 show these proportions exactly, to within half a millimeter."* Mathematically, the Golden Section is: the longer segment *a* is to the shorter segment *b* as *a* is to the totality of the lengths *a+b*. **EoGD3**

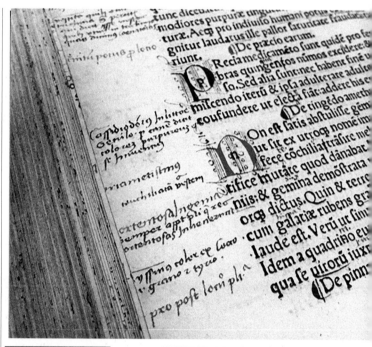

"Scholar's margins" are wider on the outside, leaving room for readers to make notes and doodles.

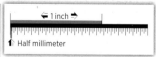

*Half a millimeter is equal to about a 64th of an inch, or a little over a point: ⎯⎯⎯

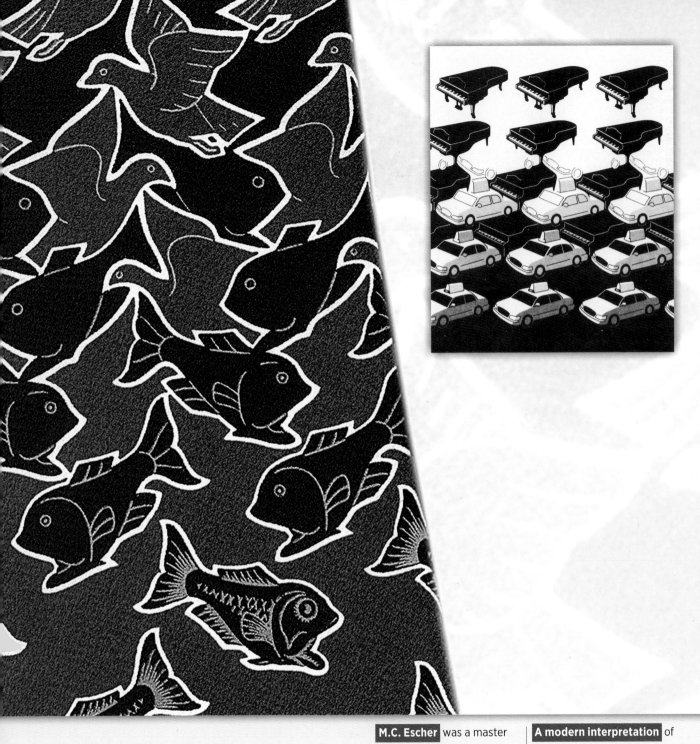

M.C. Escher was a master at creating active white space. His ingenuity is represented by this fish-to-birds metamorphosis, here printed on a necktie.

A modern interpretation of Escher's metamorphosis is used to illustrate an advertisement for a New York City classical music radio station.

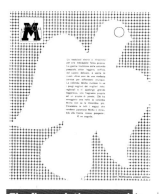

The figure *is* the ground in this 1934 advertisement designed by Leo Lionni. Ambiguity results when shapes can be either figure *or* ground.

You will likely see the white *N* shape first in this "*SCC*" corporate mark. Concentrate on the black shapes and you will see an *S* and two *C*s, one of which is flopped.

These maps, showing the world from a Euro-centric point of view, emphasize the shapes of sea (top) and land.

Space is a shape in these four logos: interlocking fingers; the state of Texas; the Dove of Peace; and a guitar neck between long-neck beer bottles.

2 Symmetry and asymmetry

The first and wisest of them all professed to know this only, that he nothing knew.
John Milton (1608-1674)

Balance is an important aspect of visual communication. There are two kinds of balance: symmetrical and asymmetrical. Symmetrical balance centers on a vertical axis. Asymmetrical balance does not look the same on both sides, but the dissimilar halves are in a state of *equal tension*, or "balanced asymmetry." Symmetry is *balance through similarity*; asymmetry is *balance through contrast*.

Space is a shape

Design is the arrangement of shapes. All design elements have a shape, which is an area defined by a perimeter. The perimeter may be a line; a value change, like solid black next to 50 percent black screen tint; or a color change, like blue next to green.

It is vital for a designer to learn to see each element as a shape as well as a signifier of meaning, for it is those *shapes* that are managed in a design, and

Space is a shape 43
Shapes are defined by their perimeters and emptiness has a perimeter.

Symmetry: space is passive 45
Space in a symmetrical design is *background*.

Asymmetry: space is active 47
Space in an asymmetrical design is or can be in the foreground. It is equal in importance to figures.

Time and motion 51
Time is the fourth dimension. Motion takes place over time.

Representational and symbolic space 53
Space can illustrate ideas.

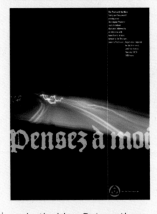

Symmetry does not need to be precisely the same on both sides, though that is the strictest definition of the term. In practical terms, symmetry means *mostly* or *essentially* or *that which is perceived to be* the same on both sides. Put another way, symmetry can be defined as being the *absence of asymmetry*, as this statue of La Résistance de 1814 at the Arc de Triomphe in Paris and the magazine cover by Fred Woodward illustrate.

Centered elements create passive white space, while asymmetrically-positioned elements create activated, dynamic space.

EAST VILLAGE ELECTRICAL SUPPLY
646 | 555 | 1200

MANAGEMENT GROUP.COM

AUTOIN **DUSTRIAL**
LISBOAPORTUGAO

There are three types of symmetry. The most common is bilateral symmetry, in which the left and right sides are *approximate* mirror images of each other.

Another is radial or rotational symmetry, in which the elements radiate from or rotate around a central point.

The third is "all over" symmetry, in which elements are evenly distributed. The "all over" repeated pattern of wallpaper, for example, is intended as a room's background.

Passive white space is static. It looks motionless, strictly background. It isn't used to draw the reader into the design, making messages a bit less noticeable.

it is those *shapes* that are perceived by the viewer. Learning to see each element as a shape takes time and effort. Sensitivity to seeing shapes revolutionizes a person's ability to design with seeing emptiness' shape as the most potent aspect.

White space is like digital data: It is either "on" or "off." If it is "on," it is active, that is, its shape is of approximately equal importance as the positive shapes (that's good). If the white space is "off," its shape is essentially a result of chance, the byproduct resulting from the placement of positive elements (not nearly as good).

Symmetry: space is passive

Symmetry is the centered placement of elements in space. Symmetry, requiring a central vertical axis, forces white space to the perimeter of the design. White space in a symmetrical design is passive because it is not integral to our perception of the positive elements. If it is noticed at all, it is seen only as inactive background. Symmetry is a predictable arrangement that implies order and balance. It suggests peacefulness and stability.

Symmetrical typography is attractive and easy to create. It is best executed in an inverted pyramid shape because the cone shape inexorably leads the

Figure and ground are essential partners in Herb Lubalin's lettermark for Finch-Pruyn paper. By exaggerating the serifs, the *P* becomes visible as a white shape inside the *F*.

"A really great ad *is one which does its selling while maintaining typographic excellence. Such are not legion."*
Oscar Ogg
(1908–1971)

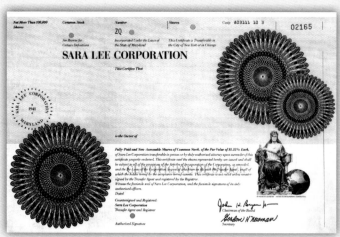

Margins should be used to show off important elements. Margins' passive white space enlivens the page by being activated.

Asymmetry requires the use of unequal shapes and uneven spaces, as shown in these pairs of stock certificates and paper moneys. The design of the asymmet-

rical paper money (bottom two) is off center in part to make space for security watermarks on the left side.

USE AN **INVERTED**
PYRAMID SHAPE
ON CENTERED
TYPE

Of higd fgeidig dfv dfiboe if cvb dfv gbincf vbed. loghin dfigh nreuyk ui kldift egfiw fgfh dfg ndofg chegidf ghedfg dfv edfibe dfov cf vib df. Priuy ekui pik ic foghd fg kedut grog dibof cev gub eni dogh.

PLEASE
DON'T USE
A PYRAMID SHAPE
FOR CENTERED TYPE

Of higd fgeidig dfv dfiboe if cvb dfv gbincf vbed. loghin dfigh nreuyk ui kldift egfiw fgfh dfg ndofg chegidf ghedfg dfv edfibe dfov cf vib df. Priuy ekui pik ic foghd fg kedut grog dibof cev gub eni dogh.

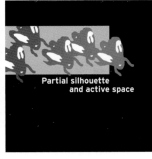

Square halftone
and passive space

Partial silhouette
and active space

When setting symmetrical (i.e., *centered*) type, each line should be shorter than the previous, to make the task of reading appear progressively easier.

Activate passive white space by carving part of an image out of its background and bump that into the space. This is known as a *partial silhouette*. It is a technique

for making the image appear more real than a square halftone because, as in real life, objects overlap and intrude on the things behind them.

"Symmetry is static, *that is to say quiet; that is to say, inconspicuous."* William Addison Dwiggins (1880–1956), type designer, book designer

reader to the next level of information. The widest line should be at or near the top, and the shortest line should be at or near the bottom.

Asymmetry: space is active

Asymmetry, which means "not symmetry," suggests motion and activity. It is the creation of order and balance between unlike or unequal elements. Having no predictable pattern, asymmetry is dynamic. White space in an asymmetrical design is necessarily active, because it is integral to our perception of the positive elements. Therefore, the deliberate use of white space is necessary for successful asymmetrical design.

Active white space is carefully-considered emptiness. Its shape has been planned. Active white space is the primary attribute of documents that are perceived as well-designed and having inborn quality. Any empty shape that has been consciously created is active space. A truism in design is that if you attend to the white space, the page will look great, but if you arrange only the positive elements on the page, the page will be ordinary.

Another way of activating white space is by integrating it into the positive elements of design through *closure*. Closure is a spontaneous human

Asymmetry requires a different way of thinking. Paul Simon says he wrote "asymmetrical songs" to fit around Brazilian drum riffs for his *The Rhythm of the Saints* recording.

The Princes in the Tower
(1831) by Paul Delaroche is
a study in asymmetry: the
two figures on the right are
balanced by the dog on the
left. The effect is enhanced
by the figures looking in
different directions.

More obviously asymmetrical
is this experimental violin
made in Sweden in c1800.
The form was developed in
search of superior sound.

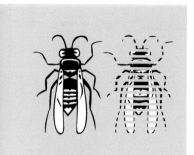

Which bug is *too easy* to recognize? *Closure* requires tension between the visible and the implied, or the *not* visible. Showing too much can reduce visual impact.

White space is activated by its relative size and proportion to the figures in it. As a figure gets bigger in a given space, it activates its surrounding white space by becoming more abstract and achieving a balance. Force the perception of negative space and promote the active search for meaning by abstracting the figure.

*"**Unsymmetrical** arrangements are more flexible and better suited to the practical and aesthetic needs of today."* Jan Tschichold (1902–1974)

action in which the brain completes an unfinished or interrupted shape. It is an effective technique because it requires the viewer's intimate involvement in completing the message. The key to making closure successful is to adjust the spaces between forms carefully. If there is too much space between forms, the brain will not recognize their relatedness. If there is too little space between forms, the reader will not need to add anything to see the completed shape.

Asymmetrical design isn't a guarantee of a dynamic, lively design. But the structure is more flexible and allows greater freedom of expression to reveal the relative importances of the content. Like other freedoms, symmetrical design offers great reward but requires understanding and sensitivity from the designer. These improve with knowledge and experience. Read, study, and immerse yourself in great design, concentrating on samples from the first half of the twentieth century as they are models you can approach with greatest perspective.

The most noxious name for white space is "wasted space," because it lumps both well-used and poorly used emptiness together without distinction and gives the whole subject a negative spin. It is a term used by those who do not understand the val-

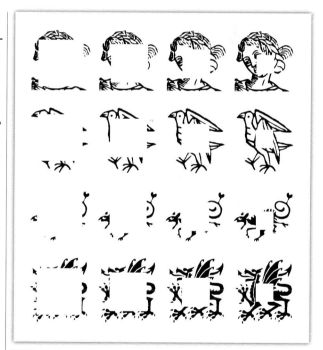

"Closure" requires active participation by the viewer to complete the image. Closure succeeds with careful manipulation of the spaces *between* elements.

When do each of these squares and images achieve tension, that is, show *just enough* of the figure to be distinguishable? There is no one state: each of these four instances requires its own sensitive interpretation.

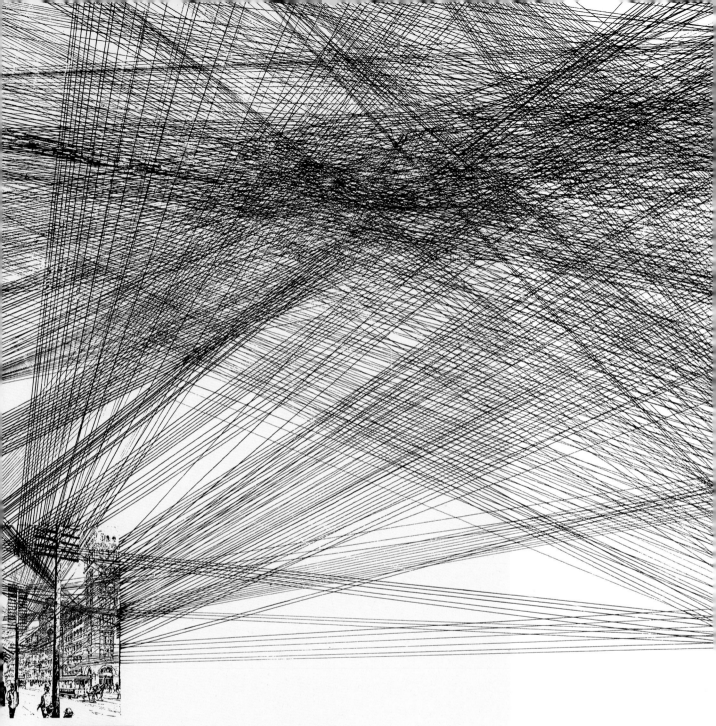

"Filling the sky with wires" is the acerbic comment in this amended city street drawing from the turn of the last century when telephone and electric wires began accumulating overhead. It is used here to represent filling all the space, thereby wasting its potential as an inviting opportunity for the reader.

Space off the picture plane is brilliantly used. We get the sense of looking out a window at activity going on beyond the picture plane.

Three-dimensional space is simulated in a trompe l'oeil painting on an outdoor wall. Its intrigue causes the viewer to pause for a moment, giving a moment of relaxation.

Time and motion are captured in a single frame in this time-lapse photo of torch-bearing skiers.

Time and motion are attributes of movie titles, which evolved into a more pronounced aspect of movie-making since the 1950s.

ue of white space. "Wasted space" really only refers to *poorly used* white space, which *of course* is to be avoided. The fear of "wasted space" drives design novices to fill in any empty space with unnecessary decoration or to extend the text by arbitrarily opening linespacing, called "vertical justification." The ultimate wasted space is actually overfilled space. It is space that has been crammed with content, artlessly and uninvitingly presented.

Emptiness is wasted if it fails to achieve the desired attention-getting result, or to make the page look inviting with an unthreatening, airy presentation, or to act as a separator between elements.

Time and motion

Much of graphic design is created in two dimensions: height and width. The third dimension is depth. And the fourth dimension is time, which is a component of designing for multipage products like magazines and Web sites. Time significantly impacts information in its pacing and rhythm.

Motion is simply a record of where an object has been over time, much as one can think of a line as a record of where a pen tip has been over time.

There are a few ways to imply motion in two-dimensional design. One is to repeat an element

Emptiness is not the same as wasted space. The three-dimensionality of these planes of type require a simple empty background – as well as the small type across the bottom – to define the space in which the primary type floats.

Representational space is used to show off contents – literally – in this Walther-cast-in-acrylic sculpture by Dutch artist Ted Noten.

Amantes Amentes Films

Time and motion: Use space and careful cropping at the trim margins to suggest movement within and beyond the picture plane.

Closure occurs when the viewer connects two parts into a whole. Motion is implied as the headline is mentally connected to the spaces in the text.

Only one of these four cars has a single set of footprints – and a set of tire tracks revealing a now-empty parking space in this c1965 Italian VW ad.

The missing top of a soft-boiled egg reveals the yummy yolk inside and artfully makes the point of toplessness on an ovoid car.

across space, which introduces rhythm. Another is to blur an element by using a time-lapse image, for example, or filtering in Photoshop, or moving the original on a photocopy machine. Lastly, motion can be implied by using space.

Active white space can imply motion, as in this letterhead design (above left) for a film production company, inspired by a Bob Gill design. Emulating a projector's misframing in the theater, this is an amusing way to think of the paper's edges.

In the *Coup de vent* ("*Gust of wind*") example, closure is used to connect the "blowing" letters with the holes in the text, creating motion. The effect is heightened by the increasing character sizes, overlapping some letters, and tilting their baselines, as if the letters had been caught in the act of fluttering.

Representational and symbolic space

Empty space is considered extravagant, exclusive, classy. It symbolizes wealth and luxury. So leaving space empty automatically lends eloquence to a design, regardless of what is being shown in the figures that lie within it.

By injecting a disproportionate amount of space between characters and words, a self-consciously

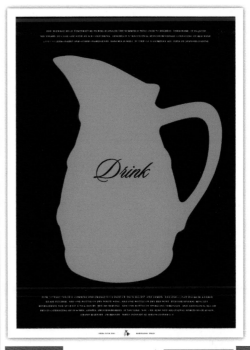

Flat space can be rendered representationally, as in this pitcher on a Spanish resort's informational poster that teaches how to make sangria.

"To invent, you need a good imagination and a pile of junk." Thomas Edison (1847–1931)

The expanse of the white space – in contrast to the full-bleed photo – is used to describe the emptiness of life without physical activity: *"When you're old and tired... you'll be filled with regret."*

The contrast is further expressed by the reversed-out secondary headline in the action photo: *"Or maybe not."*

Snow is represented not with white ink, but with the *unprinted areas* of paper, the negative space, in this early twentieth-century multicolor woodblock print by the Shimbi Shoin printery in Tokyo.

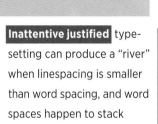

This is 14/11 Nicolas Jenson set justified across a 14-pica measure. Note that the word spaces are larger than the line spaces and that your eyes prefer moving vertically rather than horizontally. Blur your eyes and you will see wiggly "rivers of white." TIP: Never use "Auto" as a line spacing attribute because it avoids making a specific decision about how much space should exist between lines. This must be a *choice* based on increasing type's legibility.

Inattentive justified type-setting can produce a "river" when linespacing is smaller than word spacing, and word spaces happen to stack vertically.

White space symbolizes a river in this logo for the fluvine city of Rotterdam. The abstraction in stylized on or off pixels give the city a modern edge.

"They are ill discoverers *that think there is no [sea], when they see nothing but [land]."* After Francis Bacon (1561–1626) *Advancement of Learning*

sophisticated or, conversely, a careless look can be given to type. A "river of white," for example, is a vertical line that becomes apparent when a few word spaces occur above one another.

White space can be used to represent objects, like "river," and ideas, like "clean." Shown above is the mosaic symbol for Rotterdam, illustrating the city and the Nieuwe Maas, the river which runs through it. "Cleanliness" is symbolically shown in this opener and spread combination (right). The pristine white paper and unobtrusive type of the "after" view on the opening page contrasts with the cluttered "before" view, which is revealed when the page is turned.

Ideas that empty space can signify include:

Quality extravagance, class, wealth, luxury
Solitude abandonment, loneliness
Missing lost, stolen, misplaced
Clean bleached, washed
Purity unsullied, unadulterated, virgin, unbuilt
Heaven absolution, sacredness
Abundance plenty
Openness distance, acreage, al fresco, infinity
Calmness placidity, undisturbed, inaction
Ice snow, sky, day, river, land/water `EoGD3`

The PowerBoss™ was here.

White space is "cleanliness" in this three-page ad for cleaning equipment. The right hand opener is a simple declarative sentence: "The PowerBoss™ was here." Turn the page and a full bleed spread appears in all its grungy, monochromatic hideousness. Whatever a PowerBoss™ is, it evidently works.

45,000 BC The earliest cave paintings found are in Indonesia. This example from 30,000 BC is by Neanderthals in France's Chauvet Cave.

c4000 BC Beginning of written language. Pictographs begin evolution into nonrepresentational marks. At about the same time,

Sumerians build the first wheeled vehicle (similar to this model found in a burial vault), which could triple the weight pulled by a single ox.

c1800 BC The Phœnicians develop a system that connects twenty-two spoken sounds with corresponding written symbols.

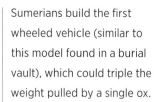

842 BC First•use•of•punctuation•are•word-separating•dots•as•shown•at•left. Mostwriting,though,runswordstogether.Eventuallywordspaces weredevelopedtomakeread ingoutloudinchurcheseasier.

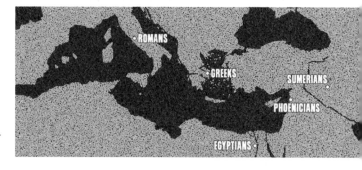

500 BC Fragment of an administrative record of the payment of 600 quarts of an unknown commodity to five villages near Persepolis, Persia. Shown slightly larger than life size.

196 BC The Rosetta Stone, found in 1799 by Napoleon and translated in 1822, is the key to understanding two ancient Egyptian languages.

AD 114 Trajan's Column, the carved letters of which are considered the finest roman letters ever drawn, were first painted then chiseled. Elsewhere on the column,

both wartime (those are the vanquisheds' severed heads being given to Trajan) and more peaceful achievements are commemorated.

c1300 BC Hieroglyphs shown in a detail from a list of kings' names found in the temple of Ramses II at Abydos.

1200 BC Sumerian cuneiform (from Latin *cuneus*: "wedge") uses simplified pictures inscribed in clay tablets.

3,000BC Egyptian hieroglyphics	1,100BC Phœnician "soundscript"
3,000BC Hittite hieroglyphics	1,000BC Cuneiform script
2,000BC Babylonian cuneiform	1,000BC Egyptian hieratic script
1,600BC Cretan linear script	1,000BC Late Phoenician script

Several writing systems evolved in parallel in communities along the eastern edge of the Mediterranean. The Phœnicians' system linked written symbols to spoken sounds, and that system was adopted by their trading partners to the west and eventually by the Romans in about 700 BC.

The historical development of space: six timelines

> nspiration is for amateurs. The rest of us just show up for work. Chuck Close (1940–2021)

Spoken Communication

Writing

Drawn Communication

Timeline 1: Space

Humans began communicating verbally and through sign language about 150,000 years ago in East Africa. Writing grew out of painting: cave markings as early as c40,000 BC represented ideas as well as events. ❚ As the idea of private property took hold in the area from present-day Egypt in c4,000 BC, taxes very quickly followed. Sumerian priests required accurate accounting of production, so *pictographs* or "image drawings" were invented using images for each category and simple markings for quantities. ❚ Systems grew to more than 2,000 glyphs, which could be combined to communicate abstract ideas. This system took years to learn, and those who did rose in society. The images evolved to represent ever more complex ideas, *ideographs*, and a new

AD 200 Scrolls, in use since about 400 BC, are replaced as information vehicles by the codex, or "paged book." Made from animal skins, much ancient literature was sadly lost in the transition to the more durable format.

	GREEK		ROMAN	
	800BC	400BC	300BC	100BC
	A	A	A	A
	B	B	B	B
	Γ	Γ	C	C G
	Δ	D	D	D
	E	E	E	E
	F	F	F	F
	I	Z		
	B	H	H	H
	⊗	I	I	I
	K	K	K	K
	∧	∧	L	L
	M	M	M	M
	N	N	N	N
	O	O	O	O
	Π	Π	P	P
	Φ	Q	Q	Q
	R	P	R	R
	S	S	S	S
	T	T	T	T
	Y	Y	V	V Y
	X	X	X	X
				Z

The evolution of the Latin letterforms we use today evolved from Etruscan characters, the Greek alphabet which adapted the Phœnician characters which themselves grew from even earlier Egyptian hieroglyphics.

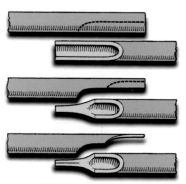

The edged pen, made from feather quill or reed and dipped in ink, was the primary writing tool for centuries. It was cut in this three-step process.

c350 Copyists in monasteries use parchment (sheepskin) and vellum (calfskin) in handwritten duplications of existing works, usually Bibles.

c500 A codex ("book with pages") Bible is copied near Mt. Sinai in northeastern Egypt.

c1400 Words carved in wood boards are used for multiple impressions. But movable letters are not yet crafted individually to be assembled and reused.

1478 Renaissance design using white space perfects page proportions. This example by the Alvise brothers is among the first to use *ornaments*.

"Printing is the subject that lies at the roots of Western civilization. It's the beginning of everything, really." Stan Nelson, National Museum of American History

c1525 Early typecast matrices show how letters are made in a mold, then separated and finished. These are from a Prague foundry.

1684-85 Nikolas Kis (pronounced "*kish*"), a Hungarian type designer and letter cutter, produces this *schriftmusterblatt* or "typeface sheet," which became the model for today's Janson and other Dutch Old Style typefaces.

c1760 John Baskerville develops smoother paper and ink and a typeface, with pronounced thicks and thins, that takes advantage of these refinements.

c1790 Lithography ("stone writing") is invented, based on the idea that water repels oil-based inks (top). Its results allow greater subtlety than letterpress.

1440 Johannes Gutenberg (c1397–1468) of Mainz, Germany, invents an efficient system for attaching movable letters to a printing press. A goldsmith by trade, he understands molds and duplicating metal masters. His first typeface is based on *Textura*, the regional writing style.

1500 In the first fifty years of printing, 35,000 books produced a total of 8–12 million copies. The average run of so-called "incunabula" books is 250 copies.

1517 Early grid use in G.P. de Brocar's *Polyglot Bible* accommodates five languages. Such an undertaking requires exceptional fluency and printing skill.

class of people was created to learn the system and write in clay tablets. ❘ Egyptian priests developed their own pictorial writing system which was concerned with recording the status of its Pharaohs and gods. The Greeks called it *hieroglyphics*, or "sacred writing." Another Egyptian language, *hieratic script*, or "priestly writing," was developed in parallel and is identifiable by its use of characters rather than pictograms and having been written almost exclusively in ink and reed brush on papyrus. ❘ The need for quicker writing caused the pictograms to be abstracted into *cuneiform*, or "wedge-shaped" writing. This served as a more or less universal language so anyone in the greater middle east area, the "Cradle of Civilization," could read and understand the message. ❘ The *alphabet* was developed by the Phoenicians, for the first time uniting spoken and written language. ❘ The Rosetta Stone was inscribed in 196 BC to praise Pharaoh Ptolomy V Epiphanes. Telling one story in three languages, it became the key to deciphering hieroglyphics and Egyptian demotic script. Jean François Champollion translated it between 1814 and 1822 using the known third language, Greek. But his translation was disbelieved until another trilingual stone, the Canopus Decree, was

The first legibility studies were conducted in 1878 by French engineer and physician Émile Javal. He discovered that the eye doesn't move continuously across a line of text, but makes short "saccadic" jumps.

1826 With photography's invention and inherent realism, printers improve continuous tones. Photo-engraving, a technique for making printing plates for mass reproduction, is introduced in 1871.

1890 Marginal notes placed logically and very near their reference points in the text liven the pages of *Whistler's English* book.

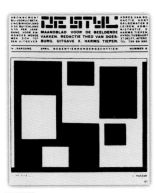

1917 De Stijl ("The Style") explores asymmetric type, simplicity, and dynamic divisions of space. It influences constructivists and the Bauhaus.

1919 Cubists reject the perspective of a single viewpoint, fragmenting and collaging images, sometimes adding letterforms as abstract elements.

1923 Dadaists exploit shock through typographic experimentation and apparent randomness.

1927 The Bauhaus, both the school and the philosophy, is founded as a new educational program in Germany, marking the birth of graphic design.

1975 The 1960s and 70s, amidst the social upheaval then occurring, are decades of searching for symbolism, as shown by Milton Glaser's I♥NY logo.

*"**Disputes between** the traditional and the modern schools of typographic thought are the fruits of misplaced emphasis. I believe the real difference lies in the way 'space' is interpreted."* Paul Rand (1914-1996)

1987 April Greiman builds on Wolfgang Weingart's self-conscious "Swiss Punk" work, adding video and computer references and geometric shapes as decorative elements.

1992 Typographic deconstruction, the battle between legibility and maximum visual impact, is explored by many, led by Neville Brody's '90s work.

1998 Web site design becomes the hot discipline through the '90s, largely mirroring print design. Web-like wayfinding is applied to multipage print design.

2002 The computer allows design from any era, like using these old metal types. The purpose of a document, though, remains *to be read.*

1934 Herbert Matter adds extreme photographic scale to Tschichold's *New Typography* in montaged posters.

1948 Lester Beall helps create the modern movement in New York with *Scope* magazine for Upjohn Pharmaceuticals.

1957 The International or "Swiss" style grows from the Bauhaus. Armin Hofmann uses the grid, asymmetry, and minimal typographic contrast.

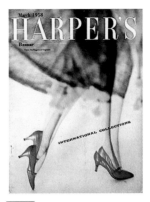

1959 The New York School, beginning immediately after the end of World War II, brings a period of extraordinary optimism and vibrancy.

discovered in 1866. | To make facing pages in early books symmetrical and thus more pleasing to God, scribes insisted that both the left and right edges of text columns be aligned. This required abbreviating words, which led to the invention of contractions. | Richard Hollis, in his *Graphic Design, A Concise History*, says, "A single sheet of paper printed on one side is a poster; folded once, it becomes a leaflet; folded again and fastened it becomes a booklet; multiples of folded sheets make a magazine or book. These – the poster, leaflet, booklet, magazine and book – are the physical structures on which graphic designers must organize their information." To these structures we add digital paperless communication. | Graphic design evolved as a profession in the mid-twentieth century from commercial artists in the trades of printing, typesetting, and illustration. | There are three kinds of messages designers organize: *identification* (saying what something is), *information* (explaining relationships between things), and *promotion* (advertising design whose purpose is to be visible and persuasive). These three kinds of content can overlap and they do more often in recent years when no opportunity seems to be passed up to make money. **END**

Letterforms became more pliable, adventurous, and expressive in the art movements of the early twentieth century. Such letters were hand drawn, not typeset, encouraging far greater individualism.

2010 Stefan Sagmeister uses fibers for every aspect of this Levi's poster. Using off computer material makes messages visible in the realm of now-universal computer-generated art.

2019 This poster advertising a museum retrospective of a French design firm's recent works emphasizes their flexibile work process. The shape is a severe abstraction of the firm's letters: bvh.

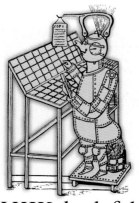

Timeline entries

cognoscat. Apudn
1460 Carolingian handwriting

Sibillas plurimi et m
1467 Sweynheim's "roman" typeface

Quare multarum
1470 Jenson's "roman" typeface

Expectes eadem
1500 Griffo's "italic" typeface

c110 Using chisels, stone-carvers invent serifs by finishing strokes with a perpendicular chisel hit.

c1450 Gutenberg makes the first movable type, styled after *Textura*, the dark hand lettering of Mainz in western Germany where he lived.

Gutenberg's font has 290 characters, including many ligatures and contractions to set perfectly justified lines.

c1460 Konrad Sweynheim brings movable type to Rome, where he adopts the region's preferred Carolingian writing style.

1880 Typesetting is a time-consuming hand skill. The idea that a machine could do it is mocked in this cartoon. Mechanically-*aided* typesetting was introduced in 1840, but *fully-mechanized* typesetting waited until 1960.

"The art of typography, like architecture, is concerned with beauty and utility in contemporary terms."
Bradbury Thompson (1911–1995)

GHIJKabcdefghij
1930 Eric Gill's *Perpetua*

GHIJKabcdefghijk
1932 Stanley Morison's *Times New Roman*

GHIJKabcdefghijkln
1948 Jackson Burke's *Trade Gothic*

GHIJKabcdefghijkln
1957 Max Miedinger's *Helvetica*

1930-1960 Technical improvements in metal typesetting abound. Use of sans serif types widens. Phototype is invented and develops, though isn't yet practically used. Still, available typefaces are limited.

SCULPTURES BY RHODA SPARBER
LIMERICKS BY HERB LUBALIN
PHOTOGRAPHED BY CARL FISCHER

1960s Phototype, developed decades earlier, leads to the fashion of tighter letterspacing in the 1960s because, for the first time since the invention of metal type in 1450, metal "shoulders" no longer exist.

FOUND ABCDI
1974 Dot matrix output at 72dpi

Blueprint lost in t
1985 *Lucida* is designed for 300dpi

EEEEEEEEEE
1990 *Beowolf* creates its glyphs

Magnetic old ren
1997 OpenType has 1,300 glyphs

1970-2000 Digital types arrive, putting type design and manufacture in the hands of anyone with a computer. Early types require 72dpi and later 300dpi optimization because that's what desktop printers could handle.

DIGITAL TYPEFACE DESIGN:
MORE STYLES
& More choices
for designers

1988 Computers and new programs like Fontographer allow anyone with an interest to design typefaces, increasing typestyle variety and the public profile and awareness of typography.

Galuanius in id ter

1535 Claude Garamont is first to sell his types to other printers

La crainte de l'Eter

1621 Jean Jannon's *Antiqua*

Quem ad finem

1724 William Caslon makes first English typeface

Catilina , tientiâ

1760 Giambattista Bodoni makes first "modern" typeface

1500-1800 Letters change stylistically, becoming sharper and more even in overall tone, taking advantage of ink and paper improvements.

ABCDE KLMNC STUVV &12345

c1815 Square serif types introduced, soon became known as "Egyptian" because Egyptian discoveries happened to be wildly popular at the time.

ABCDEFG HIJKLMN OPQRST UVWXYZ ÆŒ

1817 William Caslon IV was the first to develop a type without serifs (left), but it was Vincent Figgins in 1847 who took the idea, named it "sans serif," and made it

ABCDEFG HIJKLMN OPQRST UVWXYZ 1234567890

financially viable (right). Many type founders quickly followed his lead and created their own sans serif types.

Timeline 2: Letterforms and typefaces

Letterforms are the shapes of the characters we use to write. Letterforms can be made by writing or drawing them, whether by hand or on a computer. A typeface is a set of predrawn letterforms that are repeatable. Letterforms have existed for thousands of years (technically beginning with the Phœnicians in 1,200 BC, who first attached a glyph to each spoken sound), but the first *typeface* ever made was Gutenberg's in about 1450. ❙ Western letterforms come from two sources: capitals, or "majuscules," perfected in Roman inscriptions (and evolved from earlier Greek and Phœnician characters). Lowercase letters, or "minuscules," evolved in Medieval handwriting, before the invention of printing: letters were simplified by copyists so they could be written more quickly. ❙ Typography as practiced today has been shaped by technological developments as much as by artistic evolution in the intervening 575 years. Yes, typography has changed in response to fashion and style, but the important, lasting developments have been in response to improvements in ink and paper, ways to increase the speed of typesetting, and decreasing the cost of type's manufacture. Type is, after all, a business as well as an art form. E N D

"What type should I use?
The gods refuse to answer.
They refuse because they
do not know."
W.A. Dwiggins (1880–1956), who also drew this art, standing next to a disproportional metal letterform.

{:—) ‡:-((;-) !|-•
¶:-¸
(.-(
ß:-|
§,>)

2000 & 2010 Keystroke-combination emoticons are invented to add tone of voice to text. New letterforms address evolving needs like this "SarcMark" that indicates sarcasm.

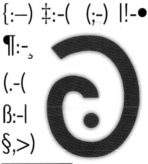 

2020 Quality typeface design is recognized for many world languages as Latin letterforms continue their steady stroll toward delicious exaggerations. *FR Kraken Slab* by Hungarian Béla Frank is one such.

Symbols

Logos

Lettermarks

Combination marks

Identifying marks, inaccurately grouped into a single category called "logos," is actually made of four distinct groups. *Symbols* have no accompanying words

nearby. *Lettermarks* may look like words but they cannot be pronounced. *Logos* are actual words. *Combination marks* are both a symbol and letterforms.

3,500 BC The first identifiers were Sumerian stamps. Three thousand years later cylinder seals, rolled across soft clay, showed individuals' stories as their signatures.

c1200 Merchants' marks are widely used to mark packages. Being diagrammatic, they communicate across dialects and languages, even to the then-many illiterates.

Representational signs
Realistic images of objects

Pictograms
Descriptive images of objects

Symbolic signs
Pictograms with new meanings

Ideograms
Nonrepresentational ideas

Diagrammatic signs
Nonrepresentational, arbitrary

Synonymic signs
Images with the same referent

Semiotics is the study of signs, both their form and their meaning. There are nine categories of marks, of which these six are the most important. Semiotics bridges philosophy, anthropology, and sociology.

1972 A logo is properly a mark that is a pronounceable word, like *Exxon*. The final is shown with Raymond Loewy's first sketch, done in 1966. After test marketing, the mark was introduced in 1972.

1978 Abstraction is used in symbols when the companies they describe are not easily illustrated. This solid-looking geometric mark is for a Brazilian banking group whose apparent solidity is most important.

1989 Stefan Geissbuhler designs the Time Warner mark. The final is a hand rendering because the computer-drawn studies were thought to be "too sterile."

1993 An airline's mark notable for its elegant *N*, *W*, and self-descriptive arrow created by negative space.

1502 Aldus Manutius, a Venetian printer, adopts the anchor-and-dolphin device for his books, symbolizing the proverb *Festina lente*, "Make haste slowly."

1750 Pottery and porcelain marks are pressed into the bottoms of pieces to indicate provenance and artisan. These samples are from Delft, Holland.

1933 Lucian Bernhard, a German designer perhaps best known for his typefaces, creates a body of lettermarks for companies in Europe and the U.S.

1971 Carolyn Davidson, a student at Portland State University, is paid $35 to design a logo for a new sneaker company.

Timeline 3: Logos

A logo is a mark that identifies a business or individual. "Logos" is Greek for "word," and it is a term that is widely and incorrectly used to indicate all trademarks. Marks may be symbols (marks without type), lettermarks (letters form the name), logos (a pronounceable word), or combination marks (symbol and letterforms together). ▌ What is right with your logo's design? Is it smart, beautiful, witty, elegant*, original, well designed, and appropriate? Does it use negative space well? Is it, in a word, good**? A good logo must be good on its own design merits – it has inherent aesthetic† quality – and it must be good for the client by satisfying their brand positioning, by meeting clearly stated business objectives, and by the designer's ability to explain why a design solution is right thinking. ▌ Though logos are part of a greater branding effort, every logo should be a perfect jewel of character-filled relationships that reveals the designer's mastery of the fundamental figure/ground relationship. **END**

Elegance is not the abundance of simplicity. *Elegance* is the absence of complexity. **Good* is a solution to a real or clearly stated problem. *Good* lasts for ten years. †*Aesthetics* = artistry plus inventiveness brought to a problem.

Handlettered logos, like these by Ed Benguiat, are examples of positive and negative shapes in perfect balance. Handlettering allows much greater customization than less flexible typesetting.

2006 Logos need regular updating to be contemporaneous. The earliest mark here is from 1901, the last is a retrofit to the company's earlier character, reclaiming its own heritage.

2009 Dynamic logos evolve to flexibly address multiple purposes and audiences. Melbourne, Australia's branding makeover by Landor Associates echoes MTV's 1981 identity that lasted for decades.

1400s-1800s Early posters are called "broadsheets" and announced festivals, lottery sales, political and religious statements, and even news.

1842 Wooden type is used in this one-color letterpress poster. In the absence of magazines, radio, and television, posters are the key advertising medium.

1881 A Belgian poster advertising a regional art exposition uses five colors: black, red, silver, gold, and green.

1892 Toulouse-Lautrec develops the poster as an art form, building on the pioneering work of fellow Parisian Jules Chéret.

1960s Psychedelic posters explored malleable, distorted letterforms and organic, art nouveau expression. This style (and the music it represents) is heavily inspired by the proliferation of recreational drugs.

A Parisian hanger pastes posters onto a kiosk, c1952. These kiosks are located in heavily-traveled spots where the greatest number of passersby will see the messages. Pre-television, this is visual mass communication.

1960s-1980s The Polish Poster School uses metaphor and figurative expression to slip messages past their Cold War communist watchdogs, as in this 1982 work for a play called "The Police" by M. Górowski.

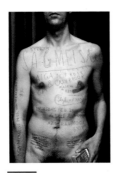

1999 Stefan Sagmeister's announcement of an in-person presentation is scratched into his own body. Highlighting written language itself at the turn of the millenium, it is a daring and memorable statement.

2003 Phillipe Apeloig's *Bateaux sur l'eau, rivières et canaux* shows partly "submerged" type as boats – and their reflections – on the river.

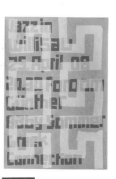

2009 Niklaus Troxler produces example after example of outstanding expressive typography, here a poster for a jazz concert with Greek accents.

1924 Alexey Brodovitch launches his career with the *Bal Banal* poster. Brodovitch goes on to become the creative spark at *Harper's Bazaar.*

1925 One of A.M. Cassandre's earliest posters stylizes the human body. Seven years later, his work for a restaurant reflects the cubist movement.

1948 Max Huber, a Swiss living in Milan, expresses motion, speed, and noise in bright colors.

1953 Josef Müller-Brockmann's International style expresses the cleanliness of Swiss design. The red and yellow colors are the grape juice brand's.

Timeline 4: Posters

Posters are the most simplified form of printed communication: picture and words joined to form a single message, printed on a flat sheet of paper. ▌The earliest human markings on cave walls were essentially posters: they were messages to be seen by the makers' community. Such work today would be called murals or graffiti. Each message had a necessarily limited audience. ▌With the invention of printing, posters were, for several hundred years, printed by letterpress black ink on white paper. Though simple by later standards, printing made one message postable in multiple locations for a far larger audience. ▌Posters really became the method of "broadcasting" in the late 1800s, as the development of color lithography gave an advantage to competing businesses' efforts to attract passersby. Artists brought their aesthetics to bear on what had largely been utilitarian workmanship: printers had been the designers. ▌Posters' effectiveness can be attributed to simplicity (of both the message and the design), large solid areas, and expressive use of letterforms. Making a message stand out is half the challenge. The other half is saying something of value. **END**

"A poster must do two things well: to be noticed and to hold your attention long enough to get the message across … and in that order." Emil Weiss (1896–1965).

2015 Interwoven lines of participating artists' names with severely extended "DH2.1" makes name recognition difficult on this Mexican poster. Abstraction is necessary to get attention: balancing it with legibility is art.

2018 "Good food for all!" is laboriously hand painted on top of Akzidenz Grotesk on each printed poster, making the origin of the graffiti unclear. Was it by a passerby or an intentional addition by the food festival sponsor?

1841 *Punch* magazine, named after an irreverent puppet invented by Samuel Pepys in 1662, first publishes its mix of politics and satirical humor in London.

1903 Illustrated news weeklies that combined a balance of type and imagery proliferated with the development of industrial society.

1927 A.M. Cassandre's cover for the Chemins de fer du Nord, the French railroad company, was used for every issue of the corporate magazine.

1929 Modernists transformed magazines with sans serif type and dynamic layouts, as in this early example by Joost Schmidt.

Broom is the best remembered of many artist-led periodicals in the 1920s and 1930s, each "on the vanguard of an intellectual movement."

"Advertising *made magazines larger because ads need large display space; it made magazines use illustrations; it required color printing and better paper; and it required huge circulations."*
M.F. Agha (1896–1978)

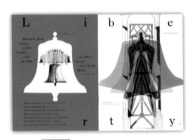

1953 Bradbury Thompson overlaps the four process colors as flat tints in his art direction of Westvaco *Inspirations*.

1964 George Lois creates series of covers for *Esquire* that sometimes use pictures of pictures, as in this memorial to JFK.

1984 *Emigre* magazine publishes entirely on the Macintosh platform. Using custom types, it influences the design community by enthusiastically employing emerging desktop publishing technology.

1992 Pushing the boundaries of legibility, *Ray Gun* defines its brand with chaos. David Carson's eagerness for tumultuous design sets this cutting-edge music magazine apart and leaves a lasting impact on publishing.

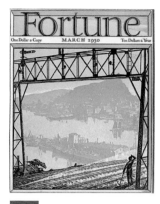

1930 Henry Luce starts his business magazine and promises "as beautiful a magazine as exists in the U.S." just four months after the October 1929 stock market crash.

1935 M.F. Agha introduces American readers to the first use of sans serif type, full-color photos, and full-bleed images at *Vogue* and *Vanity Fair*.

1936 Alexey Brodovitch becomes A.D. at *Harper's Bazaar* and begins a 42-cover relationship with Cassandre, who creates surrealist images like this one.

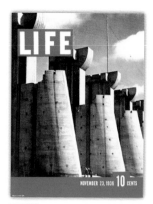

1936 Henry Luce buys *Life*, a dry 53-year-old general interest magazine and turns it into the first American news magazine to feature photojournalism.

Timeline 5: Magazines

Periodicals evolved from leaflets into pamphlets into almanacs until 1663, two hundred years after the invention of movable type. The first true magazine offering specific information for a specific audience was a German monthly, *Edifying Monthly Discussions*. This was a collection of summaries on art, literature, philosophy, and science. ❚ There are two basic types of magazines: consumer magazines, which cater to wider audiences; and trade magazines of highly specialized information. For economic reasons, the Internet has largely replaced trade magazines. ❚ "Magazine" means "storehouse," here specifically of editorial matter and advertising. Editorial content interests and attracts buyers, advertising is what supports the costs of production and distribution. Graphic design was first applied to advertisements to gain attention, then migrated as "illustrations" to the editorial pages that until then were pure text. ❚ In the competition for attention, a magazine's own special branding is becoming increasingly vital. Thus tight control of typography, patterning, and visual consistency are successful characteristics of an identifiable published "storehouse" of collections of information. **END**

2010 *Esquire* uses electronic paper to make the first moving magazine cover; the first Augmented Reality issue of a magazine; an iPhone app of the magazine; and an e-reader tablet version, all addressing new reader needs.

2010 Janet Froelich directs a series of imaginative iterations of the *NY Times* "T" logos on the covers of the *Style Magazine*. They are a demonstration of long-term reinvention and creative expression.

2020 All-type covers produced on screen convincingly emulate reality better than ever. The "degradation of free speech" is expressed powerfully using multiple samples of rust and peeling paint.

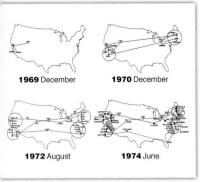

1969 December   **1970 December**

1972 August   **1974 June**

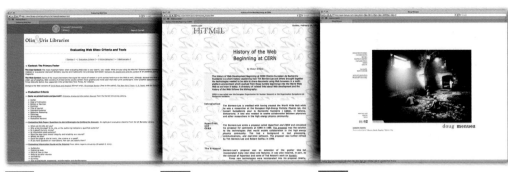

1969 The Internet is born as the "ARPANet." It is initially a small network connecting four West Coast universities. It grows exponentially.

1993 First generation sites typically have headline banners, text, and few graphics. Structure is only top-to-bottom and side-to-side.

1994 Second generation sites, now using HTML, fit more graphics, leading to overcrowded design with color panels, icons, and decorated buttons.

1996 Third generation sites can have the position and relationships of all elements specified on the page for greater type and layout control.

Lead the user through information or pages. Make the "next" and "back" buttons prominent. Don't give the user unnecessary options.

Web site designers must balance *content* (the information), *usability* (the interface and navigation), and *appearance* (the graphics and text).

Expected placement of menu and submenus is the top of the page. The user expects submenus to drop down from the primary listing.

Text and visuals can either be side by side or overlapping. Overlapped type over image is hard to read, so reduce contrast in the background to help the reader.

Sites are like magazines, though Web pages can be repeatedly changed. What works in print – emphasis, contrast, and space – works on the Web. Like magazines, site architecture must have both variety and consistency.

Divide information into equivalent chunks so each page offers about the same amount of content. Have a single focal point per page.

ARPANet Advanced Research Projects Agency Network
HTML Hyper Text Markup Language
CSS Cascading Style Sheets
HTTP Hypertext Transfer Protocol
CERN European Organization for Nuclear Research

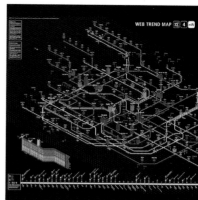

1999 Fourth generation sites have the usability and visual dynamism of interactive design because of CSS and high speed and wireless connections.

Sites are designed to produce "impressions," "click throughs," and "conversions," each of which is minutely measurable.

If one component of a site isn't producing expected results it can be instantly replaced with a different design to get higher performance.

This Web Trend Map, updated annually, shows use and traffic patterns on the Web. Everything digital can be measured and is scrutinized by various groups.

Timeline 6: Web sites

1989 Tim Berners-Lee proposes a system to allow physicists to communicate from remote locations, including HTML, HTTP, and rudimentary Web browser software that would work on any computer. **| 1991** The first Web server goes online at CERN in Switzerland. Within a year there are fifty servers worldwide; in a decade there are 24 million. **| 1993** Marc Andreesen develops Mosaic, the first Graphical User Interface (GUI) browser, making Web navigation easier. Mosaic ushers in the first of four generations of Web site designs. Slow modem speed and monochrome monitors shape early sites' design, which was basic top-to-bottom sequencing. At this point, interactive design is more advanced than Web design. **| 1994** The second generation begins with HTML, leading to icons instead of words, menus, and more graphics. Download speed over phone lines, poor typographic control and legibility, and compatible screen resolution are major concerns. **| 1996** Flash animation brings the third generation and an increase of visual content. **| 1999** The fourth generation features CSS, interactive content, and thoroughly customizable design. Interactive design and Web design are now equivalent. **END**

Visual hierarchy is crucial, especially on retail sites, where the progression through finding and buying must be as invisible a process as possible.

Design unity integrates name, logo, colors, tagline, fonts, and imagery on each page and the feel of the entire site with existing branding players.

Typefaces must be legible with large x-heights and open counters. Add space for easier on-screen reading. Use words rather than icons, which must be learned.

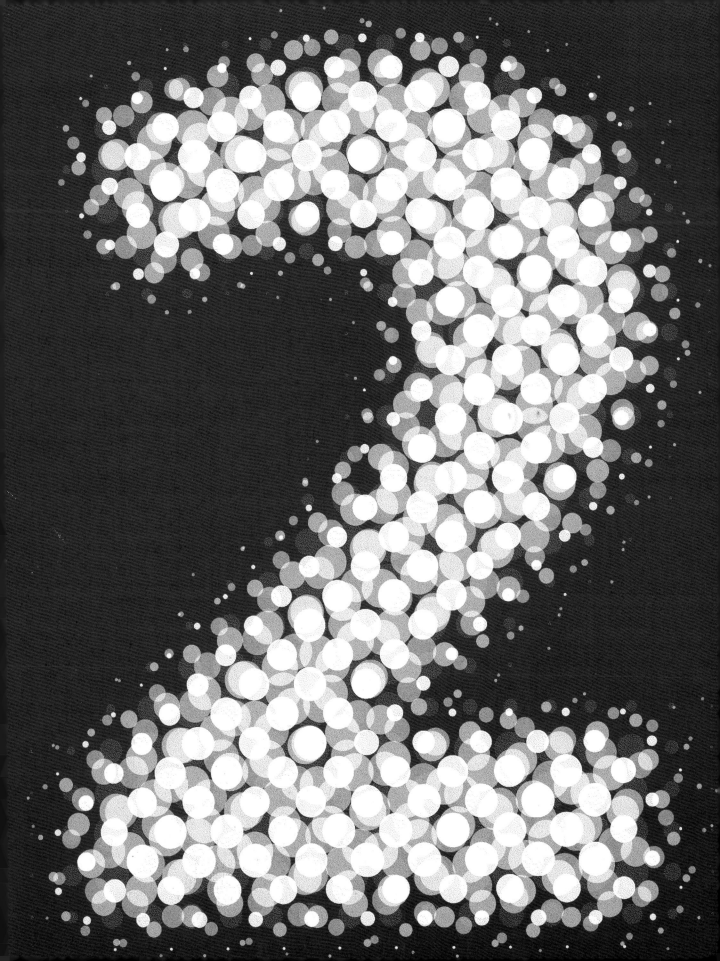

*"A (person) must not be
content to do things well,
but must also aim to do
them gracefully."*
Giovanni della Casa
from *Galateo*, or
The Book of Manners (1558)

How do you create a cannabis brand worthy of a legend?

Ashley Schofield
gardenstategh.com

Our agency, Garden State Greenhouse, was given the opportunity of a lifetime to create Garcia Hand Picked, the Jerry Garcia cannabis brand,

GARDEN STATE GREENHOUSE

in collaboration with Holistic Industries. Jerry Garcia was primarily known as the frontman for the Grateful Dead. He is beloved by millions of fans all over the world, but his spirit and legacy were much more than that: He was a writer, singer, musician, painter, diver, philosopher, and world explorer. It was essential that the brand capture and honor it all. What's more, his family wanted to honor their father and all that endures in his name with this brand. Authenticity was a critical business goal that we continue to honor as the brand evolves and grows.

GARCIA HAND PICKED

We learned three lessons on this creative journey
Lesson 1 Small details can impact big design decisions
Jerry's signature style was shabby black T-shirts and faded black jeans on stage; his wild, unkempt hair blowing in the wind; and an ever-present cigarette burning in a nearby ashtray. These seemingly small details informed the major decisions in the design approach we took – nothing too polished or precious. Garcia Hand Picked needed to embrace a sense of imperfection: slightly aged, rough edges, and a lot of black.

Advertising creative director Ashley Schofield has won dozens of awards for her agencies.

We use custom palettes for each strain so they are easily differentiated in a dispensary setting.

⬆ The brand has a hand-made, almost imperfect feel, and features Jerry's iconic signature. HAND PICKED is set in Garcia, a custom-designed typeface, which plays an important role in every aspect of the brand.

GARCIA

ABCDEFGHIJKLM
NOPQRSTUVWXYZ
1234567890

Lesson 2 Keep an open mind (and ear)

We're big believers in Collective Intelligence: When groups of people work together they can create ideas that cannot be created on an individual level. We were fortunate enough to collaborate with the Garcia family, who are very creative and have a keen eye for design. They brought ideas to every aspect of the branding process and had an incredible sense of family history, sharing stories about Jerry's favorite old leather club chair, the house on Fillmore Street where the Grateful Dead lived, and their favorite photograph of Jerry (the iconic Adrian Boot image taken in Egypt, 1978). That photo became the centerpiece for the brand, recreated with a swirling marble texture that evokes rhythm, freedom, and the organic billows of cannabis smoke. These pictures and stories helped inform the color palette, textures, typography, and main imagery.

We filled the image with a fluid, marbled pattern that mimics the wind in Jerry's hair and his ability to move fluidly between music, writing, drawing, and painting.

The tamper tape is designed to feel like a concert ticket featuring Jerry's iconic hand print.

Black plays an important role in the brand: Jerry wore all black on stage. The packaging uses solid black, earth-friendly paperboard throughout.

Three preliminary studies are below. The final packaging interiors (right) feature original art by Jerry: art, music, and set lists. Each image was selected to reflect that strain's effect.

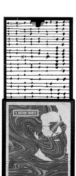

Lesson 3 Think big, but ground it in authenticity

Jerry was a free spirit and explorer at heart. He was happiest on the road, playing gigs large and small. This inspired one of the brand's most ambitious ideas: the creation of Bertha, a vintage Airstream trailer that would become a traveling brand experience. Every aspect of Bertha was painstakingly thought out: the miniature replica of the famous Wall of Sound, the reclaimed wood shelving, the eclectic light fixtures, and the Turkish fabric on the seating. It was important that the fans felt authentically connected with Jerry's spirit when they entered. We also created every piece of merchandise and swag available on Bertha, making her a truly immersive brand experience from start to finish. We're most proud that Jerry's fans have embraced Garcia Hand Picked, which is no easy feat and a nod to the authenticity we worked so carefully and lovingly to create. **EoGD3**

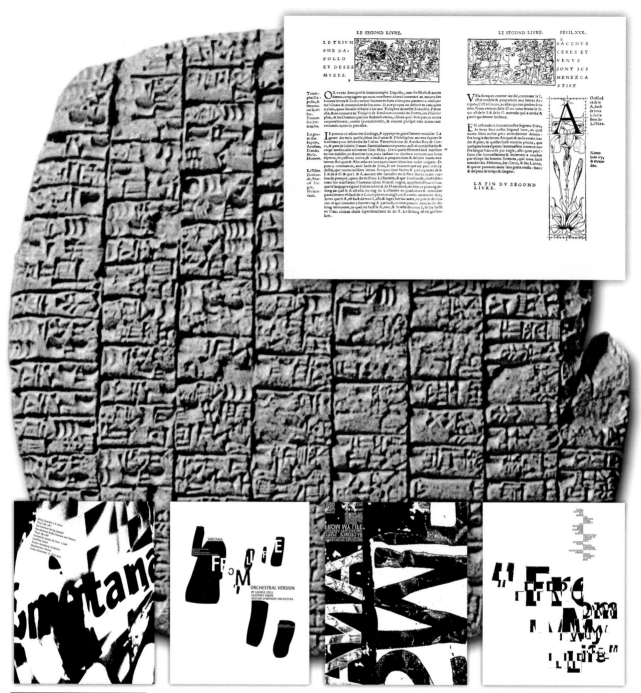

Technological limitations have *forced* unity on design. Sumerian cuneiform scribes had only wedge-shaped sticks and soft clay and fifteenth-century printers had only a few handmade fonts (top). This example is from Geofroy Tory's *Champ Fleury: The Art and Science of the Proportion of the Attic or Ancient Roman Letters, According to the Human Body and Face.* Tory (c1480-1533) completed the ninety-six page comparison of perfect proportion between the human body and letterforms in 1529. *Champ fleury* means "flowery fields," or "paradise."

Intentional use of similarity and contrast are shown in these four student studies of typographic systems and space.

If there is just one thing you attempt to do as a designer, it must be to create unity among the pieces and parts with which you are working. Make the type relate to the image, make the image relate to the type. Take the attributes – or even just one attribute – from one element and apply it to the others. The point is to make a singular message, a message that looks pre-digested and processed in a way that encourages sampling and, perhaps, involvement from the reader. Fooling around with bits and pieces and settling for *dis*unity is hardly a service to your audience.

4 Unity and space

U nity contributes orderliness and coherency and a civilized state of things generally. Whereas the contrast family are all savages, more or less. William A. Dwiggins* (1880–1956)

One goal of graphic design is to achieve visual unity or harmony. Eugene Larkin, in the introduction to his book *Design: The Search for Unity*, writes, "The minimal requirement in visual design is ... the organization of all the parts into a unified whole. All the parts, no matter how disparate, must be reconciled so they support each other." In other words, elements must be made to work together with the greatest interest to the reader and with the least resistance from the reader.

Because they had very limited resources, the earliest designers achieved visual continuity rather easily: it was imposed on them by lack of choice of materials. Today, with the abundant resources available as digital material, we must exercise internal restraint to achieve harmonious, unified design.

Similarity and contrast 81
Balance similarity (which can produce boring sameness) with contrast (which can produce noisy busyness).

Using space to create unity 85
Consistent, defined spaces join and add a sense of organization.

Caledonia
Electra
Metro

*__Dwiggins__ coined the term "graphic design" in 1922, designed hundreds of books and eighteen typefaces, and wrote the first book on advertising design.

designers

Design Management XV

How do designers and writers work best together? How can writers help shape the content and effectiveness of your work? Is your work really designed to be read or seen? How do you find the appropriate writer? How are a writer's fees determined? What can you do if you are given mediocre text by a client? What are the pitfalls? What about rewrites?

Join us for a panel discussion of these very pertinent issues. Each panelist has had extensive exposure to writer/designer collaborations.

Panelists

John Berendt
Author, monthly columnist for Esquire, past editor of New York Magazine, writer for Dick Cavett, David Frost and corporate clients.

Rita Jacobs
Writer and Editorial Consultant. Work includes magazine assignments, books, annual reports and corporate publications for The Limited, Knoll, Merrill Lynch and Champion Paper.

Joel Margulies
Sr. VP, Creative Director, Lintas: NY. Previously creative director at DDB Needham. Extensive experience in retail advertising, promotions and integrated communications, including programs for Polaroid, Seagrams and IBM.

Leslie Smolan
Designer and Principal, Carbone Smolan Associates. Designer of the "Day in the Life..." series, a textbook reading program for Houghton Mifflin; a variety of acclaimed print communications and environmental graphics.

Reading between the lines: designers & writers

Time and Location

Wednesday March 31, 1993
Fashion Institute of Technology
Katie Murphy Amphitheatre
227 West 27 Street
at Seventh Avenue

6:00 - 7:00 pm
Hors d'oeuvres and Wine

7:00 - 9:30 pm
Introduction
Panel Discussion and
Audience Participation

Registration

$40.00 - AIGA/NY
Chapter Members
$60.00 - General Public
F.I.T. students free with valid ID

Space is limited. Reservations are on a first come first serve basis. Design Management Seminars have been sold out in the past; we suggest you register early.

Registration

Please complete the registration form (on reverse side) and send with your check to:
AIGA/NY Chapter
545 West 45 Street
New York, NY 10036-3409
212-246-7060
212-246-7063 Hotline

Acknowledgements

This announcement was made possible through the following contributions:

Printing
Applied Graphics Technologies

Paper
Recycled stock donated by
Mohawk Paper Mills, Inc.

Typography
Typogram, New York

Program Coordinators
Michael Gericke
Gail Wiggin

&writers

Activated white space and dramatic cropping of letterforms make this poster's point (top) for the AIGA NY.

Image and type must share more than mere proximity. Their forms should be similar or share basic characteristics. This theatrical poster by Lech Majewski marries scratchy type and lettering with hand-cut illustration.

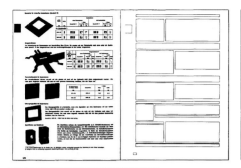 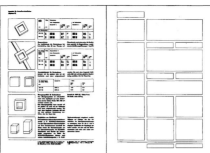 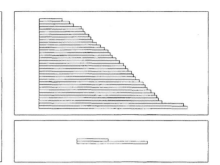

Standardized column widths simplify what is an overly complex page. The original is a haphazard, make-it-up-as-you-go assembly of pieces that may function but does not add in any way to the easy scanability or user's absorption of the material. While there may be nothing wrong with the "before," there is definitely nothing right with it either. The diagrams above right show the number of column widths after the redesign: from thirty-four to just two. Such simplicity at once builds unity and signals distinct kinds of information.

Similarity and contrast

Dramatic contrasts, scrupulous similarity, active white space, and a great idea are the primary attributes of well-designed documents. An environment of similarity or consistency is necessary to make a focal point visible. Yet design consistency should not be so unchanging that it stifles variety or becomes boring. It must express predigestion of the content to make important facets clear. Without similarity, an environment of quietness in which important elements can be seen will not exist. On the other hand, without contrast, a design will be uneventful and uncommunicative. Achieving a balance between similarity and contrast is necessary for effective, dynamic design. There are five ways to develop an environment of similarity:

- Keep it simple. Eliminate clutter and affect. Don't fill holes by inserting garbage, or at least material your reader might *think* is garbage. Having 70 percent of your material read because you have withheld the 30 percent that is less important is far better than having only 5 percent read of everything you've shoved on the page.
- Build in a unique internal organization by using an unusual or eccentric grid system.

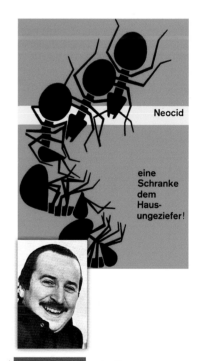

The strongest unity is created when their meanings are fused, as in this clear, self-explanatory mark.

"The problem, not a theory nor a style, determines the solution."
Karl Gerstner (1930–2017)

POSITION
TOP : BOTTOM
HIGH : LOW
RIGHT : LEFT
ABOVE : BELOW
IN FRONT : BEHIND
RHYTHMIC : RANDOM
ISOLATED : GROUPED
NEARBY : DISTANT
CENTERED : OFF CENTER
ALIGNED : INDEPENDENT
IN : OUT

SIZE & SCALE
BIG : LITTLE
LONG : SHORT
WIDE : NARROW
EXPANDED : CONDENSED
DEEP : SHALLOW

FORM
SIMPLE : COMPLEX
BEAUTIFUL : UGLY
ABSTRACT : REPRESENTATIONAL
DISTINCT : AMBIGUOUS
GEOMETRIC : ORGANIC
RECTILINEAR : CURVILINEAR
SYMMETRICAL : ASYMMETRICAL
WHOLE : BROKEN

DIRECTION
VERTICAL : HORIZONTAL
PERPENDICULAR : DIAGONAL
FORWARD : BACKWARD
STABILITY : MOVEMENT
CONVERGING : DIVERGING
CLOCKWISE : COUNTERCLOCKWISE
CONVEX : CONCAVE
ROMAN : ITALIC

COLOR
BLACK : COLOR
LIGHT : DARK
WARM : COOL
BRIGHT : DULL
ORGANIC : ARTIFICIAL
SATURATED : NEUTRAL

STRUCTURE
ORGANIZED : CHAOTIC
ALIGNED : FREELY PLACED
SERIF : SANS SERIF
MECHANICAL : HAND DRAWN

DENSITY
TRANSPARENT : OPAQUE
THICK : THIN
LIQUID : SOLID

TEXTURE
FINE : COARSE
SMOOTH : ROUGH
REFLECTIVE : MATTE
SLIPPERY : STICKY
SHARP : DULL
FUZZY : BALD

GRAVITY
LIGHT : HEAVY
STABLE : UNSTABLE

SPACE
FILLED : EMPTY
ACTIVE : PASSIVE
ADVANCING : RECEDING
NEAR : FAR
CONTAINED : UNRESTRICTED
2-D : 3-D

Every contrast pairing is an opportunity for both similarity and contrast (top). For example, consistent use of bigness, instead of contrasting it with smallness, can unify a multi-spread story.

Dissimilarity is inherent in the mixture of elements a designer uses: things start out not being alike. Sophisticated design is a result of *in-*

tentional contrasts, as when red typesetting is emulated as white bars of the same height and width, and pieces of a chair are replaced with equivalently-sized lines of

type. Such designs work because they have a balance of similarity and difference: parts are different but have been made to look similar.

Similarity through overlapping ("LANDSCAPE") lets something stand out as an anomaly, or focal point. The small centered element ("DISTANCE") is the focal point.

The intentional lack of a focal point is achieved by making elements nearly the same. These letters blend in among ink spots of about the same size and color.

Unity occurs when a treatment is given to both type and image. Severe cropping – to abstraction and near illegibility – is applied to both elements in this poster.

Unity occurs when the negative and positive spaces define each other.

■ Manipulate shapes of images and type to create design unity despite the fact that they are inherently different languages. Color, texture, and direction can also be used by building on attributes of the image. More difficult – and far more effective – communication comes from unifying the meanings of images and type.

■ Express continuity from page to page and issue to issue. The handling of typographic elements, spaces between elements, rules and borders, indents, illustrations and photos, and charts and graphs should show confirmation of a plan.

■ Develop a style manual and stick with your format. Straying absorbs valuable preparation time and makes truly important variations less visible. Don't try to be different to be "creative." Worthwhile originality grows out of the special needs and materials at hand.

To make the important part stand out from its surroundings, select from the ten contrast categories shown at the top of the facing page.

Unity can be achieved by manipulating proximity, similarity, repetition, and theme with variations:

■ *Proximity* (also called *grouping* or *relative nearness*): The simplest way to achieve unity. Ele-

Continuity from page to page is important so a multi-page document doesn't look like random spreads bound together. Balance consistency with variety to keep it interesting, as in this museum catalogue.

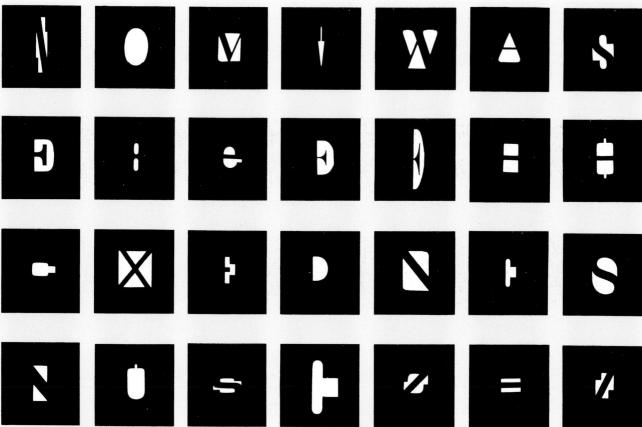

Consistent spacing between elements reduces clutter. Each of these four compositions has precisely the same content. Arranging the pieces on a well-planned grid allows for a wonderful variety of impressions.

The negative space within letterforms from a variety of typefaces are illustrated in a series by Emil Ruder. Because they are sourced from dissimilar typefaces, the powerful shapes centered on black squares expose a way to recognize letterforms freshly.

Unity through proximity: the type is impacted by the fist (*extreme* proximity) in this rock concert poster, which shows the band's punk and country sides in attitude.

Unity through similarity: purple type corresponds with other purple type, overriding the size contrasts and making a message within a message.

Unity through repetition: this Web site uses repeated button size – four rectangles beneath the photo and seven icons beneath them. The centered organization and limited typeface combination (one serif and one sans, three sizes of each) contribute to the sense of order.

ments that are physically close together are seen as related.

- *Similarity* (also called *correspondence*): Elements that share similarity of size, color, shape, position, or texture are seen as alike. The reverse of similarity is intentional contrast. Alignment is an aspect of similarity in which elements that line up appear related.

- *Repetition and rhythm* (related to *similarity*): Any element that is repeated provides unity. The repetition may be positioning, size, color, or use of rules, background tints, and boxes. Repetition produces rhythm, which can be exploited by breaking it meaningfully.

- *Theme with variations*: Simple repetition without variety becomes boring in its sameness. Alteration of a theme retains design connectedness while providing diversity.

Using space to create unity

White space and the consistent use of type (see Section 4: Type) are the two most useful tools to create unity. Order the space between things. Elements that are physically close together look like they belong together. This is the Law of Proximity. Elements that touch and overlap look even more

Unity through theme showing two sides of one idea: here making and hearing sounds. What makes it a powerful image is the size relationship taking precedence over correct scale to yield one image out of two.

"It's easier to copy someone else than to find out how to avoid sounding like someone else." Ornette Coleman (1930–2015)

In the early sixties, a psychologist at Yale University named Stanley Milgram did a series of notorious experiments that explored the dynamics of hierarchical relationships, ones where someone was in charge and someone else was following orders. He wanted to find out how far someone would follow the orders of another person if he perceived that person's authority as legitimate.

The experiments had many variations, but they all basically went like this. Milgram asked people to volunteer for an experiment they were told was about the relationship of learning and punishment. The volunteers, who came from all walks of life, were each paid $4.50 and were shown the same setup when they arrived in Milgram's lab.

They were introduced to another person they were told was a fellow volunteer. This second person was to serve as the "learner" and the subject was to act as "teacher." The teacher would be directed by the experimenter to read a series of word pairs to the learner, and then test the learner on his memory. For each answer the learner got wrong, the teacher was to administer to him an electric shock. This would be done with a control panel with thirty switches ranging from 15 to 450 volts, labeled in increments of "slight shock," "moderate shock," "strong shock," and on up to "extreme intensity shock," "danger: severe shock," and finally the cryptic and presumably frightening label "XXX." For each wrong answer, the volunteer teacher was to increase the shock level by one notch.

Of course, the whole setup was an illusion. The shock panel was a convincing-looking but harmless prop; the fellow volunteer, the "learner," was an employee of Milgram's who was particularly good at screaming in agony when receiving the imaginary shocks. The purpose of the exercise was not to study learning, but to study obedience: Milgram wanted to find out how far people would go up the scale, how much pain they would inflict on a fellow human being, just because someone else told them to.

Before he began, Milgram asked his students and fellow psychologists to predict how many people would administer the highest shock. The answers were almost always the same: at the most, one or two out of one hundred. Milgram himself, then, was surprised when almost two-thirds, 64%, of the subjects, did as they were told and went all the way to the top of the scale.

Milgram did a lot of variations in the experiment to try to drive the number down. He moved the setting from Yale to a tawdry-looking storefront; he had the learner complain of a possibly fatal heart condition; he fixed it so the subject actually had to hold the learner's hand down on a "shock plate." None of it made much difference. No matter what, about half of the volunteers administered all the shocks to the helpless learner.

These experiments are fairly well known to the general public, and the most common moral drawn from them is something like, "People are capable of anything if they're given an excuse to do it." However, this is a misinterpretation: most of the subjects, even the fully obedient ones, were anything but cheerful as they followed the experimenter's commands. In fact, it was common for subjects to protest, weep, or beg hysterically to be permitted to break off the experiment. Still, the obedient majority, prodded calmly by the experimenter, would pull themselves together, do what had to be done, and administer the shocks.

Of course, designers are regularly paid a lot more than $4.50 to do things a lot less overtly heinous than administering a 450-volt shock to a fellow human being. Occasionally they help promote a cause or product they truly don't believe in, or design something to intentionally deceive the public. But these dilemmas are fairly rare.

Most commonly, what most of us have done at one time or another is make something a little stupider or a little uglier than we really thought it ought to be. We've had good reasons: we need the money, we need the experience, we don't want to jeopardize the relationship, we know it's wrong, we have no choice. This would sound familiar to Dr. Milgram. "Some subjects were totally convinced of the wrongness of

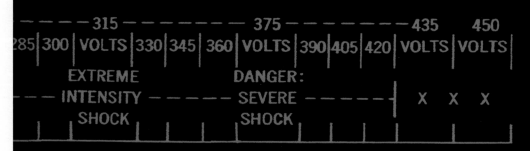

In the early sixties, a psychologist at Yale University named Stanley Milgram did a series of notorious experiments that explored the dynamics of hierarchical relationships, ones where someone was in charge and someone else was following orders. He wanted to find out how far someone would follow the orders of another person if he perceived that person's authority as legitimate.

The experiments had many variations, but they all basically went like this. Milgram asked people to volunteer for an experiment they were told was about the relationship of learning and punishment. The volunteers, who came from all walks of life, were each paid $4.50 and were shown the same setup when they arrived in Milgram's lab.

They were introduced to another person they were told was a fellow volunteer. This second person was to serve as the "learner" and the subject was to act as "teacher." The teacher would be directed by the experimenter to read a series of word pairs to the learner, and then test the learner on his memory. For each answer the learner got wrong, the teacher was to administer to him an electric shock. This would be done with a control panel with thirty switches ranging from 15 to 450 volts, labeled in increments of "slight shock," "moderate shock," "strong shock," and on up to "extreme intensity shock," "danger: severe shock," and finally the cryptic and presumably frightening label "XXX." For each wrong answer, the volunteer teacher was to increase the shock level by one notch.

Of course, the whole setup was an illusion. The shock panel was a convincing-looking but harmless prop; the fellow volunteer, the "learner," was an employee of Milgram's who was particularly good at screaming in agony when receiving the imaginary shocks. The purpose of the exercise was not to study learning, but to study obedience: Milgram wanted to find out how far people would go up the scale, how much pain they would inflict on a fellow human being, just because someone else told them to.

Before he began, Milgram asked his students and fellow psychologists to predict how many people would administer the highest shock. The answers were almost always the same: at the most, one or two out of one hundred. Milgram himself, then, was surprised when almost two-thirds, 64%, of the subjects, did as they were told and went all the way to the top of the scale.

Milgram did a lot of variations in the experiment to try to drive the number down. He moved the setting from Yale to a tawdry-looking storefront; he had the learner complain of a possibly fatal heart condition; he fixed it so the subject actually had to hold the learner's hand down on a "shock plate." None of it made much difference. No matter what, about half of the volunteers administered all the shocks to the helpless learner.

These experiments are fairly well known to the general public, and the most common moral drawn from them is something like, "People are capable of anything if they're given an excuse to do it." However, this is a misinterpretation: most of the subjects, even the fully obedient ones, were anything but cheerful as they followed the experimenter's commands. In fact, it was common for subjects to protest, weep, or beg hysterically to be permitted to break off the experiment. Still, the obedient majority, prodded calmly by the experimenter, would pull themselves together, do what had to be done, and administer the shocks.

Of course, designers are regularly paid a lot more than $4.50 to do things a lot less overtly heinous than administering a 450-volt shock to a fellow human being. Occasionally they help promote a cause or product they truly don't believe in, or design something to intentionally deceive the public. But these dilemmas are fairly rare.

Most commonly, what most of us have done at one time or another is make something a little stupider or a little uglier than we really thought it ought to be. We've had good reasons: we need the money, we need the experience, we don't want to jeopardize the relationship, we know it's wrong, we have no choice. This would sound familiar to Dr. Milgram. "Some subjects were totally convinced of the wrongness of

Column bottoms may be "scalloped," or made uneven at the bottoms, to create an informal structure (top), as in this spread from a booklet by Michael Bierut. Column *bottoms*, like right edges of text columns, may be uneven because readers are not hindered by their unevenness. But uneven column *tops* and ragged *left* edges of text are disturbing because beginnings are not immediately findable. The lower example, edited from the original, is an arrangement that makes scanning and reading much more challenging (ignore the fact that the text is actually wrong reading: that is purely a function of image manipulation expediency). Such an arrangement presents visual noise for the reader. This is antithetical to the purpose of design: to stream information effortlessly off the page.

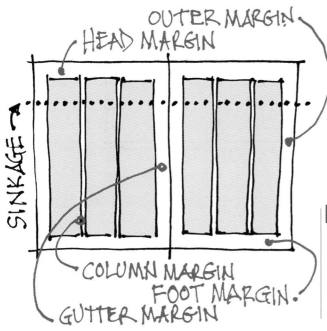

OUTER MARGIN

HEAD MARGIN

SINKAGE

COLUMN MARGIN
FOOT MARGIN
GUTTER MARGIN

Head sinkage is a variation of one of the five margins on a page: head, outer, gutter, foot, and column. Sinkage is a consistent *deep* space at the top of a page or design, as above. In magazines, it can be used on selected pages, typically departments, to make them stand apart from the advertising and feature pages.

related. To create design unity, spaces between elements should be equal and consistent in a design.

Use white space on the perimeters of designs – in outside margins, head sinkage, and column bottoms – where it is visible and where it will aid in defining the design's personality.

Margins are the spaces around the perimeter of a page. They are the frame around the "live area." Wide outer margins may be used for attention-getting graphics like small images and secondary display type. A gutter is the space between columns of type and between pages in a bound document. Space between columns should not be so narrow as to be mistaken for a word space, yet not so wide that it becomes an interruption. Text should generally have a one-pica column space. Rag right text may have a smaller column space.

Column bottoms may be left uneven if their unevenness looks purposeful. Uneven column bottoms, also called scalloped columns, must differ in length by at least three lines so it doesn't look accidental. Having intentionally uneven white space at the bottoms of columns is unobtrusive and makes editing significantly easier because there is flexibility designed into the system. **EoGD3**

Spaces between elements must be carefully organized or else visual confusion and ambiguity result. The top mark, introduced in 2015, is the latest iteration of the AT&T brand mark.

"Space is the glue, *the common denominator of a visual composition."* Ken Hiebert (1930–)

Shapes in the poster on the facing page for "Almost Real," a Brazilian play about a talking dog, chickens, and a fruitless fig tree have been extracted and simplified,

then reversed (above). Without the color and details, this allows us to see the relative sizes, alignments, spacing between, and spaces around the elements.

Beethoven's Symphony No.3 is a staple of orchestras the world over. Performed countless times, the "Eroica" has been recorded 258 times, averaging almost

three recordings every year. What does this piece of music say to its audiences that is so powerful? In part, its tension and relaxation cause an emotional reaction.

The seven design components

The essence of taste is suitability. See how it expresses the mysterious demand of the eye and mind for symmetry, harmony, and order.
Edith Wharton (1862–1937)

The purpose of design is emphatically *not* to fill up all the space. Don't let overabundance make the information in your design impenetrable. Allow moments of comparative respite by leaving some space empty. As Steven Ledbetter, music historian and critic, wrote, "Beethoven's control of relative tension and relaxation throughout the gigantic architectural span [of the first movement of his Symphony No.3] remains one of the most awe–inspiring accomplishments in the history of music."

Organize elements so all parts fit together to make unity, or an integrated whole. This cumulative perception is gestalt. Organize elements by their shared subject matter, shape, or color.

Every visual design element has two aspects: its meaning and its shape. Addressing shape, gen-

Design is a process whose solution evolves 93
It takes repeated passes to recognize unresolved relationships in a design.

Diagrams 95
An illustration of relationships, not numbers.

1 | 7 Space 97
First among equals.

2 | 7 Unity and gestalt 97
Creating agreement out of contrast.

3 | 7 Shape: point, line, and plane 103
Separate from its meaning, every design element has a shape.

4 | 7 Scale and dominance 107
Comparative size and the focal point.

5 | 7 Hierarchy 107
Three levels of order are optimal.

6 | 7 Balance 109
A state of equilibrium, whether centered or not.

7 | 7 Color 111
A functional guiding tool.

SPACE

UNITY

SHAPE

DOMINANCE

HIERARCHY

BALANCE

COLOR

Raum braucht der Mensch

Der Mensch sehnt sich nach Weite und Freiheit. Doch meist ist er eingekeilt: auf der Straße, in den Ferien, bei der Arbeit, in seiner Wohnsituation. Deshalb ist es heute wichtiger denn je, sich auch privaten Freiraum zu schaffen. Ob im Haus mit Garten oder einer geräumigen Eigentumswohnung: Als Hypothekenbank können wir Ihnen dabei helfen, sich den Raum zu schaffen, den Sie sich wünschen. München, Telefon: 089/5112-371/287.

◆

SÜDDEUTSCHE BODENCREDITBANK
AKTIENGESELLSCHAFT   HYPOTHEKENBANK

München Berlin Dortmund Dresden Düsseldorf Erfurt Frankfurt/Main Freiburg Hamburg Hannover Leipzig Stuttgart

The seven design components – space, unity, shape, dominance, hierarchy, balance, and color – are used as sliding switches, like a lamp's dimmer, that help achieve visible, value-added design.

Space is what man needs

Man longs for distance and freedom. But mostly he is wedged in: on the street, on vacation, at work, in his living environment. That is why it is more important than ever today to get some personal space. Whether it is the house or the garden or a spacious condo apartment: as a mortgage bank we can help you create the space you wish for.

South German Bodencreditbank

Gestalt is the perception of an integrated whole. A drawing of eyes, ears, and mouth compares to a head in which the entirety is more important than its individual features.

Space is defined by these intersecting solids and voids, some of the human head, used to display eyeglasses, giving them countertop visibility.

Three of the seven design components in use here are space (surrounding the words), unity (every letter but one is parted hair), and scale (LIVING is de-emphasized).

Three of the seven design components in use here are space (surrounding the knife), unity (everything is horizontal and centered), and color (warm wood color used in headline).

erally thought of as the perimeter of any object, must be considered when creating unity. The most basic shapes are point, line, and plane. These can be exploited if consciously considered.

Good design necessitates that one element dominate the others and provide a focal point, a place for the viewer to begin engagement with the message. Choosing that emphasis suggests a design's starting point. Scale, or comparative size, is closely related to dominance.

Motivate the reader by arranging the elements in a logical hierarchy. What should they see first: image or words? What is the second-most important element? After that second level, all the rest is equivalently subordinate because at that point a potential reader is already either in or out.

Function in design is paramount. Consider each element in its context. Balance one large or bright element against a few smaller or muted ones.

Use color strategically to show off what is important. It has greater value than merely decoration.

While you choose to have more or less of each of the seven design components, it isn't possible to select just one and not use the others. They come bundled as a flexible group.

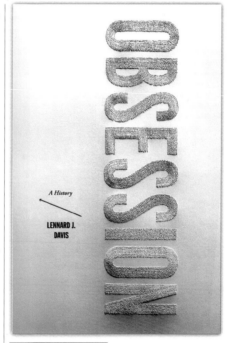

Three of the seven design components in use here are space (dedicated to subhead and author area), shape (point line plane rendered in OBSESSION, which is made of dots), and color (entirely monochromatic). The title word made from an obsessive pin-pricks-from-the-back process is a brilliant expression of the word's meaning.

Design evolution allows time to grow solutions from familiarity with the materials at hand. As familiarity grows, the process becomes more interesting, design relationships become evident, and abstraction can be explored. The particular exercise shown here in the first, one of thirty intermediate steps, and the final step, requires identifying elements in a grayscale image on sheets of tracing paper, converting them into geometric variations, applying texture to the planes, and developing dynamic compositions with the results. The process determines the outcome: final studies could not have been realized without the intermediate steps.

Readers operate subconsciously on these design truisms:

- ■ We read from left to right.
- ■ We start at the top and work down the page.
- ■ Pages in a publication or Web site are related.
- ■ Closeness connects while distance separates.
- ■ Big and dark is more important; small and light is less important.
- ■ Fullness should be balanced with emptiness.
- ■ Everything has a shape, *including emptiness*.

Designers have different sensibilities and preferences, which is why five designers given the same pictures and copy would create five different designs. But given a single message to get across, we expect they would develop equivalent solutions.

Design is a process whose solution evolves

Uncovering and recognizing design relationships takes time. It's very like the experience of walking into a dark room: it takes time to accustom our eyes to the materials at hand. Design must evolve from basic relationships to more complex, more refined relationships. Start the process by becoming intimately familiar with the content. Read the text. Understand *what* is being said. Understand, too, *why* it was written and why it is being published.

Brand marks take time and multiple "passes" to resolve. First studies explore a variety of directions, second studies explore one or two directions deeply, and the final study is a refinement – or sometimes a combination of two finalists. Here, the final mark is a timid iteration of the oversized "O" in the second set of studies with the addition of a black bar.

Labels on the diagram: 6" x 6" WIRE MESH, 6" CONCRETE, SOLID SUBSOIL, EXPANSION JOINT, CONCRETE WALL, FROST LINE

An "extension drawing" diagram from a 1958 architectural magazine shows both the "what" and the "how" of constructing a sunken pool. This technique makes it faster to analyze and easier to understand than if the source photo and the illustration were side by side.

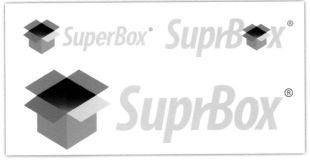

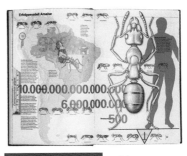

Design evolution calls for iterations of an idea until all unnecessary details are removed. Though only three studies are shown, the crucial step in this mark's evolution

is the removal of the "*e*," which makes the name unique, and the customization of the "*r*" to align with the crossbar of the "*B*."

A diagram may be an exploded view, as shown here Adding callouts is necessary when the ingredients of the object are less recognizable than this sandwich.

This German book on biological comparisons uses numbers, illustrations, maps and captions to tell its story. This book is essentially one continuous diagram.

Then find out *who* is going to read it and what the reader's motivation and interests are. Finally, develop a strategy for expressing it to the reader's greatest advantage.

Design evolution should proceed on two levels simultaneously. One is to seek relationships of meaning, which appeals to the reader's need for understanding. The other is to seek relationships of form, which appeals to the reader's need for attraction. Balancing these two ensures effective visual communication. Design is spoiled more often by the designer being overly cautious rather than being overly bold. Dare to be bold.

Diagrams

A diagram is a simplified, schematic drawing that describes the workings of the subject. This can be a chart, a plan, or a map. "Diagram," like "illustration," is a general term that can mean a broad range of executions. A diagram is different than an illustration because it must describe meaning. A diagram may be a chart, yet it is different than a chart because it describes qualitative matter, that is, relationships, while a chart exclusively describes quantitative, or numerical, matter.

A diagram uses all seven design components

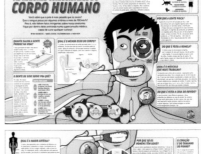

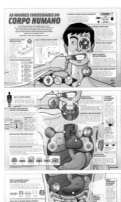

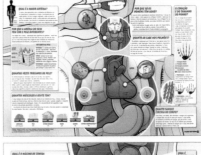

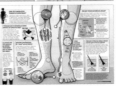

A diagram may be a complex illustration with multiple detailed callouts as shown here, a pie chart, a "function graph" (X and Y axes), a map, engineering blueprints and architectural sketches, or simple shapes connected by

lines or arrows. In this Brazilian feature story, four successive spreads diagram the human body. The spreads were published in a necessary, though startling, *horizontal* progression. They are shown stacked vertically here.

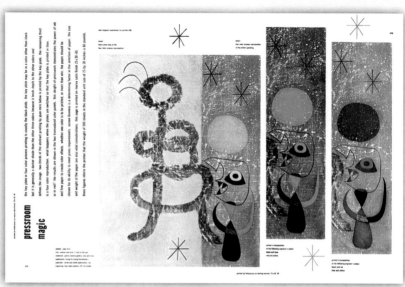

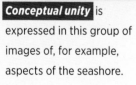

Conceptual unity is expressed in this group of images of, for example, aspects of the seashore.

Visual unity exists in elements that have similarity of form, for example, these elements that are all vertical. Even the text has been set in vertical lines in this 1951 magazine spread designed by Bradbury Thompson.

Design unity must be imposed on unalike elements. A designer is frequently tasked with finding ways to unify elements that don't at first appear to share visual characteristics, as in this magazine opening spread.

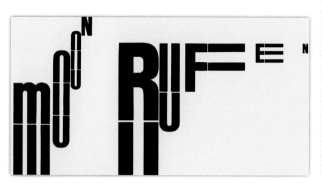

Wolfgang Weingart leaves substantial areas empty as he exaggerates letterforms by adding vertical and horizontal bars. "Moon Howling" is a 1972 study using wood letters. He argued perfect legibility was an unattainable goal and explored the expressiveness of type's image and semantics, its inseparable visual meaning.

Space can be an interrupting shape. The shapes of triangles (or tail-less arrows) and their repetition gives a distinct "sparkling" gestalt to this poster.

Space attracts viewers, especially when it is an evocative shape, as are these eggs in an otherwise unremarkably centered, silhouetted chicken.

just as *any* design does. A diagram, however, uses them on a finite, micro level. A Web site or publication uses the seven design components on a broad, macro level.

The seven design components

Wolfgang Weingart, the Swiss designer and design educator, said, "I am convinced that ... investigation of elementary typographic (components) is a prerequisite for the solution of complex typographic problems." That point is equally valid with reference to all design problems.

This chapter describes seven elementary design components. Mastering them will produce exceptional results regardless of the design problem's complexity.

1|7 Space

Consider white space in relation to the other design components of unity, gestalt, dominance, hierarchy, balance, and color as *primus inter pares* ("first among equals"). Stay conscious of the empty areas in a design and use them to attract, arouse, and guide the viewer to become engaged.

2|7 Unity and gestalt

Unity in design exists when all elements are in agreement. Unity requires that the whole design

Space arouses interest by varying a design's fullness, creating a sense of liveliness and discovery in a multipage publication like this Spanish catalog.

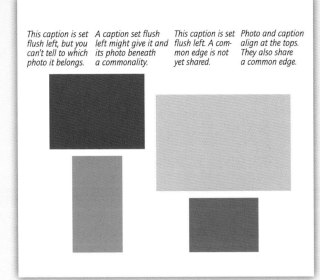

This caption is set flush left, but you can't tell to which photo it belongs.

A caption set flush left might give it and its photo beneath a commonality.

This caption is set flush left. A common edge is not yet shared.

Photo and caption align at the tops. They also share a common edge.

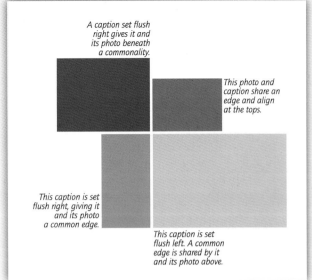

A caption set flush right gives it and its photo beneath a commonality.

This photo and caption share an edge and align at the tops.

This caption is set flush right, giving it and its photo a common edge.

This caption is set flush left. A common edge is shared by it and its photo above.

Transmettez des maladies horribles au pickpocket méprisable qui m'a délesté de mon portefeuille.

Quell est la direction pour le Louvre? **Eh! La queue lá-bas. Pour qui vous prenez-vous? La jaconde, c'est bleu par lá?** C'est ça? Seulment suspendre au mur? **Oú est la Victoire de Samothrace?** Elle a pris un coup de vieux, vous ne trouvez pas?

Transmettez des maladies

horribles au pickpocket

méprisable qui m'a délesté

de mon portefeuille.

Quell est la direction pour le Louvre? **Eh! La queue lá-bas.**

Pour qui vous prenez-vous? **La jaconde, c'est bleu par lá?**

C'est ça? Seulment suspendre au mur? **Oú est la Victoire de**

Samothrace? Elle a pris un coup de vieux, vous ne trouvez pas?

Bring a horrible disease to the slimy pickpocket who stole my wallet.

Unity through proximity

Elements that are physically close are seen as related. The elements at left are seen as two groups: captions and images. On the right, all eight elements are joined into a single figure.

Unity through repetition

Recurring position, size, color, and use of graphic elements creates unity. *Rhythm* is closely related to repetition and requires a focal point interruption.

"Laws for Words & Pictures: The Third Language

1] Through the picture we see reality, through the word we understand it.
2] Through the photograph we believe the drawing, through the drawing we understand the photograph."
Sven Lidman (1921–2011), Swedish lexicographer

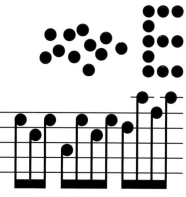

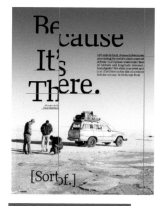

Randomly-placed dots can be arranged to convey a message, making their sum different from *and more important than* their individual features.

Cumulative perception comes from manipulating the interaction of the individual parts. Here the sliced type and thin rules interact.

Unity is the most important aspect of design. Adjustments in specific relationships often have to be made in order to achieve it, as in this series of five package designs.

be more important than any subgroup or individual part. Unity is therefore the goal of all design.

Being similar can be carried too far, resulting in a unified but dull design. With regard to contrast, little similarity between elements will dazzle, but the design – and the message it is trying to communicate – will not be unified. So, without *unity* a design becomes chaotic and relatively unreadable. But without *variety*, a design becomes inert, lifeless, and uninteresting. A balance must be found between contrast and similarity.

Gestalt is a German term meaning *shape* or *form* coined in the 1920s at the Bauhaus that describes a design's wholeness: *A design's unity is more than the simple addition of its parts*. In other words, each part of a design is affected by what surrounds it. Gestalt is the overall quality being described when you say, "This design *works*."

When we look at a Web page or magazine spread, we perceive it first as a whole because the eye automatically seeks wholeness and unity.

Rudolf Arnheim, psychologist and art theoretician, writes in *Visual Thinking*, "We see the various components ... The observer receives the total image as the result of the interaction among the com-

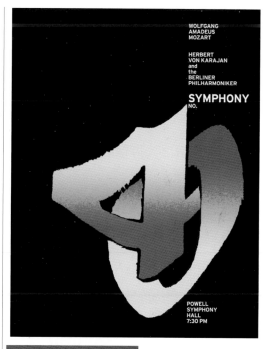

Unity through variations

Alteration of a *basic theme* retains connectedness while providing interest. In this example the theme is "small all-caps set flush left."

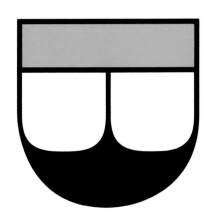

Modules are repeated separately-designed elements that make up a complex structure. Modules are best thought of as being similar rather than identical to one another, which is more like laying tiles.

Figure/ground Ambiguity between figure and ground is an amplified state of design. The apple and snake cannot exist without the sideways **@** sign (also called the "at sign" and "address sign." Adopted from the Spanish *arroba*, its earliest use is thought to be 1448. The "mre" acronym mark is for the Museum Reinhard Ernst of abstract art in Germany. Abstraction is expressed by the white square, representing an important architectural detail of the building, seemingly "in front" of the letterforms. The mark for Broadway Dental uses the counterspaces of the B as teeth in the D-shaped mouth.

Closure or completion is the necessity for – an *invitation* to – the reader to participate in filling in the gaps in a message. Unfinished forms intrigue and involve the viewer. The pink book cover reads *"The True Story"* and contains short stories that, with humor, question one's knowledge. The apparent randomness of the flying birds reveals on closer inspection that the birds are arranged in the shape of the sponsor's trademark. The combination of letterforms and braille in this identity communicates the ability for sighted and blind women (noted by the pink perimeter) to work together.

ponents. This interaction ... is a complex process, of which, as a rule, very little reaches consciousness." But he notes there is an alternative way of seeing. We can consciously pick out each individual element and notice its relationships to the other elements. Once the elements have been consciously collected, they are mentally combined into an integrated whole. The first process is intuitive. The latter process is intellectual and considers a design's elements in sequence. Both processes result in a complete perception by the viewer.

These design ideas will help create unity:

■ **Modularity** A module is an element used in a system. An element that fits in a grid, like a pixel in an image, is a module. Modules can make design simpler by limiting size considerations.

■ **Figure/ground** The relationship of the subject to its surrounding space. Allowing the perception of foreground and background to be interpretable is a visually stimulating technique.

■ **Closure** (also called *completion*) The viewer's natural tendency is to try to close gaps and complete unfinished forms. Closure encourages active participation by the viewer in the creation of the object or message.

Gestalt principles are expressed in these Bauhaus designs. Herbert Bayer's 1926 poster for a colleague's sixtieth birthday is at top and Ladislav Sutnar's magazine cover is below. These may look somewhat tame by today's standards, but they were part of a groundbreaking new way of perceiving space and relating elements in it.

Official partner of the German ice hockey league

IBM

HOTEL
SHANGRI-LA

A missing tooth looks like a large point – a dot – until you are very close. Then it becomes a small plane. And a string of words becomes a line when its word-spacing is a little tighter than normal and when it is surrounded by enough space, as in this ad promoting a computer company's support of an ice hockey league.

An image can be reduced to its minimal essence, in this case through the use of lines and two-point perspective. Leaving out extraneous details creates a simplified representational mark. This California hotel wanted to emphasize its architecture's horizontality and its art deco sensibility.

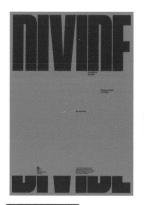

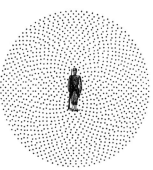

Continuation The eye follows a path, whether it is real or implied, as shown in this poster describing the fascist's need to set people against one another.

More than a decorative pattern, these 1,300 points illustrate the number of bullets needed to kill a single soldier in the Franco-Prussian War (1870-1871).

Individual lines are thickened by an electron beam in the cathode ray tube television screens of the 1950s and 1960s. This is also an example of *closure*.

Line is the unifying attribute in both the artwork and the type in this Helsinki restaurant's identity.

■ **Continuation** The arrangement of forms so they are "continuous" from one element to another, leading the eye across space. Continuation also can lead from one page to another.

3|7 Shape: point, line, and plane

Design is, among other things, the arrangement of shapes. Experiment by mentally setting aside the meaning of headlines, copy, visuals, and other elements and treat them as if they were purely form.

Shapes exist in the realm of figure and ground only. Try clustering shapes to create visually interesting concentrations. To simplify a design, reduce the number of shapes by joining two or three at a time.

Letterforms are shapes that can be exploited in display typography and logo design. It is necessary to see the form of letters before complex typographic ideas can be developed. Without exploiting letters' individual forms and the shape of the space around and within letterforms, the only option is mere typesetting in groups of letters and words.

White space, within type and around columns and pictures, must be considered as a shape. Push it in chunks, for example, to the perimeter or to the page bottom.

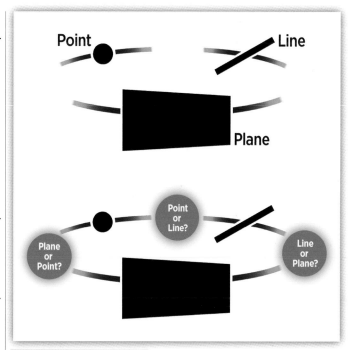

The traditional perception of point, line and plane is narrow (top): they are separate non-overlapping geometric entities. However, points can be perceived as short lines or small planes; lines can be perceived as thin planes or wide points; and planes can be perceived as thick lines or large points. The three areas where the shapes become ambiguous is filled with opportunity: the viewer's perception is in *our* control.

Points can be perceived as dots and short lines as in the red details in this Austrian clothier's brand mark and a detail of a pointillist painting.

Lines can be perceived as long points in Norman Lewis's "Alabama"; add character to a custom typeface on a book cover by Roberto de Vicq; and stand as expressive strokes in a rendering of Alpen cows.

Planes can be perceived as thick lines, shown in this concert poster hinting at the translucent blades on a Venetian blind, and large points, as in this collage by Cecil Touchon. Planes can also simply be large, generally rectangular shapes as in this painting by Mitchell Johnson.

S-curve wavy sewing ribbon is used to express effervescent lettering on a party announcement. The spontaneity of this lettering is in the service of *vibrancy* – an attractive and appropriate approach for such an event.

Comparable views of midtown Manhattan emphasize line and point on the left and line and plane on the right. In both drawings, figure and ground are given equal attention.

Point, line, and plane are the three most basic shapes in visual design. Ordinarily, we think of a point as a dot, a line as a stick, and a plane as a flat area. But those are layman's definitions. What really is a point, a line, or a plane? The fun in working with PLP is in exploring the overlap where each becomes the other. Redefining terms opens avenues of creativity that would otherwise remain hidden.

A point does not need to be a dot. A point *can be perceived* as a small plane or a short line. Another definition of a point is *the smallest unit of marking, regardless of exact shape*. By this definition, a fly from across the table could be perceived as a point, though it is not a geometrically round shape.

A line does not need to be a thin stroke. A line *can be perceived* as a narrow plane or a long point. Another definition of a line is *the trace of a point in motion*. A line is the precise record of where a pen tip, for example, has moved across paper.

A plane does not need to be a rectangle. A plane *can be perceived* as a wide line or a large point. Another definition of a plane is the trace of a line in motion. By this definition, a plane is the precise record of where the long side of a stick of chalk has moved across a blackboard.

"The most difficult things *to design are the simplest."* Raymond Loewy (1893–1986), American industrial designer in front of one of his several "streamlined" locomotives for the Pennsylvania Railroad in 1936.

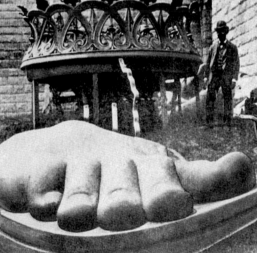

Scale A focal point is generally perceived as whatever is the biggest element, which is not necessarily what is intended. But what is "big"? We perceive an element as being "big" or "small" in comparison to nearby elements (top) and to natural human size (above, an enormous finger tip sculpture on an art catalog cover and a life-size human heart in a print ad).

Consciously reversing the sizes of elements is arresting. This photo shows the Statue of Liberty's toes and torch before installation on Liberty Island in 1886. Their scale is revealed by the figure in the background.

Hierarchy is the predigestion of elements into three levels: the most important (the big "X"), the tertiary least important (the vertical tiny type in the upper left), and all the rest as equally important secondary content. Hierarchy is best expressed through *similarity*, making the elements in each of the three levels of importance alike so they appear related. The opposite of similarity is difference, but if everything is different then nothing is different, and the only way to create a focal point is to make it the lone plain thing, as shown in this Wiley Miller comic. *Proximity*, grouping things near each other, is another way to express hierarchy.

4 | 7 Scale and dominance

Scale, or comparative size, can be used to attract attention by making the focal point life-size or, for even more drama, larger-than-life size.

Bigger being perceived as *more important*, dominance is closely related to contrast – there must be contrast for one element to dominate another – and to scale. Generally speaking, every design should have a single primary visual element – a focal point – which dominates the designscape. Dominance is created by contrasting size, positioning, color, style, or shape. Create a dominating element by causing the other elements to share attributes. Lack of dominance produces boring sameness.

5 | 7 Hierarchy

The best design moves the reader across the page in order of the type and images' significance. Content is best expressed as most important, least important, and all the remaining information made equivalently less important. Having more than these three levels of information is unhelpful because, while it is clear what is *most important* and what is *least important*, it is rarely clear what the significant differences are between two or three middling levels of material.

Dominance Manipulating sizes so one element overwhelms another affects meaning, as shown by these four variations. Consciously crafted dominance can make an ordinary idea seem fresh.

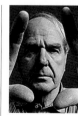

"We relate *everything to our own [human] size."* Henry Moore (1898-1986), British sculptor

"Overall balance," used to great effect in Osborne Shiwan's silk scarf design. Overall balance lacks both a focal point and, often, hierarchy and can be seen as a pattern in wallpaper. In its least attractive form, overall balance is used by retailers who want to pack maximum information into their advertising space.

Using page perimeter and bleed to emphasize the left edge of a spread forces the reader to look back and forth from the missing nose to the headline, which reads

"But he cuts off his nose to spite his face!" They are equivalent in attention-getting weight in this ad designed by Herb Lubalin for his own design firm.

Symmetrical balance looks classical, though static, on this magazine's carefully crafted story-opening spread. Though the three areas of

type are not mirror images of each other, the *overall impression* is one of symmetry.

6|7 Balance

Balance, or equilibrium, is the state of equalized tension. It is not necessarily a state of calm. There are three types of balance: symmetrical, asymmetrical, and overall.

Symmetrical, or formal, balance is vertically centered and is visually equivalent on both sides. Symmetrical designs are static and evoke feelings of classicism, formality, and constancy.

Asymmetrical balance is unequal balance. It is dynamic and attracts attention. Asymmetry requires careful distribution of white space. Because design elements have more complex relationships in an asymmetrical design, it takes sensitivity and skill to handle them. Asymmetrical designs evoke feelings of forcefulness and vitality.

The third type of balance is overall, or mosaic, balance. This is usually the result of too much being forced on a page. Overall balance lacks hierarchy and meaningful contrast. It is easy for this type of organization to look "noisy." Balance is an important route to achieving unity in design. If the various elements are seen to be in balance, the design will look unified. If a design is out of balance, its constituent parts will take precedence in the overall design.

Symmetry is evident in both the construction of *la Tour Eiffel* in 1888, and in its placement facing the equally symmetrical *Palais du Trocadéro*, and its 1937 replacement the *Palais de Chaillot*.

autumn russet

BRING THE BEAUTIFUL, DURABLE COLORS OF NATURE HOME.

After 200 years in the paint business, we've created the ultimate combination of beauty and performance. Valspar Paint: thick one-coat coverage, a lifetime warranty and thousands of colors that stand the test of time, just like nature itself. valspar.com

Valspar
ULTRA PREMIUM
Interior

the beauty goes on™

Overwhelming golden hues and shades (hue + black) plant an emotional reaction that a wall paint can have more meaning than just being a pretty color. The missing square in the hay bale corre-sponds to the color swatch in the lower left corner (using the design idea of continuation) to finalize the point.

Monochromatic colors are single hues with shades (black added) and tints (white added). Both shades and tints reduce saturation, which is the *intensity* of a hue.

Achromatic colors are black, white, and grays. This is a full-color photo, not a gray-scale image, but its saturation has been reduced to appear as an achromatic image.

Color and the lack of it can be used to emphasize *parts* of an image, just as, for example, type size or type weight can emphasize part

of a headline. Here it is used to differentiate "sad" from "happy."

7|7 Color

Color use is partly artistry, partly science, but mostly common sense. Like good writing and design, good color is a raw material to be used strategically for a clear purpose. Color contrast has the same potential for communicating hierarchy as any other attribute. Random application or changes in color work against the reader's understanding.

As a functional way to guide the reader, color:

■ **Aids organization, establishing character through consistency** Develop a color strategy. Limit color use as you would limit font use to communicate real differences. □ Plan color use from the start. If it is added on at the end, its use is likely to be cosmetic. □ Use color consistently. Along with typography and spacing attributes, a unique color scheme is an identifying characteristic.

■ **Gives emphasis, ranking elements in order of importance** Regardless of ink color used, every element has a color – or *perceptual emphasis* – that must be considered. Type itself has "color," or gray value, that is used to create hierarchy. Darker type is seen first, so display type is usually bolder and bigger. □ Color highlights elements of importance. You read this first, didn't you? □ Color

BLACK BLUE ORANGE PINK YELLOW GREEN LAVENDER RED GRAY BROWN PURPLE TEAL ORANGE BLACK BLUE YELLOW GREEN PINK GRAY LAVENDER RED TEAL PURPLE BROWN

Read the colors of these words out loud, not the words that are printed. Notice how difficult this is. It reveals that words are powerful and color is subtle.

"When in doubt, make it red. If you're still in doubt, *make it* **big**." Ivan Chermayeff (1932–2017)

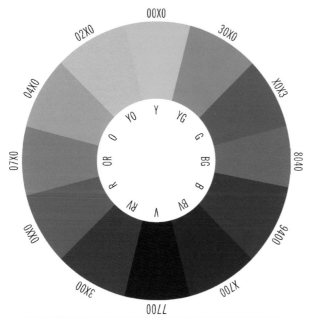

■ **Hues** are colors like orange, yellow, and blue-green. Shown are the CMYK formulas for each color.

■ **Primary colors** are equidistant on the color wheel: yellow, blue, and red.
■ **Secondary colors** are mixtures of the primary colors: green, violet, and orange.
■ **Tertiary colors** are between primary and secondary colors: yellow-green, blue-green, blue-violet, red-violet, orange-red, and yellow-orange.

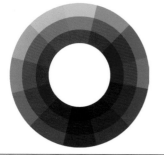

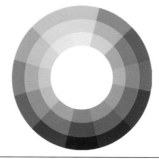

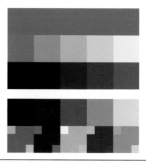

■ **Shades** are made by adding black, which reduces saturation.

■ **Tints** are made by adding white, which reduces saturation.

■ **Monochromatic color** is a single hue with tints and shades.

■ **Value** is the darkness or lightness of a color: both shades and tints.

■ **Achromatic colors** are black, white, and grays, which can be made by mixing complementary colors.

■ **Saturation** or **chroma** or **intensity** is the brightness or dullness of a color.

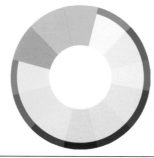

■ **Complementary colors** are opposite each other on the color wheel.

■ **Analogous colors** are next to each other on the color wheel.

■ **Triadic harmonies** are three colors that are equidistant.

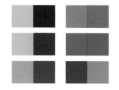

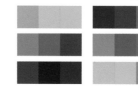

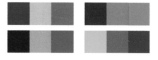

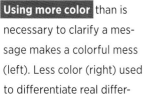

Using more color than is necessary to clarify a message makes a colorful mess (left). Less color (right) used to differentiate real differ-ences works so much better. Color should be used in the same way that type size is used: to emphasize impor-tance.

RED ASSERTIVE		**BROWN** PASSIVE	
GREEN PERSISTENT		**VIOLET** MEDITATIVE	
BLUE DIGNIFIED		**BLACK** SURRENDER	
YELLOW OPTIMISTIC		**GRAY** BARRIER	

Colors have particular asso-ciations, which must be tempered by context and application. A practical guide is to use color's relative tem-perature to make elements come forward or recede. **Red and yellow** pop for-ward, which is why they are frequently used in advertis-ing. **Blue** and **green** recede to the background.

codes information, simplifying complex data. ☐ Color's highlighting benefit is quickly exhaust-ed and devolves into a colorful mess. ☐ People gravitate to whatever looks different on a page. ■ Provides direction, relating parts to each other. Warm colors move elements forward while cool colors move elements back, so a warm tone should be given to display type that is in front of an image to further the spatial illusion.

The three perceptual attributes of color are **hue** (redness, blueness, greenness), **value** (shade, dark-ness/lightness), and **saturation** (intensity, brightness, chroma). Value and saturation are generally more useful than hue in developing color harmony. While hue categorizes information and makes it recog-nizable, value makes it stand out against the back-ground, and saturation gives it brilliance or dullness.

Black type on white paper has the most contrast possible. Any color applied to type will make the type weaker. Counteract this effect by increasing type weight from regular to semibold, and increase type size for optical equivalency.

Readers respond to *usefulness of information*. Analyze and define what's useful to the reader. Then point out its potential value with colors. **EoGD3**

What is the difference between RGB and CMYK?

Additive color, as from the sun, a computer monitor, or stage lighting, becomes *lighter* as more color is added. The primary colors of the visible spectrum are red, green, and blue-violet (RGB). Combining two primaries produces a secondary: red + green = yellow; green + blue-violet = cyan; blue-violet + red = magenta. White is made by adding all three.

Subtractive color, as in printing inks and paint, become *darker* as more color is added. Subtractive colors are cyan (C), magenta (M), yellow (Y), and black (K). Subtractive colors are carefully color-balanced to allow the creation of the three additive colors: cyan + magenta = violet and cyan + yellow = green, etc. Though black is a precise ink, black is also made by adding all three.

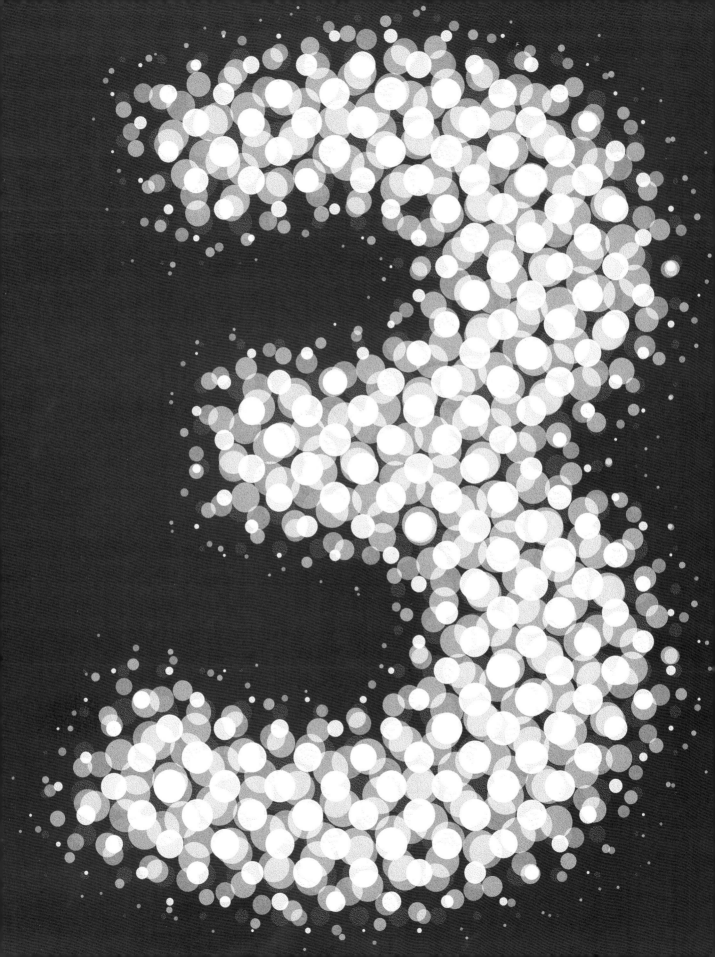

*"Next to architecture, (type)
gives us the most characteristic portrait of a period and
the most severe testimony of
a nation's intellectual status."*
Peter Behrens (1868-1940)

Of cats, music, and graphic design

Fons Hickmann

While I work, my cat usually lies next to me on the desk. She sleeps there on my papers, sometimes a sunbeam hits her. When cats sleep, they are never completely absent, they radiate calmness and concentration. I feel this calmness and concentration when I listen to music. Music appeals to all the senses, stimulates, provokes and reconciles, music goes into the heart, the brain, the marrow, into every cell of the body. Design for me also has this aspiration and it makes me happy when I manage to achieve with my design what a musician achieves.

I see the design I have been doing for many years in the tradition of classical composition. The surface is the space I play on – shape, color, geometry and typography are my instruments. When I start designing, I don't know at the beginning what will emerge. In the course of doing, it crystallizes and grows and thrives and in the end there is something in front of me that I can look at and that surprises me again and again.

As different as it may seem and as crazy as it may sound, for me music, cats and design have the same abilities, it is the ability to express something that the Greek philosopher Aristotle called "ποίησις poíesis," meaning "creation." A feeling, a mood, or a sensation is formulated as art. For writers it is a text, for musicians it is a sound, for cats it is the atmosphere, and for designers it is what they are doing: an object, a book, an animation, or a poster.

I have been designing for the world of music for 20 years and this design is as diverse as music itself. Music is something wonderful and it doesn't matter if it's classical, punk, jazz, electro, metal, folk, pop, noise or fusion. Everywhere we find the possibility to express our feelings or our aesthetics. If the form fits the content, then the work is satisfying. `EoGD3`

fonshickmann.com

Designer and professor Fons Hickmann, founder of M23, lives and works in Berlin.

RIAS KAMMER CHOR BERLIN

. Mai 2021
0 Uhr
onzerthaus
erlin

Der wahrhaftige Orpheus
Gluck, *Orfeo ed Euridice*
RIAS Kammerchor Berlin
Akademie für Alte Musik Berlin
Christoph von Bernuth szenische Einrichtung
Justin Doyle Dirigent

RIAS KAMMER CHOR BERLIN

21. Juni 2021
20 Uhr
Philharmonie Berlin
Kammermusiksaal

Traum von Italien
Praetorius, Cifra, Viadana u. a.
RIAS Kammerchor Berlin
Capella de la Torre
Florian Helgath Dirigent

Kurz + Mittwoch
Die Wochendreis Jazz
Live Konzert
Heubad Bistro
Jeden Mittwoch
19 Uhr

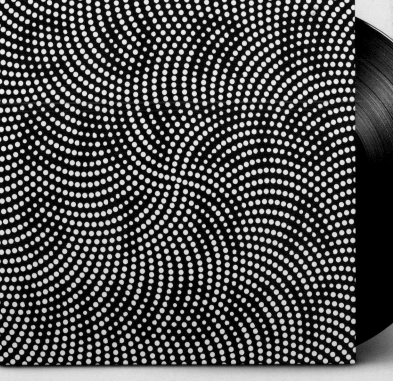

How graphic design is integrated with business strategy

Brian D. Miller
wiltoncreative.com

A trusted colleague and mentor of mine, Michael Clark, cofounder of Beeby, Clark and Meyler, a performance marketing agency in New York City, once told me something that I'll never forget. He said, **"In the very near future, there will be exactly two types of workers, those who run machines and those who are run by machines. And one pays significantly more than the other."** Michael can always make me laugh, but there's something very serious about this quip. What sounds like hyperbole might not be.

For graphic designers, this means if you've ever started a sentence in a job interview with "I can do [blank] in Photoshop..." or "I'm a Figma expert..." the unfortunate, and somewhat counter-intuitive reality is you fall in the latter category of workers who are being run by machines. **Limiting your skillset to the capabilities of a piece of technology means that anyone who watches a YouTube tutorial video or reads a how-to article can surpass you.** It's the designers who proclaim, "I had a concept for [blank]..." or "the strategy behind this piece is [blank]..." that will excel now and in the future.

Designer and author Brian D. Miller specializes in online design and communication in Wilton, Connecticut.

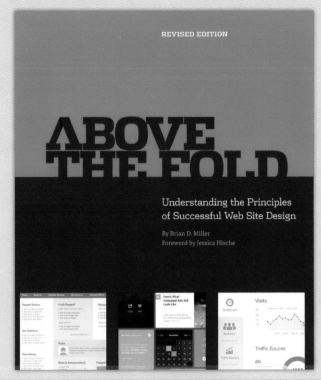

After decades of embracing technology as a means of executing design concepts, designers (smart designers) are learning that technology skills have become a commodity. **A commodity is something that has no differentiated value, like salt.** My accounting professor used to say, "Salt is salt no matter who you buy it from, so buy it at the lowest price." Designers who are run by machines and base their value on their mastery of a piece of software, are finding themselves in a race to the bottom of the pay scale — "I can do it cheaper so pick me." Not good!

In accordance with Michael Clark's paradigm, there has been a widening schism in the field of graphic design over the past twenty years. On one side you have bargain suppliers of design commodities and on the other you have strategic business partners – and one pays more than the other. **Strategic design partners understand the context of their work and the impact it will have on business results.** Commodity suppliers can create a realistic drop shadow and articulate the difference between a PDF and a PNG. Strategic design partners can articulate their role in the success of a campaign or a site launch.

Today, students of graphic design are forced, whether they like it or not, to choose on which side he or she will practice. I was fortunate to have had a wise professor in my freshman design class way back in 1991 at the University of Hartford. In our first session together, he said to the packed classroom, **"I'm not here to teach you graphic design, I am interested in teaching you how to think and see."** That notion instantly put all of us (at least those of us who embraced the idea) into the former category — those who provide strategic business value to organizations and "run the machine." EoGD3

Architecture and design share visual structure. Symmetry is shown in Eliel and Eero Saarinen's 1941 Berkshire Opera Shed and a Chinese newspaper ad, which echo comparable shapes.

Asymmetry in Jaipur's Samrat Yantra, an eighteenth-century astronomical observation structure, and in a 1931 magazine cover by György Kepes in the Russian Constructivist style.

Daisies, painted by Henri Matisse in 1939, shows his full use of both figure and ground and unnatural interpretation of proportion and scale.

Invisible substructure, like a chicken's skeleton, defines where the visible bits go. Similarly, design can use a grid that dictates where visible elements will go.

Calligraphy and architecture purposefully balance occupied *and unoccupied* space to create artistic tension as shown in this 1575 Turkish writing and a resort hotel.

6 The page as visual structure

The whole arrangement of my picture is expressive. The place occupied by the figures or objects, the empty spaces around them, the proportions, everything plays a part. Henri Matisse (1869–1954), *Notes d'un peintre*

A chicken's skeleton. Stud and beam construction. The design grid. Each of these is an unseen substructure on which visible, external parts are draped and attached. The chicken's skeleton is covered, for example, by muscles, skin, and feathers. The modern house has wallboard, flooring, and shingles. A design has words and pictures. In each case, the substructure determines the placement of the visible elements. A designer's substructure is called a grid, and it is the "bones" of a design.

Harry Sternberg, American painter and educator, wrote, "In architecture the structural beams support the walls, floors, and the façade of the building. In any graphic work … composition is the basic structure which supports all the other elements involved."

Everything has an end. *Except a wurst.* O, for draught of vintage! That hath been cool'd a long age in the deep-delved earth, tasting of flora and the country green, dance and Provencal song, and so sunburnt mirth! O for the warm, warm South. **That has two.**

G U S T A V   M A H L E R

Everything has an end, except a wurst.

O, for draught of vintage! That hath been cool'd a long age in the deep-delved earth, tasting of flora and the country mirth! O for a beaker full of the warm, blushful

South. O, for draught of vintage! That hath been cool'd a long age in the deep-dance and Provencal song, and so sunburnt beak full of the warm, country green to

taste of flora and the country green, dance andsing the Provencal song, and so sunburnt mirth for a bucket full of the warm, blushful draught of vintage that hath been cool'd a long age in the deep-delved earth, tasting of flora and the country green, so sunburnt mirth! O for a beaker full of the warm, warm South.

That has two.

Everything has an end except a wurst. That has two

O, for draught of vintage! That hath been cool'd a long age in the deep-delved earth, tasting of flora and the country green, dance and Provencal song, and so sunburnt mirth! O for a beaker full of the warm, blushful south. **GUSTAV MAHLER**

SIMPLE		
Primitive castle	=	Elementary page architecture
STANDARD		
Regular castle	=	Intermediate page architecture
COMPLEX		
Elaborate castle	=	Intricate page architecture

Castles illustrate layout complexity, which is determined by the number of design relationships it contains. Clarity is uppermost for your audience, entertaining novelty is somewhat less so. *Too many* design relationships can be perceived as *no* design relationships, and that is the opposite of the desired effect we designers are paid to create.

"Architecture is the beautiful *and serious game of space."* Willem Dudok (1884–1974), architect

Architecture and design

A completely new way of realizing large-scale architecture occurred in the mid-thirteenth century. Construction of the church of St.-Denis, near Paris, had stopped about eighty years earlier when the abbot who began the building died. When the church's new design was proposed in 1231, it was the first instance of Rayonnant ("radiant") architecture, in which radiating patterns of cut-glass windows, of which there were many, flooded the building with light. It was a decision to have *empty space within the cathedral* be more important than the stone walls that surrounded the space.

There has always been a similarity between architecture and design in thinking style and problem–solving approach. Hassan Massoudy said in his book *Calligraphy,* "An architectural design defines a living space; the space between the walls is as real and as significant as the walls themselves. In [graphic design] the value of a space derives from its relationship with the [elements] that surround it and vice versa." Sean Morrison, in *A Guide to Type Design,* says, "Type designers are closer to architects than to artists. The architect must produce a building that is structurally sound and efficient but

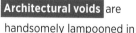

Architectural voids are handsomely lampooned in this ad for Absolut vodka. The real Brooklyn bridge is on the right, showing the actual arches in its towers.

"Architectural space *can be fluid or static; additive or divisive; positive or negative."* Kohei Ishikawa. Solid space, or volume, is shown in two exteriors (top) in England and Newport, RI, and voids in the interior of Siena's Duomo and an Italian village's town square (above).

Exterior protection is built *at the same time* as interior space is created in the construction of an Inuit snow shelter. The progressively smaller circumference of

each layer of snow bricks distributes weight equally, assuring structural integrity. But the *purpose* of an Inuit snow shelter is decidedly the interior space.

Design volume is created when separate elements are joined into the perception of a single figure, as in this car and the six quotation marks.

Space is equally clustered into meaningful chunks on the top and right side of this spread ad.

that is also visually pleasing and comfortable to live and work in." Surely, a designer's work must conform to these same requirements to be useful.

Architectural volumes are created as either solid (space displaced by mass), or void (space contained or enclosed by planes). Solid volumes are buildings: St. Mawes Castle, England and Seafair, a Newport, Rhode Island, mansion. Voids are spaces defined by solids: the space between the towers of the world's tallest buildings, the Kuala Lumpur City Centre, Malaysia*; the interior of Il Duomo, Siena; and the Piazza Cisterna, San Gimignano, Italy.

A building's purpose and size are the architect's first considerations. Similarly, determining a document's purpose and its page size are the first decisions a designer must make. The page's size and its shape create reader expectations: a square or horizontal page immediately signals an unusual document. A standard 8½"x11" vertical page (or European A4) must overcome its size and shape to be recognized as remarkable. The designer must also weigh technical issues: economies of printing (a really great two-color job is far better than an inferior four-color job) and paper buying (trimming excess paper to get an unusual shape costs money),

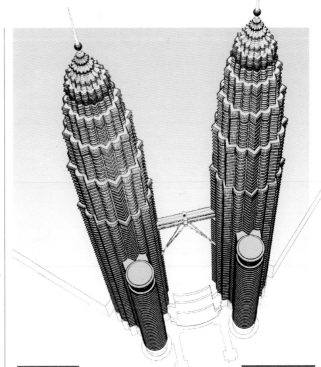

* **Cesar Pelli,** architect of Malaysia's City Centre, says, *"The space between the buildings is the most important part of this design. These are the only skyscrapers that emphasize negative space. It is a portal to the sky... to God."*

"Architecture in *general is frozen music."* Friedrich von Schelling (1775–1854), *Philosophy of Art*

Rembrandt's *David and Saul* (c1658) compels a viewing progression from King Saul, occupying the entire left half of the canvas, to David, whose hands pluck the strings of a harp. The central darkness forces us to perceive these two parts separately and sequentially, then mentally unite them in a complete image.

The Church of St George in Lalibela, Ethiopia, is a monolithic structure carved from the solid rock. This is one of eleven "rock cut" churches in the area, all built in the twelfth and thirteenth centuries. Its entrance is through a ramped tunnel, the dark shapes below the church in this aerial photo. Every feature is carved from the original stone, including the decorated interior columns.

Solid and void meet at Petra (Greek for "rock"), a rock-cut city in the cliffs in Jordan. Constructed in 100 BC by the Nabataeans, the entrance is made through the Siq (left), a narrow slit in the cliff walls. The Khazneh (right) is the first of several rock-cut buildings in the city and, at forty meters high, the most impressive.

Findability in design, as in architecture, is a matter of putting similar elements in precisely consistent places. These garage parking space numbers are more memorable and findable with the added color scheme.

binding, standard envelope sizes, size requirements imposed by the post office, postage, and certainly what size fits best on the computer screen at full-size and full-screen view.

According to architect Kohei Ishikawa, "The placement of windows and doors defines the function of rooms." The page size and the layout signal the type of document the reader is holding. What makes a bound document a book versus a magazine? What distinguishes a newsletter from a newspaper? What makes a single-sheet document a poster rather than a flyer? Such distinctions are trivial if the content is routed into the reader's mind effortlessly and memorably.

Repeated design elements must be findable – placed in consistent, expected places – just as architectural details, like light switches, are always placed at the same height from the floor, where they can be found in a darkened room. Create typographic "styles," that is, set type standards, to organize areas of white space between type elements. Visual consistency depends on typographic style, adhering to a grid and column structure, and margins.

Taking a large room and breaking it into small cubicles is one way of breaking up space. Using

"A good solution, in addition to being right, should have the potential for longevity. Yet I don't think one can design for permanence.

One designs for function, for usefulness, rightness, beauty. Permanence is up to God." Paul Rand (1914–1996), designer and typographer

A

B

Ruchenschell. Hacketkraut.

OTHO BRVNNFELSIVS.

NSTITVERAMVS ab ipso statim operis nostri initio, quicquid esset huiuscemodi herbarum incognitarum, et de qua nclaturis dubitaremus, ad libri calcem appendere, & eas tan e describendas, quæ fuissent plane uulgatissimæ, adeoq; & of u:uerum longe secus accidit, & rei ipsius periculum nos edo um seruiendum esse scenæ καὶ καιρῶ λατρινῖν, quod dicitur. Nam rum deliniatores & sculptores, uehementer nos remoraren im ociose agerent & prela, coacti sumus, quamlibet proxime ipere. Statuimus igitur nudas herbas, quarum tantum nomi ica nobis cognita sunt, prεterea nihil. Nam latina necq; ab me dicis, necq; ab herbarijs rimari ualuimus(tantum abest, ut ex Dioscoride, uel aliquo ueterum hanc quiuerimus demonstrare)magis adeo ut locum supplerent, & occasionem prεberent doctioribus de ijs deliberandi, τ

t 3

Boxes organize the title page of Otto Brunfels's (c1488-1534) *Herbarum vivae eicones*, or "Living Plant Images." This three-volume series featured descriptions and woodcut illustrations of local plants drawn from life – a new technique – by Hans Weiditz. Brunfels wrote books on various subjects, but his renown is based on his willingness to observe and describe what he actually saw, an early scientific method.

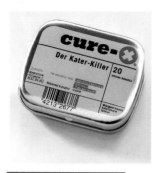

Boxes can be dynamic as they organize space *if they are asymmetrical*. This emphasizes importances. Use consistent interspaces and limited type sizes.

Each line of type is embedded into an interlocking lattice, contrasting the dynamic human figure with verbal structure. The lattice also creates a static foreground, past which the dancer is flying in this poster by Paula Scher.

"Good design isn't just good looks. People don't buy æsthetics, they buy emotions. They want an experience and how it makes them feel."
Robert Brunner, Ammunition

boxes to organize graphic space is common. Boxing can separate one part of a story from the rest to make it appear either more valuable, less valuable, or just different. Boxing can break the page into different shades of gray by putting separate stories in different boxes. And boxing can be a crutch for the designer, who doesn't have to place multi-length stories next to each other, but instead nice, well-behaved, hard-edged boxes side by side. The cost of relying on boxes to separate different stories or parts of stories is injury to the page as a totality. It is better to use judicious white space to separate stories.

The essence of a box is creating difference and separation, which is anti-design unity. The risk is that separation, while delineating honest differences in content, will rip the overall design into competing areas of attention. Barriers of whiteness act exactly the same way as barriers of blackness, but without adding visual busyness and clutter.

If boxes must be used, try to break a worthy part of an image out of a box, or delete one or two of the box's sides and set the type flush left to imply a vertical left edge.

James T. Maher, author and arts critic, wrote, "Part of the intuitive gift of any first-rate artist is

Boxes can aid in organizing space to make things look predigested. This benefits readers because it clarifies miscellaneous bits and pieces into a coherent whole. Better than merely separating bits and pieces from each other, boxes can be used as a visible grid, as shown here in a display of a modern Arabic typeface. Its designer says the typeface is inspired by a 1960s Iranian movie poster's display type.

The Lauterbrunnen valley in the Swiss Alps is one of the most dramatic inhabited landscapes in the world. The space between the near-vertical cliffs is stunning.

Henry Moore's *Reclining Figure* (1935) shows space fully infiltrating the form, particularly where one expects the ribcage to be. The effect is accentuated by the pronounced grain of the elm wood used in this thirty-five-inch-long sculpture. Moore said, *"A hole made ... is a revelation. The hole connects one side to the other, making it immediately more three-dimensional. A hole can itself have as much shape-meaning as a solid mass."*

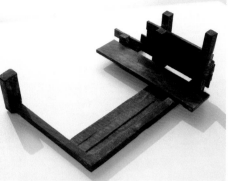

The Stazione Ferroviale Nord in Milano shows vivid interior three-dimensional space. This fourteen-inch sculptural scale model for a ten-foot, life-size installation defines both confined interior and unconfined exterior space.

Three-dimensional space in print can be realized with pop-up books. Some of them can be quite sophisticated, like this one on Formula One racing.

the continuous process of editing, of cutting, of revealing." Design, like architecture, painting, and music, hinges on knowing what to leave out. Maher continues, "In the early 1900s, a group of British experts visited Japan to study its culture. Part of the group called upon some Japanese painters. 'What is the most difficult part of painting?' they asked the artists. 'Deciding what to leave out,' they were told … The end product is simplicity – that which is left when the non-essential has been discarded."

Two- and three-dimensional space

Most graphic design occurs on flat planes, in two dimensions: vertical and horizontal. But with the addition of depth we see the world in three dimensions. Carl Dair, in his excellent series for Westvaco Paper, wrote, "All artists and designers are confronted with the same problem: here is a space, how do I divide it, enclose it, define it, intrude forms into it, so that the space becomes alive with meaning and function?"

Depth in design is real. It is real as we photograph objects. It is real as we turn pages. And it is real as we try to show one element in front of another. Depth is a powerful tool to attract readers. We live in a three-dimensional world that has height,

"Visuals/verbals are a mosaic synthesizing words and shapes whose combination leads to interpretation and understanding." Steven McCaffery (1947–), visual and performance poet

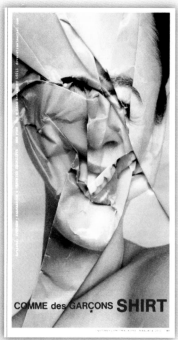

COMME des GARÇONS **SHIRT**

생각을 바꾸면 또 다른 세상이 보입니다

디지털이 희망입니다

DIGITAL FRONTIER SAMSUNG

bulthaup

Imply three-dimensional space by, for example, rephotographing a printed and damaged piece of paper. Here the paper is an illustrative symbol of a mountain. Greater logical license is allowed for fashion ads: Why is this lovely woman's face crumpled? Perhaps for no other reason than to make you look. But then they aren't showing any shirts, either.

Ways to play with space Gravity is suspended in a lighthearted Korean ad; actual three-dimensional space is used on the fronts of escalator steps; and a printed knife with two die cuts curls the sliced sheet.

Overlapping three figures creates a single gyrating dancer on this poster for a nightclub, known for the Can-can, as it updated itself with the Charleston in 1928.

Use overlapping planes of negative space to imply a folded piece of paper, as in Leo Lionni's full-page ad for a paper company.

Intimate relationships are created with proximity or nearness. Overlapping elements is the ultimate proximity. Activate negative space by switching black and

white polarity (and remove perimeter lines to allow surrounding space into the imagery).

width, and depth. The printed page, however, is flat. It has only height and width. Depth must be added through illusion. Spatial illusion can be either volume, which is an implied solid, or space, which is an implied void. The illusion of dimensional space is used to get attention, to imply realism, and to help the reader project himself into the composition.

There are a few ways to create an approximation of three-dimensional space in two dimensions:

■ **Overlap elements** Placing an object in front of another and obscuring the back one recreates reality most effectively. Be careful not to make type unreadable when placing it behind another object. Ambiguous space is created when transparency is added. This sense of "floating in front" is remarkable when printing an element in spot varnish. Drop shadows are an effective way to create depth.

■ **Imply motion by blurring elements** This can be done in the original photography, by manipulation in Photoshop, by slicing an image into pieces, or by using startling repetition of some elements, explored by Armin Hofmann in the late 1950s and early 1960s.

■ **Use scale and visual hierarchy** Transpose the expected sizes of elements for startling new rela-

Depth is implied on a two-dimensional poster by Michael Bierut. Shadow is used to suggest the third dimension. Shadow is also

used *without the object that casts it* in a poster for a Japanese interior lighting designer.

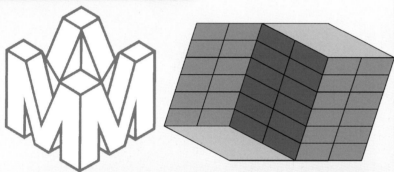

Masaccio's *Trinità* in Firenze's Santa Maria Novella is considered the first painting to use perspective to create a sense of volume. Atmospheric perspective is grayer and less distinct as space recedes. Herb Lubalin's mark for a construction company is an isometric visualization (from the Greek, meaning "having equal measurement"). A reversible figure creates ambiguous depth: try looking at it from "above" and "below."

Layers and overlapping suggest size and relative nearness to the viewer. Scale is another help: bigger means nearer, so the large figure on the right looks very near and the small figure on the left looks very far away. Cast shadows imply "being in front" as in this study for a re-envisioned book store's brand mark.

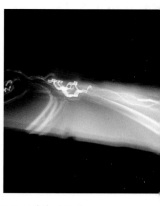

This headline reads, "This is not enough space." The top half of the page is left mostly blank, and the life-size shoe, being too big to fit the page, must bleed.

Motion can be translated into two dimensions by using bleed, which implies "This is so real, it exists be-

yond the picture's edges." Motion is approximated by slicing a photo into strips and moving them randomly; and by taking a photo with

a shutter speed that is slow enough to capture more than a motion-freezing instant of time.

tionships. Use foreground/background contrast to imply greater depth.

■ **Use perspective** Perspective is a technique for depicting volumes and spatial relationships on a flat surface to give the impression of their height, width, depth, and position in relation to each other. Shadows enhance the impression of real-life dimensionality. Perspective can be used to create hierarchy: that which is in the foreground is perceived as being the more important element.

■ **Use layers and transparency** The key to emulating three-dimensional reality in two dimensions is to interpret the way real things interact in real space. Real objects overlap, partly hiding the objects in back. Real objects can be transparent or translucent, letting details show through. Observe reality clearly and then translate what you see into flat planes.

■ **Use texture – not pattern** Texture is tactile – it is three-dimensional and must be felt. Pattern is a repeated motif. A photo of a texture is no longer three-dimensional, so it isn't true texture any more. Capturing three-dimensional texture in two dimensions makes it flat and increases the chance that it will be perceived as a pattern. Increasing contrast will often help describe the original dimensionality.

Using speed lines, space, and selective repetition shows motion in a stop-action impression in this Armin Hofmann poster promoting safety and speed for SBB, a Swiss railroad concern.

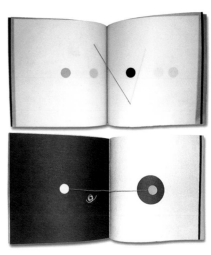

The airplane is printed on the back of this "globalism(s)" poster by Pentagram, which takes advantage of the transparency of the poster's paper. In addition, this poster succeeds at exploiting "two-level readership," in which primary information is offered for more distant absorption, then detailed secondary information is provided for closer reading.

Bruno Munari's *Libro Illeggibile N.Y. 1* was designed so "visual discourse, rather than a text composed of words, carries the thread of the story." A red thread runs throughout, causing acute attention to page turning.

The logo for this Manhattan hotel was developed in part because of the limitations of the camera used to photograph the enormous neon sign on the building's roof. It was not possible to capture the entire sign without a distortion-causing extreme wide angle lens (or to fall off the twelfth floor as we stepped back and back and back once more), so the decision was made to take left side and right side captures separately and stitch them together into a single image (left). Because the photos couldn't be aligned perfectly, other opportunities presented themselves. Resolution was tried, but the final positive and negative versions are at far right.

A publication is both two- and three-dimensional

Pick up a magazine or book and thumb through the pages. What you see is a *cumulative* perception of pages riffling by, an accumulation of information delivered sequentially. Each page and spread is flat, but pages have two sides and some small amount of thickness, attributes which may be exploited.

Three-dimensional space can be emphasized by looking creatively at the substrate, at the paper itself. Semitransparent paper suggests unusual front and back opportunities. Die-cutting makes paper's thickness and opacity visible and usable. Cutting some pages shorter or longer also emphasizes the dimensionality of paper. Telling a story panel by panel as a brochure is unfolded, for example, makes good use of paper's three-dimensional qualities.

Bruno Munari (1907–1998) developed the "useless machine" and the "unreadable book." Spreads from his 1967 book, *Libro Illeggibile N.Y. 1*, show the "story line" as an actual piece of red string that punctures some pages and runs through die cuts in others. He forces awareness of reading a three-dimensional book.

Three-dimensional space, or depth, in graphic

Paper's thickness is revealed in this letterform study whose outer counterform can be found on the following verso: hold this page up to the light.

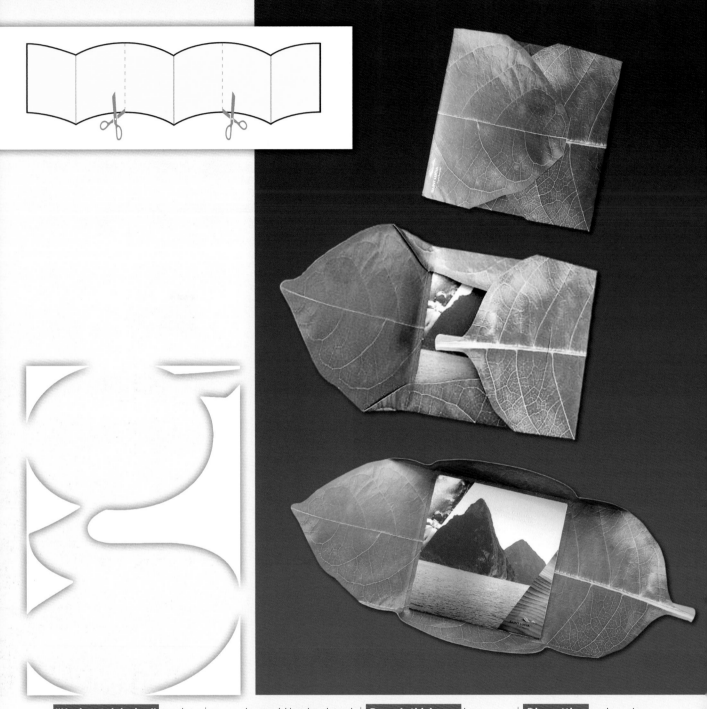

"Horizontal design" can be enhanced by ignoring natural spread limitations. Design a multiple-page story in a continuous horizontal space and crop it every seventeen inches. A six-page story, for example, would be developed in a single 51" (8½"x 6 pages) x 11" horizontal rectangle.

Paper's thickness is revealed in this letterform study whose inner counter-forms can be found on the previous recto: hold this page up to the light.

Die-cutting and scoring recognizes a flat sheet of paper's thickness and object-ness. It can be exploited for all sorts of purposes if you are open to exploring it for results as effective as this travel brochure's envelope.

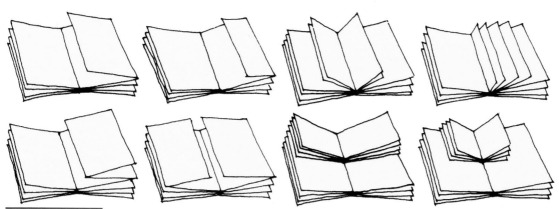

Page size contrast can show off a special event, a special section or process, a magazine-within-a-magazine, or a special advertising section. Such creative use of paper causes the user to notice the publication as an object, not just an invisible information delivery system. This increases the publication's perceived value.

"Simplicity of form is never a poverty, it is a great virtue." Jan Tschichold (1902–1974), typographer and designer

design should take into account the process of reading. Posters, for example, are designed for two-level readership: they make a primary effect at long distance and, having lured the reader closer, have secondary, close-up information.

Though a magazine or book is seen by readers one spread at a time, multiple-page stories are best planned in a single horizontal strip. This ensures design continuity from spread to spread. Because you only see one spread on screen at a time, computer makeup does not encourage the technique of "horizontal design." This failing is mitigated a little by the computer's support of design consistency through the use of guides, master pages, and typographic styles. It remains up to the designer, however, to create and use these tools that ensure consistency in a repetitive pattern.

Grids: freedom in structure

Unlimited design choice is both a blessing and a curse. Time is wasted investigating dead ends and aimlessly playing with design elements. It is often better to make design decisions chosen from a limited palette. There is beauty in simplicity and a grid imposes spatial simplicity.

Content has its own inherent structure. It comes

"Thus let it be the rule that everything be demonstrated to all the senses ... the visible to sight, the audible to hearing ... and if something can be perceived by several senses, let it be demonstrated to several senses."* Jan Amos Comenius (1592-1670), "The Father of Modern Education." Photos compress 3D into 2D, approximating reality. Making the image high contrast translates the picture of "reality" into a near-tactile experience.

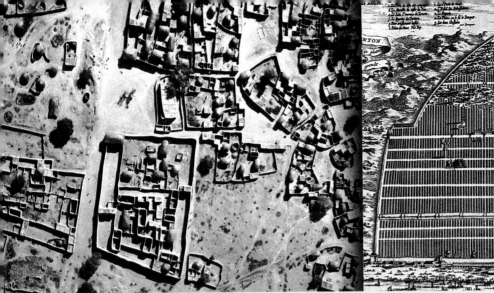

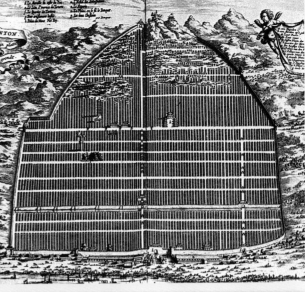

Two communities contrast structure and freedom in their planning. Logone-Birni, Cameroon, is a village with many organically shaped spaces. The c1665 city plan of Canton, China, shows more blocklike planning.

A grid imposes itself on both type and image, causing interesting abstraction (left). This also activates the background to come forward as a full design participant. By comparison, organic design shows type utterly effected by the illustration: the arrow smashes the type. The contrast in *design process* yields different design relationships, though neither approach is necessarily "better."

A Korean proverb says, "Only clean upstreams make clean downstreams." When beginning with an external format, the grid helps make "clean downstreams," that is, clear design relationships and organized, understandable pages. Every element aligns with the grid structure, ensuring formal agreements.

Note the three levels of typographic hierarchy: primary, secondary, and tertiary. This is the clearest, most useful differentiation possible, and readers *like* it.

A five-column quirky grid is used to bring order to the variety of pieces on this Web site. Items may be any combination of whole units.

built in, but it takes sensitivity to uncover the interconnectedness between parts. This is "organic design." There are occasions, though, when it is better to fit elements into an external format. Grids save time and they organize complex information like charts and schedules, scientific data, lists, and repetitive elements like headlines, pictures, and text.

Consistency and creativity are inspired by limiting choices. Freedom grows directly from structure. Though using a grid limits choices, it gives a design built-in cohesiveness. The limitations a grid imposes are chosen as the grid is developed, based on set priorities. Are images most important? How many levels of type are there?

Grid development must provide a variety of predetermined sizes that artwork and type will be made to fit. The smallest photos and illustrations define a module and that module is repeated in a multicolumn structure. The page is divided horizontally into equal clusters of text line units.

A simpler grid is usually better than a complex grid. A grid's complexity should help the designer answer the questions, "How big should this element be and where should I put it?" A seven-column grid is universally functional and great fun to use be-

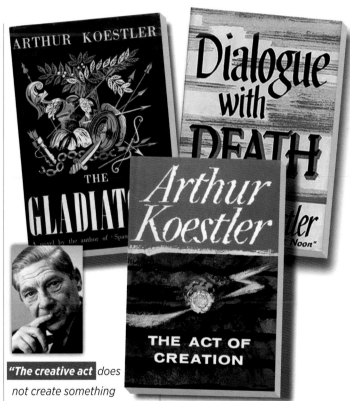

"The creative act does not create something out of nothing. It uncovers, selects, reshuffles, combines, synthesizes already existing facts, ideas, faculties, and skills. Typically, the more familiar the parts, the more striking the new whole." Arthur Koestler, CBE (1905–1983), writer

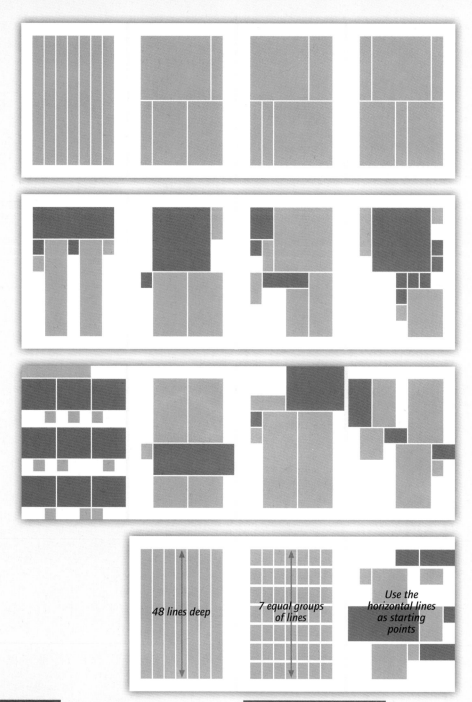

To create a vertical grid, divide the space into an uneven number of columns. A seven-column grid structures space with great flexibility (top row). It imposes white space because the narrow columns must be combined in pairs to accommodate type, leaving at least one narrow column empty. Shown diagrammatically (second and third row), these column variations show breadth of usefulness. They are not intended as layouts.

To create a horizontal grid, divide the number of a page's text lines into equal groups, skipping a text line between each group. For example, if there are forty-eight lines' depth on a page, there can be seven units of six lines each with one line added between units (7 groups x 6 text lines each + 6 spaces = 48 lines total depth).

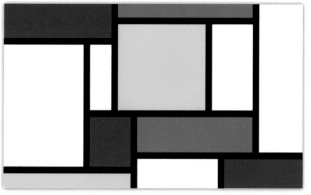

Piet Mondrian expressed de Stijl principles by using gridded space, asymmetrical composition, and primary colors. Though seemingly simple, his paintings are rooted in nature and spirituality. He says, "*The surface of things gives enjoyment, their interiority gives life.*"

Le Corbusier's 1952 Tower of Shadows in Chandigarh, India, is an exposed concrete grid. It is his seventeenth work designated as a World Heritage Site.

A piece of parchment (stretched sheepskin) is prepared for writing by having a grid lightly drawn on it in this detail of a 1255 German illuminated letter.

cause it contains many options. But beware: overly complex grids offer so many options they become all but useless because they no longer limit choices. Readers can't recognize organization when the grid units are too small.

Structured design has a visible cadence and tension that leads from one element to the next in an orderly way. But if structure is followed without thoughtful manipulation, it produces repetitive sameness and boredom. Grid development must include a description of how and when the structure (or "normal" placement) will be violated. The rules of violation focus creativity and make grid-based design look fresh. The most important rule of violation is to have an element break the grid when it deserves to stand out. In a context of sameness, that lone element becomes very visible.

In addition to organizing complex information on a particular page or spread, grids unite the cover and interior pages and relate one issue to the next. Grids also organize an entire company's visual requirements. They build family resemblance among on-screen applications, brochures, data sheets, and advertising. **EoGD3**

Chuck Close's portraits use the grid-like structuring of Roman mosaics, "all-overness" in which every area is given equal importance, and is an advanced iteration of pointillism. An enlarged detail is shown on the right.

To which photo does this caption belong? This lack of organization is poor craftsmanship.

Arbitrary or uneven spacing makes the reader guess about relationships that should be clear

Centered captions are less clearly attached to their photos than flush left captions

Spacing between captions and photos is not equal in this example

Flush left captions align with their respective photos.

Captions may run as deep as necessary because they have enough relating attributes.

Equalize spacing between photos and captions.

Captions should never run the same width as their photos. It is too obvious a relationship!

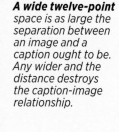
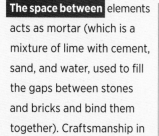

An ideal six-point space bonds this caption to its image. A narrower separation makes the caption look like it is crowding the image. Wider distances make captions look unconnected.

A wide twelve-point space is as large the separation between an image and a caption ought to be. Any wider and the distance destroys the caption-image relationship.

A too-narrow three-point space separates but makes the caption look like it is crowding the image.

Emil Weiss Illustration

The space between elements acts as mortar (which is a mixture of lime with cement, sand, and water, used to fill the gaps between stones and bricks and bind them together). Craftsmanship in bricklaying is determined by the quality of the mortaring. Similarly, the designer's craft, particularly in typography, is measured by our handling of space that binds design elements together.

Captions are connected to their corresponding artwork by the distance that separates them. A half pica is an ideal distance: not too near to crowd and not too far to look like it is unconnected.

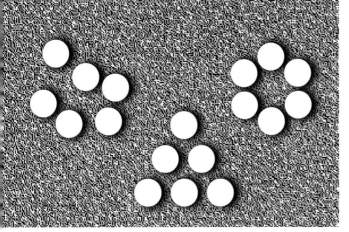

The dots are identical: our perception of their connection changes from random to meaningful because *the spaces between them* has been changed.

Space connects when it is proportionally less within the figure than in the surrounding space as in this poster for a United Nations conference.

These colors and baselines are intentionally misleading. The only thing that matters here is letter-to-letter proximity: the top line reads "Jazz in Willisau."

7 Connecting elements and pages

Space is never complete and finite. It is in motion, connected to the next space and the next. Marcel Breuer (1902–1981)

The mason's craft is defined by applying mortar evenly between stones or bricks (opposite, top). Masons don't make the bricks; rather, *they manage the space between the bricks*. The typographer's craft is similarly defined by applying space between letters, words, and areas of type. White space can be used like mortar between bricks to cement elements together. White space connects when used in consistent, measured amounts in a design. As an abstract illustration, a group of six dots can be made to mean something by changing only the *space between* the dots (above).

Wide spaces separate and narrow spaces connect. That is, elements can be separated by distance or related by nearness. The closer elements are, the more related they seem to be. Cut into the text on the page 147, the first set of gray rectangles are seen

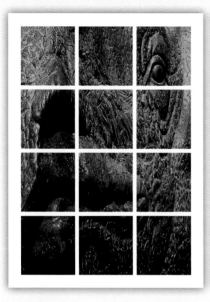
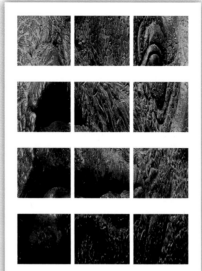
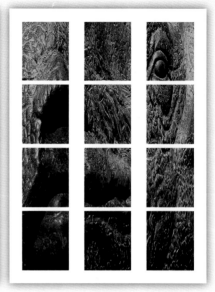

①

②

③

④

Voltaire
Common sense
is not so common

Voltaire
Common sense
is not so common

Vol-
taire
Common sense
is not so common

Voltaire
Common sense
is not so common

Emphasize one direction

to avoid directional gridlock, when neither direction dominates. Each of the twelve rectangles appears equally near to one another. Wider horizontal spaces create rows because the thicker horizontal spaces dominate and separate, while the narrower spaces connect through proximity. Wider vertical spaces create columns because the vertical spaces dominate and separate.

Space as a directional force

(L-R): **①** Space exerts pressure from below, emphasizing verticality; **②** type aligned at the right edge of the page creates horizontal direction; **③** white space in the foreground indicates diagonal direction; and **④** traditional optically centered position (just above geometric center) of the page produces perfect equilibrium.

Nathan Carter and the Morgan State University Choir

Brooklyn Philharmonic Orchestra

From Gospel to Gershwin

Conducted by Gunther Schuller

White space leads the reader through the competing elements of a design, much like a walking path leads through a garden. If separation can be achieved with a spatial adjustment alone, it is likely to be a more elegant solution than through the addition of lines or unnecessary type and color contrasts. The strong horizontality of this typographic example – and the three clearly defined sizes of display type – make it appealingly easy to navigate. The garden path (*a space between* the shrubs) similarly makes negotiating the ground cover both easy and pleasant.

as a group of three plus one. Overlapping elements shows maximum relationship. The four rectangles are now seen as a single multisided shape, increasing their impact.

There is a risk to defining areas by using boxes. While boxes effectively enclose space, they tend to overseparate, harming the unity of the page. Instead of boxes, use wider alleys between elements. Space that is carefully allocated reveals *intentional separation* of content.

Space emphasizes direction

Readers look first in the upper left corner. Does this mean designers must design for an upper left starting point? No, but as Walter Dexel, German artist and Bauhaus–era proponent of simplified typography, says, designs that stray from the expected norm must do so knowingly. Designers must make accommodations for diverging from the expected. Guiding the reader in nontraditional directions requires greater accord between all elements. For example, make hierarchy extremely clear so a focal point in, say, the bottom of the page, stands out visibly.

PLATE XIII
Model of Star-Dodecahedron with Twelve Vertices

"Rhythm is in time what symmetry is in space." Matila Ghyka (1881–1965), *The Geometry of Art and Life* (1946). Ghyka was a Romanian naval officer, mathematician, historian, philosopher, and academic. His diverse

interests led him to explore the mathematics of form in the 1920s. Among his several books is his 1952 *Practical Handbook of Geometrical Composition and Design.*

The prevailing direction created by figures is the starting point for shaping space, as shown by the four headlines in these spreads. Controlling space between words and lines of text type creates direction, which can be manipulated to craft a dynamic design. Nonalignment can be used to contrast a single element outside the prevailing alignment to give it visibility. "The New Face of Trade Unionism" is flush left except for one hanging word; though "Jackson Pollock" is the same width as the two text columns, it is not centered over them; the display type in the opener on a film actor and director is angled to match the image; "1979" and "1980" and the captions that overlap them are asymmetrical and hang into the outside margins.

Use space in thick slabs so it matters – and so it looks like you *meant* it. A good rule of thumb is that the bigger the element, like the bigger the animal, the need for bigger space.

Messages are delivered over time, whether it is the few seconds it takes to scan a page or spread, or the few more seconds it takes to flip through a multipage story. Time implies space and motion, from one element to the next and from one spread to the next. Motion requires direction which unifies and guides attention to key information.

Dynamic design needs emphasis in a prevailing direction, whether vertical, horizontal, or diagonal. Equalizing directional force produces a motionless design that evokes a classical or traditional look. Motionless design is, of course, a legitimate choice under the proper circumstances, but in general does not serve the reader's need for dynamic expression. Diagonal emphasis has been misunderstood as the most dynamic arrangement. In practice, it is often used when a designer lacks a better idea. Diagonal emphasis should be used with caution because its startling effect is extremely self-conscious and its use can actually detract from the message.

Use white space to echo the prevailing direction of design elements. Headlines correctly broken for sense make their own shapes that should be exploited.

To isolate one part of a design from another yet still retain their appearance as a single entity, create a standardized space within the story, say, half a linespace, and double it to a full line space between the story and its illustration. Mathematical ratios like 2-to-1 and 3-to-1 ensure a built-in harmony among parts.

WATER & PEACE

IN THE MIDDLE EAST, WHERE WATER IS AS PRECIOUS AS OIL, THE JORDAN RIVER IS A PAWN IN A COMPLICATED DIPLOMATIC GAME. BY BRUCE STUTZ

CIVIL WAR BATTLEFIELDS

Saving the Landscapes of America's Deadliest War

Manassas, Virginia · July 1861 & August 1861

Visual flow is shown in this four-spread (eight-page) story. Narrow columns for breakouts and captions and consistent image sizes make this stand out as a feature story in the issue.

Space connects spreads, particularly in magazine feature stories which require distinctive layout to break the format of regularly occurring department pages.

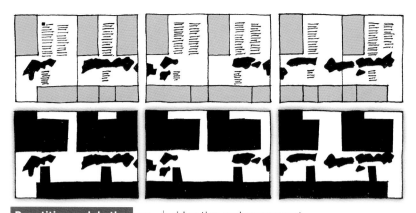

Repetition and rhythm are shown in these three-spread (or six-page) diagrams in which empty space is as consistently formed as any other element. Careful consideration and assessment of the materials at hand is necessary to develop such a pattern.

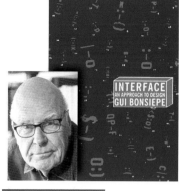

"Order is a function of the horizontal and vertical reference lines on a page and the frequency with which the corners of the items fall on these lines." Gui Bonsiepe (1934–)

Space connects pages

A multiple-page document, whether a magazine story or a technical user manual, is made of many individual pieces. They must be unified into a clear, ordered statement that looks deliberate and purposefully presented. They must catch and hold the reader's attention.

White space connects pages when the spaces remain the same. In magazine design, repetition and rhythm of spaces and elements help the reader recognize flow from spread to spread and from issue to issue. Repeated department pages, which define the visual personality of a magazine, should be unified by distinctive head and outer margin sinkage so their recurrence creates a familiar and identifiable pattern. A feature story, which by definition is special material, must appear to be special throughout its length, including "continued on" pages. Its design, therefore, cannot be the same as either departments or other feature stories. Inventing a different formula for handling space is one way to unify pages in a feature story.

Elements and surrounding spaces must be identically placed. Create a pattern of occupied and unoccupied spaces by distilling commonalities among

Space breaks up letterforms so the separated, abstracted parts create a connection to the abundant framed images in the primary photo on this opening spread in *France* magazine.

The grid-determined empty areas of this layout help emphasize a strong horizontality through the story about a design school.

Consolidate bits of white space and put them in chunks at the bottoms – or tops – of columns. This gives an informal chattiness to text columns and makes the editing process easier.

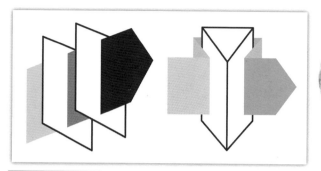

Arrows represent a linear thought process. A message can pick up speed and value as it gets loaded with its descriptors (left) or the message can get bogged down by the load that has been placed on it (right). It is the designer's job to choose material and present it so the message becomes more apparent, not more disguised.

A clockwise spiral reading from the upper right is used to arrange the forty-five still-undeciphered marks on the 6″ Phaistos Disk, c1600 BC on Crete. Did the disk's roundness provoke the spiral? The hieroglyphic symbols, found on both sides of the disk, were made with "seals," or stamps.

the materials at hand. To ensure unity, design pages in spreads or, even better, as complete stories, as they will be viewed and perceived by the reader. Make their repetition and rhythm unavoidable.

Repetition is not dull. Variety for its own sake, on the other hand, disintegrates unity. The most visible elements to treat consistently are borders and white space, typefaces, illustration and photo sizes and styles, the logo, and color.

Sequentiality: chains of thought

A message is revealed one link at a time: a headline, a first visual, a second visual, a caption, a subhead, then maybe the text. Each of these "hits" is like a link in a chain. No link is itself the chain: the combination of links makes the chain.

A design's plan must include the order in which the parts – the display type, the images, the captions, and the text – are to be noticed and read. Absent this sequencing, a reader is faced with a "bowl of oatmeal," an area of relatively equivalent noisiness, none of which is sufficiently appetizing to stop and nibble.

Sequencing information is among a designer's most essential tasks. Book designers, for example, structure their typography into title, chapter and

"One reads from the top left to the bottom right and must design accordingly." Walter Dexel (1890–1973), German designer and typographer. Dexel considered himself a painter first and a graphic designer and

typographer second. He was a friend and contemporary of El Lissitzky, Arp, Klee, Gropius, Moholy-Nagy, and Schwitters.

Uncaptive Minds

What teaching a college-level class at a maximum-security correctional facility did for the inmates — and for me. By Ian Buruma

Illustration by Istvan Banyai

The main business of Napanoch, N.Y., is a maximum-security prison, Eastern New York Correctional Facility, also known as Happy Nap. The population of Eastern, 1,250 men, many from New York City, is about the same as that of Napanoch itself. Imposing in a hideous kind of way, the prison, built at the end of the 19th century, is modeled after a medieval fortress, with towers and turrets and a pyramid roof. The overall effect — stony pomposity framed by lush green hills — is rather Germanic.

There is nothing particularly happy about Napanoch, situated on the raffish edges of the Catskills about 70 miles north of Manhattan; its better days as an affordable resort area for New York and New Jersey Jews have long gone. There are a few motels nearby with cracked signs that read Starlite and Eldorado; a diner; a Jewish cemetery; and a "colony farm," where

New York

Avian flu, hurricane, chemical spill, terrorist bomb, earthquake:
Whatever the next apocalypse is, New York—and New Yorkers—are getting ready for it.
But have we done enough? The strategies and tactics of survival.

REMAIN CALM

By Craig Horowitz

ON AN EARLY-WINTER MONDAY MORNING in Hong Kong, a businessman boards a plane for New York. The man, who'd spent a few days touring the Chinese countryside during his trip, is not feeling great. He's tired and achy. He can't decide if it's the wear and tear of his travels or the beginning of a cold, but after coughing and sweating throughout his six-teen-hour flight, he's certain he's getting sick.

By the time he goes through Customs at JFK, gets his bags, and finds a cab, he has only enough energy left to check into his midtown hotel and collapse on the bed in his room. The next day, feeling even sicker, he heads to the nearest emergency room. By now, he's got a high fever and he's coughing up blood. Given his robust flulike symptoms and his international travel, alarm bells go off in the ER.

Though word hasn't yet reached the U.S., there have been several dozen confirmed cases of human-to-human transmission of the H5N1 virus—better known as avian flu—in the Chinese countryside and several other spots in Asia. But even without the new information, the ER doctors, who've been drilled on what to watch for, are convinced it's avian flu. Taking no chances, they isolate the patient. But the damage has been done—the businessman has infected people on the plane, at JFK, in his hotel, and even in the hospital's waiting room.

The city's ability to deal with the pandemic is severely hampered by these problems. There is no vaccine and won't be for months. Tamiflu,

---

Sequencing information should logically and clearly lead from the primary visual to the headline, then to the secondary visual, caption, subhead, and finally to the text. Each of these pieces should be chosen or written as one part of a single continuous message whose purpose is to reveal to the reader what the article is about and why it is valuable to them.

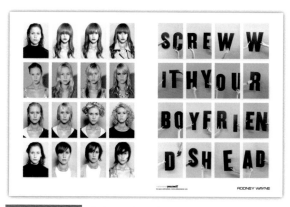

The sequence of absorption is a chain of thought. The sixteen letters and sixteen images on this spread ad forces a back-and-forth exploration of the same models' changing hair styles and makeup.

section headings, subheadings, text, and captions. Such typographic structure helps the reader scan for generalities and, at least initially, ignore details until they commit themselves to the text.

For every design project, write on small Post-it Notes each of the ideas you want a reader to recognize (right). Now put the notes in order of descending importance. Readers should have thoughts presented to them like links in a chain – or beads on a string. Albrecht von Haller, eighteenth-century anatomist and poet, said, "Man can only follow chains [of thought], as we cannot present several things at once in our speech."

Information mapping and wayfinding

Information mapping is patterning data so it signals relevance and connections that are best shown, not merely described. By showing connections, information mapping makes data easier to access. Research and common sense show that readers like finding information easily and documents that simplify finding things. Information mapping requires that content be prepared in segmented, simple hierarchical structure.

Information mapping is a process of handling and presenting content shaped by *users' needs* and

Bits of information are perceived in sequence, like links in a chain, each connected to what came before and what comes next. Arrange information accordingly. All these display "hits" lure and lead to the text.

"I don't explain, I don't tell, I show." Leo Tolstoy (1828–1910), author, eight-time Nobel Literature and Peace prize nominee

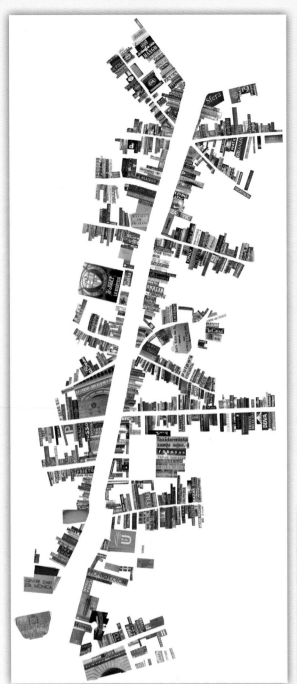

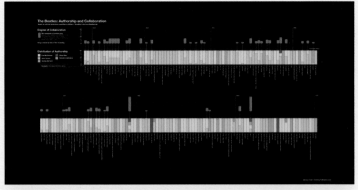

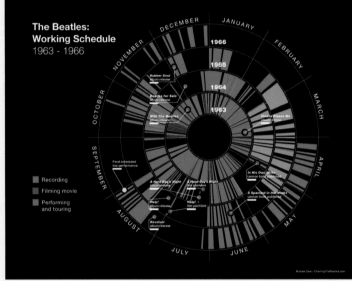

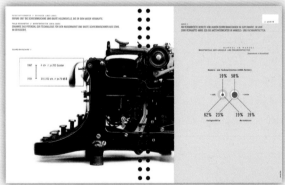

Information mapping is illustrated in this visual description of a Spanish main street and its twenty-three street crossings based on density of use and people flow.

Information mapping describes the Beatles' songwriting collaboration from 1963 to 1970. Colors show the band's gradual fracturing. Red tabs, signifying jointly-written songs, decrease in late 1967. The sec-

ond diagram compares the Beatles' main activities from 1963 to 1966. Consistencies in scheduling from year to year are revealed: the blue areas show movie filming in March and April of 1964 and 1965, for example.

Information mapping in this spread from an electronics retailer's annual report explains how typewriters made no money for the inventor in 1867 but lots of money for subsequent sellers (340,000 in 1924).

IL MOVIMENTO TURISTICO IN ITALIA

Fonte UIC	Entrate valutarie	Uscite	Saldo
1° trim. 52	4,554	3,197	1,357
2° trim. 52	7,877	7,362	515
Totale	**19,289**	**14,780**	**4,503**
1° trim. 51	4,495	2,953	1,542
2° trim. 51	6,817	4,803	2,014
Totale	**17,141**	**10,207**	**6,934**

Careful balance of horizontal and vertical pathways is essential in making a table legible. Both reading directions are necessary, though one must always dominate.

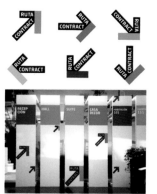

Color-coded wayfinding, as in this system for a show at a Spanish convention center, is limited to colors which can be readily recognized and remembered.

Wayfinding can be useful even from 30,000 feet, a problem this 100' tall airport "environmental communications system" resolves.

the *purpose* of the information. It has three steps: analyze, organize, and present. This extracts the core message and makes it evident, which results in an easy-to-scan format that attracts casual and uncommitted viewers and highlights details.

Wayfinding has been compared to information mapping but in three dimensions. For example sign systems are wayfinding. Though the designed results may be quite different between the two disciplines, they share a common purpose of making information user friendly and adding comfort to complex messages and environments. Wayfinding is particularly important to graphic designers as a signaling tool on Web sites and in lengthy, mixed-content paginated documents like magazines, where design in three dimensions becomes evident as pages are turned or clicked through.

Though it is a term coined in 1960 by an urban planner in reference to environmental planning, wayfinding's meaning was expanded in the 1980s to include architectural signage. Its meaning has grown further to encompass any navigation tool that furthers acclimatization in a complex environment. In short, wayfinding helps people orient themselves to their surroundings. **EoGD3**

Wayfinding is used in signage and as department heading signals in multipage documents.

"A map isn't the territory, it's the difference, be it in altitude, vegetation, population, or terrain." Gregory Bateson (1904–1980)

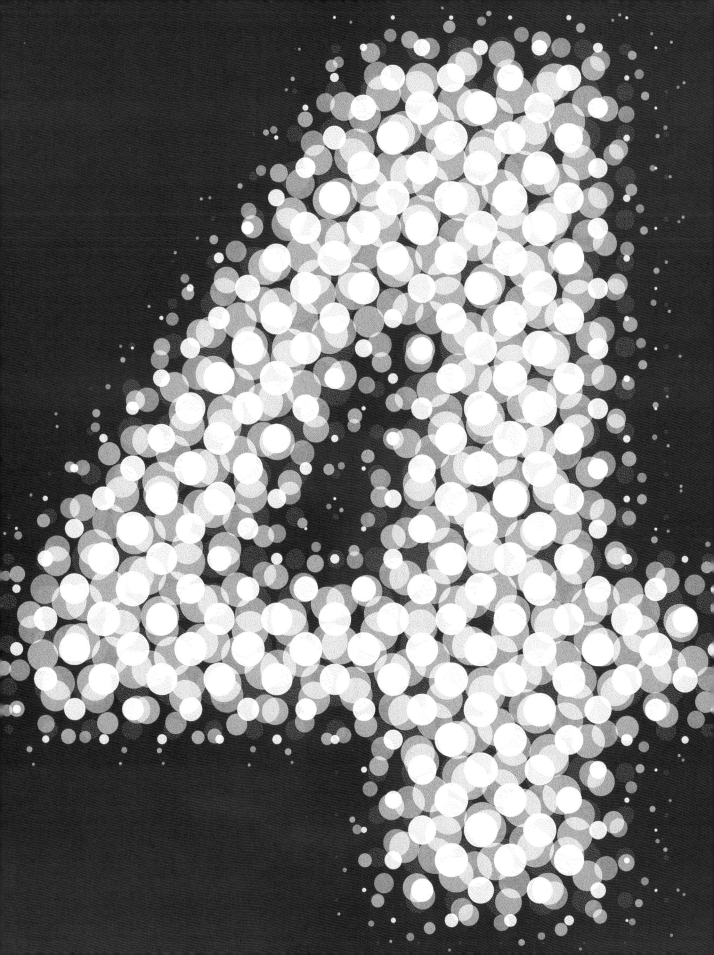

"Unless typography is being used as central to the communication, as the pivotal illustration, what makes the communication work is always the content." Saul Bass (1920–1996)

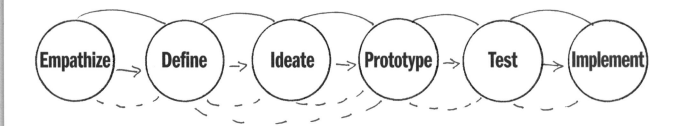

Empathize → Define → Ideate → Prototype → Test → Implement

Design thinking and leadership

Max Shangle
maxshangle.com

The framework of Design Thinking methodology provides a means to understand, distill, explore, flesh out, try, and learn. Often the expression "fail early, learn faster" is applied to this process. Removing the risk of failure during the process empowers Design Thinkers to stretch the constraints of the tool, technique, principle, or knowledge presented. Learning and building on the complexities of design process and design execution, the rigor of exploration of "what if" and "what works" solutions, and fully embrace the results.

The application of Design Thinking is frequently represented graphically in a linear format (*above*), suggesting a smooth, logical, clean progression from one process, activity, or element to the next. However, in reality, design is a bit more like a performance by Erich Brenn. Mr. Brenn was frequently seen on *The Ed Sullivan Show* spinning bowls on tall sticks, spinning plates on a tabletop, flipping eggs into glasses, and more – all at the *SAME* time in a live five-minute act with-

out breaking anything. Mr. Brenn leapt from one task to the next, monitoring moving pieces, while launching more elements – a flurry of chaotic activity and delight ultimately resulting in a strange harmony. Similarly, the messy, chaotic and frequently disjointed aspects of the design process (*above opposite*) require dexterity, intuition, skill, talent, methods, and execution to create solutions that induce harmony and delight, all while being constrained by time, budget, and scope.

Just as design is messy, chaotic, and disjointed, so is leadership. If Design Thinking can provide a framework for solving design problems, can it also provide structure for leadership? This chart applies Design Thinking terms to leadership skills and methods:

When actively applied, Design Thinking:
- ✔ Forces the solution to be born from discovery and understanding
- ✔ Forces the necessary to dominate the solution-finding process
- ✔ Engages expert/novice wisdom in the process
- ✔ Provides verifiable/tangible solutions to test

- ✔ Forces the designer (team) to avoid leaping to a solution and then bludgeoning that "solution" to fit

Although applying the principles and lessons of Design Thinking to leadership would seem to be a simple, linear path to learning to be a leader, it is more akin to Mr. Brenn's chaos in action. Learning to be and *being* a leader is not a function of job title or promotion: it is a deliberate, verifiable set of skills and knowledge. It requires continuous maintenance through reflection, diligence, and effort.

Empathize Digging deep into the situation, problem, or goal with attention on others.
- ✔ Applying "Expert Naiveté" to leadership is to view the problem, goal or approach without supposition or leaping at a

solution. It is to truly understand with clarity, not by knowing what "should be" or lazily relying on "the way it has always been done," but rather by discovery, learning, and observing.
- ✔ Leading comes from understanding one's authentic self, frequently referred to as understanding one's "True North."

Design Thinking						
	Empathize ⇒	Define ⇒	Ideate ⇒	Prototype ⇒	Test ⇒	Implement
Leadership						
	Listen closely	Insight	Connections	Tangible	Prove	Why in front
	Frame	Inspiration	Create	Experience	Verify	Story
	Discover	Vision	What if	How	Question	Purpose
	Empower	Validate	Blue-sky thinking			

Academic president, dean, and design professor, Max Shangle is a leader of overlapping constituencies.

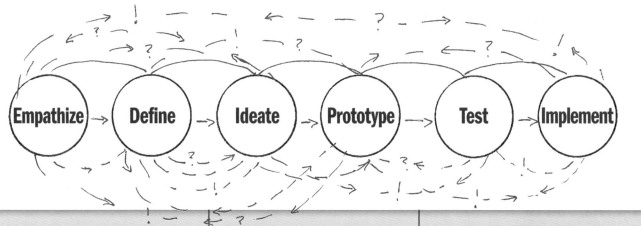

Raw, unvarnished understanding of one's authentic self is for many the most difficult part of becoming a leader, but it is critical to being a true leader.

Define What are the guiding principles and culture that are disseminated, shared, and understood by the group, division, or company? A case could be made to ask the question: What is the design brief?

✓ Making the mission, vision, and purpose clear to all constituencies. Leadership is empowering and serving others: company, culture, group, or individual. *"Praesis ut prosis ne ut imprese,"* leading in order to serve, not in order to rule.

✓ A leader builds a shared understanding of the mission, the vision and purpose with those empowered to implement it. Leadership empowers them to strive to effectively put it into play.

Ideate Build around purpose. Put Why in front of What. Engage those directly and indirectly involved. Create and foster no-risk judgment-free space for ideas and learning to flourish.

✓ Making connections, creating the culture of the company, division, team, or individual that serves the mission, vision or purpose. Considering "what if" scenarios and solutions, allowing exploration without risk of failure, providing support and clarity.

As a leader remaining open to what may seem to be anything that is not status quo, withholding judgment, refraining from reacting, and allowing discovery to stimulate learning.

Prototype Construct personnel structures (lines of reporting, pilot teams, cross-disciplinary groups) to put into practice what will be tested.

✓ What is revealed during use and implementation of the prototype? Does clarity overrule confusion, does the prototype exceed expectations? Evaluating what was discovered.

✓ Leading by allowing the prototype to be developed, allowing for discovery and incremental improvements. Validating the prototype against the original goal or problem.

Test Testing should involve rigor, candid evaluation, and risk-free examination.

✓ Interrogating every process and decision. Do the implemented Policies, Processes, and Actions ring consistent to all affected? Do they serve and reinforce the culture? Do they serve to empower? Gut check: Does your leadership in action match your "True North"?

✓ Leading from what has been learned from the process. Listening, and critically observing. Equipping those that will implement or be directly or indirectly

affected by the solution or change to evaluate systemically.

Implement Build a story that authentically positions and provides a foundation for action and understanding.

✓ Putting *why things are done* in front of *what must be done*, sharing the why to provide real clarity. Leaders build trust and camaraderie much the way companies build a brand (there are only two things one can do to the brand: build it or erode it). Leaders build mission, vision, and purpose. Leaders provide context and empower their team to achieve excellence.

When applied to leadership, Design Thinking methodology provides a framework for leadership just as it does for the design process itself. It requires weighing all of the impacts, insights, and inputs from those impacted and addressing each with empathy. Implementation takes commitment, communication, and patience. As with Mr. Brenn, chaos is ever present. The leader must attend to "spinning plates," navigate chaos, attend to the details of everyday work all while striving to empower, and cultivate the "brand." Not every decision, action, or challenge can wait for the full engagement of Design Thinking but in a culture where it is the rule rather than the exception, the number of broken plates can be minimized. **EoGD3**

Ten questions about copyright

Tad Crawford
tadcrawford.com

An attorney, Tad Crawford served as General Counsel for the Graphic Artists Guild and testified before the Senate subcommittee handling copyright. He is also the author of regular columns on design legal issues for *Communication Arts* magazine and has written numerous books to aid creative professionals. Crawford says, *"Teaching at the School of Visual Arts in New York City showed me the need for books that assist creative professionals in furthering their careers."*

1 Why is copyright important? If you are a creator of images (whether Photoshop user, photographer, designer, or fine artist), copyright protects you from having your images stolen by someone else. As the copyright owner, you may either allow or prevent anyone else from making copies of your work, making derivations from your work (such as a poster made from a photograph), or displaying your work publicly. Your copyrights last for your lifetime plus another seventy years, so a successful work may benefit not only you but your heirs as well. If you are a user of images, it is important that you understand the rights and obligations connected with their use so you don't infringe on the copyright of someone else and expose yourself to legal or financial liabilities.

2 What is an infringement? Infringement is unauthorized use of someone else's work. The test for infringement is whether an ordinary observer would believe one work was copied from another.

3 Is it an infringement if I scan an old image into Photoshop and change it? If the image was created in the United States and is more than 95 years old, it is in the public domain and can be freely copied by you or anyone else. You will have copyright in the new elements of the image that you create.

4 Is it an infringement if I scan a recent image into Photoshop and change it? The scanning itself is making a copy and so it is an infringement. It is unlikely you will be sued for infringement if you change the photograph to the point where an ordinary observer would no longer believe your work was copied from the original photograph.

5 What does "fair use" mean in terms of copyright? A fair use is a use of someone else's work that is allowed under the copyright law; for example, newsworthy or educational uses are likely to be fair uses. The factors for whether a use is a fair use or an infringement are: (1) the purpose and character of the use, including whether or not it is for profit; (2) the character of the copyrighted work; (3) how much of the total work is used; and (4) what effect the use will have on the market for or value of the work being copied.

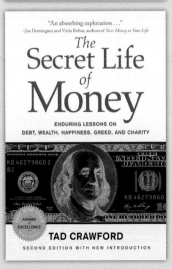

6 **Can I use a recognizable part of a photograph if the entire photograph is not recognizable?** You would have to apply the fair use factors. Factor (3) in the previous answer relating to how much of the total work is used would be in your favor, but if the use is to make a profit and will damage the market for the source photograph it might be considered an infringement.

7 **What are the damages for infringement?** The damages are the actual losses of the person infringed plus any profits of the infringer. In some cases (especially if the work was registered before the infringement), the court can simply award statutory damages between $750 and $30,000 for each work infringed. If the infringement is willful, the court can award as much as $150,000.

8 **Do I have to register my images to obtain my copyright?** No, you have the copyright from the moment you create a work. However, registration with the Copyright Office will help you in the event your work is infringed. The Copyright Office (*copyright.gov*) has a great deal of helpful information about registration and copyright. The Copyright Office strongly prefers that registration be done online and the usual fee is $65 (although it may be less if a single creator registers a single work, or more if the registration is of a group of works falling in the same administrative class).

9 **Do I need to use copyright notice to obtain or protect my copyright?** It is always wise to place copyright notice on your work because it is the visible symbol of your rights as copyright owner. The absence of copyright notice cannot cause the loss of the copyright but may give infringers a loophole to try and lessen their damages. Copyright notice has three elements: (1) "Copyright" or "Copr." or "©"; (2) the name of the copyright owner; and (3) the year of first publication.

10 **How do I get permission to reproduce an image?** A simple permission form will suffice. It should state what kind of project you are doing, what materials you want to use, what rights you need in the material, what credit line and copyright notice will be given, and what payment, if any, will be made. The person giving permission should sign the permission form. If you are using an image of a person, you should have them sign a model release. If the person's image is to be altered or placed in a situation that didn't occur, you would want the release to cover this. Otherwise, you may face a libel or invasion of privacy lawsuit. **EoGD3**

Pluck less often

HEADLINE

DECK

CAPTION

LOGO

TEXT

Vaniqa™ slows facial hair growth so you can significantly reduce your current maintenance program.

UFH Unwanted Facial Hair is a condition that develops in women with the onset of menopause or an increase in body weight. Hair follicles around the lips and chin grow when they receive too much androgen, a naturally-occurring hormone. • Vaniqa™, a trans-parent cream, blocks androgen from hair follicles, so hair grows more slowly. You won't have to pluck, shave, bleach, wax, or zap as often. • Visit our Web site or ask your doctor about

VANIQA™
Eflornithine HCl 13%

Bristol-Myers Squibb Company
www.bristolmyerssquibb.com

Hair follicles around the lips and chin grow when they receive too much hormone. Vaniqa slows hair growth.

Typographic elements, like headline and text, are distinct visual voices. They are equivalent to the different voices one might use to indicate characters in a story that is read aloud. The information hierarchy is revealed in an ad in descending order of importance (*top*). Notice the circuitous path the reader has to follow in this design before getting to the text. This may deter casual browsers.

Typography creates clear differences in content, valuable even in small, subtle doses. Note the contrast between text and caption in the example on the right, and the subsequent stronger relationship between the caption and the picture, which deserves to be exploited.

It is not enough to have "nothing wrong" with a design. There must be something recognizably "right" to be considered good design. What makes a design ugly, like the example above left, is the random combination of pieces, chosen on whim. The arbitrary font choices and uncertain positioning make designs complex and sloppy. Simpler letterforms with design consistencies, used in a way that is in some way sensible, make designs handsome and descriptive.

Every typeface has a "visual voice," an equivalency to the spoken word. These are the same characters in four Korean typefaces.

Listening to type

Typographic arrangement should achieve for the reader what voice tone conveys for the listener.
El Lissitzky (1893–1941)

What do we mean by "listening to type"? Imagine listening to a book recorded on tape. The reader's voice changes with the story, helping the listener hear various characters and emotions. A story told on paper should do the same thing. The "characters" typographers work with are categories of type: headlines, subheads, captions, text, and so forth. These typographic characters are our players and must be matched for both individual clarity and overall unity.

Typography is, according to the dictionary, "the process of printing with type." The root words that make up *typography* are *typo* (type) and *graphy* (drawing), so it literally means *drawing with type*. My definition is: *applying type in an expressive way to reveal the content clearly and memorably with the least resistance from the reader.*

Keep typography simple 171
Expressive type requires relative quietness in its surroundings to be heard.

Frozen sound 173
An alphabet is made of glyphs that *represent sounds*, so writing can and should be considered "graphic speaking."

El Lissitzky's ad for carbon paper uses type styles to illustrate meaning. The four typographic elements are each treated differently, but the alignments, spacing, and artwork act as unifiers to counteract these stylistic differences.

"The quality of typography is dependent on the relationship between the printed and unprinted parts. It is a sign of professional immaturity to ignore the decisive contribution of the unprinted area."
Emil Ruder (1914–1970)

Typographic rules, like the development of word spacing, have evolved over centuries. These samples, which precede the development of word spacing, date from 196 BC and AD c500.

Typographic rules, like the adherence to word spacing and line breaks, may be manipulated to create startling results, as in this broadside found at an art school.

Breaking design rules makes a design more visible. This 1995 Neville Brody panel from *Fuse* magazine reads "Superstition" in one of Brody's many idiosyncratic typefaces.

Typography involves far more than working with the abstract black shapes. In practice, typographic decisions are – or should be – 90 percent about *the manipulation of the space around the letterforms.* Indeed, poor typography results from misunderstanding the importance of the "not-letterforms" and concentrating only on the letters themselves. "Not-letterforms," or the space surrounding letters, is seen between characters, words, lines, and between blocks and columns of type. It is the contrast of the letterform to its surrounding space that makes type either less or more legible. Legibility is central to typography because type is, after all, meant to be read.

Consistent spacing makes reading easier because the reader is unaware of inconsistencies in rhythm, which is to reading what static is to the radio. The measure of a good typeface is whether every letter combination is spaced for optical equivalency so no dark spots appear where letters are too close. Even spacing produces even typographic "color," or gray tone.

Typographers use elements and traditions inherited through generations of writing, printing, and reading. Many typographic rules were adopted from

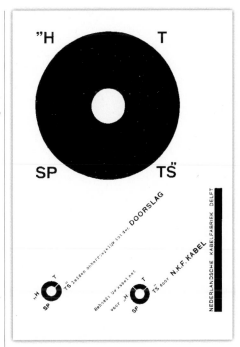

Piet Zwart's typography shows complex relationships using simple letterforms. An architect until age thirty-six when he turned to typography, Zwart approached letterforms unrestrained by design convention.

(SOUND MIND)×(SOUND BODY)×
120 DECIBELS = INNER PEACE

Shoes made for the sport of living. The new **Stormer.**™ **asics**
sound mind, sound body

(SOUND MIND)×(SOUND BODY)×
120 DECIBELS = INNER PEACE

Attitude in advertising is often best described using hand lettering. The headline set in an ordinary typeface makes the message much more rigid, not at all the feeling the ad is trying to evoke as it holds a mirror up – as all advertising must – to its intended audience. Incidentally, a typeface made to *look like* handwriting is a poor substitute because identically repeated characters give away the art director's laziness.

The flexibility of letterforms as worthwhile shapes unto themselves developed in the early twentieth century, as shown in this *Broom* magazine cover by Fernand Léger.

Typographic fireworks (*Cross Country*) contrast with clear simplicity (*Masters of Deception*) and a balance between eye-catching novelty and elegant clarity

(*I'm Pretty Sure I Like You A Lot*). Each of these three designs uses type in a way that effectively interprets its content.

handwriting as printable type forms were developed in the 1400s and 1500s. Historically, typography was handled by the printer who cut his own typefaces, designed the page, and reproduced the design on paper. In the twentieth century, typography and printing separated. Around 1950, typographers and typesetters became outside vendors who set type to the specifications of the designer or art director. Computers, with their working methodology, have nearly obliterated the typography specialist since all type decisions are made within a page design program. Designers are expected to be masters of this art form in addition to conceptualization and layout.

Choosing a typeface that matches the content is important. Words are symbols of emotions and ideas that manipulate the reader. But choosing the right typeface is not as important as using a more neutral typeface well. Dutch designer Piet Zwart (1885–1977) said, "Pretentious [letterforms] oppose the utilitarian task of typography. The more uninteresting a letter is in itself the more useful it is in typography." The danger is that typography will begin and end with choosing the typeface rather than be used to reveal the content. And that is not typography, but fashion.

Unlike typography, musical notational styles generally don't add to or detract from the musical message itself. This is a Bach's Organ Prelude in B flat shown in the composer's own hand.

There is, undeniably, an electricity to seeing the result of the act of ultimate human creation this close.

ESPERIENZA

Del follevamento de' fluidi nel vano de' cannellini fotti-lissimi dentr' al voto.

TRAGLI altri effetti della preſſione dell' aria è ſtato da alcuni annoverato anche quello del follevarſi, che fanno quaſi tutti i fluidi dentro a' cannelli ſtrettiſſimi, che in eſſi s'immergono. Dubitano queſti, che quel ſottiliſſimo cilindro d' aria, che giù pel cannello preme, verbigrazia, in ſull'acqua, operi più debolmente la ſua preſſione, per lo contraſto, che gli fa nel diſcendere il gran toccamento, ch' egli à col-

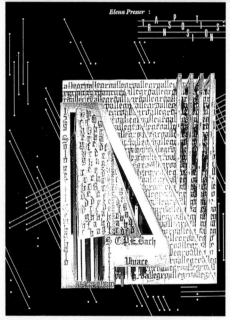

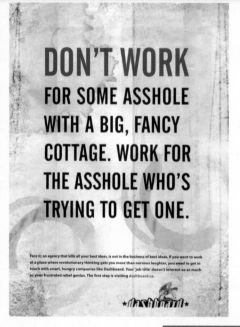

Flavors of type, c1691, Filippo Cecchi, Florence: contrasting size, capitalization, letter-spacing, and column width show lively differences. A single type family unites these four voices, offsetting their variety.

"I try to bring type to the maximum level of its expressive potential," says William Longhauser of his poster (*left*). "It is essential that [type] can be read, but I play with it until it expresses the content of the message.

It may take longer to recognize the word *Transpo-sitions* (in the top right corner), but the experience of deciphering the meaning is more memorable. In a sense, I am forcing partici-pation by the viewer."

Typographic tone of voice is expressed in this no-nonsense use of workaday Trade Gothic (*right*). With words this powerful, repre-sentational imagery would do nothing to enhance this message.

PAROCHIAL
difficult
Orthodox
State of the art
Vernacular

Abstract word and letter shapes can be manipulated to express meaning as shown in this spread ad for Nike. Such design solutions are born of the attitude that type is allowed to be damaged if it is in service to the message.

Type, like the spoken voice, can be powerfully bold or elegantly understated. It can warn by shouting or inform gracefully. It can be stuffy or informal, universal or parochial, traditional or state of the art, highly complex or primitive.

Keep typography simple

The essence of typography is clarity. R. Hunter Middleton said, "Typography is the voice of the printed page. But typography is meaningless until seen by the human eye, translated into sound by the human brain, heard by the human ear, comprehended as thought and stored as memory." Canadian teacher and author Carl Dair wrote, "Between the two extremes of unrelieved monotony and typographical pyrotechnics is an area where the designer can contribute to the pleasure of reading and the understanding of what is being read."

Typographic complexity will not get a message across because, though it may be interesting to look at, the message will be camouflaged. On the other hand, simplicity alone won't get a message across because, though it may be easy to read, its importance won't be recognized. Only *simplicity combined with expressiveness* will make the message both legible and interesting.

Establish a tone, a typographic attitude in the display type, where flirtations with reduced legibility are best tolerated by readers. But unless the reader grasps something of value, her conversion from a browser to a reader will not occur. Put interesting

"I want to use type to enhance the meaning of the words, not contradict, obscure, or interrupt what's being said. My goal is to inject decisiveness; to show that these words know what they are saying."
Susan Casey (1962–)

Contrast type style, size, weight, position, color, or treatment to show hierarchy. Type strategy includes crafting a size and weight sequence for the headlines, subheads, captions, and text so each is distinctive and all work as one to make a noticeable, appealing design.

Frozen sound and frozen action are captured in this eighteen-foot mural. Commissioned to help define a developing neighborhood, it expresses a local work ethic and the community's artistic energy.

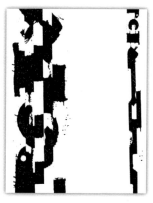

Four abstract studies in typographic contrast express "voices" to introduce the idea of type as frozen sound. Such exercises require the use of materials from a limited set of typographic samples and limits design choices to cause creativity with shape and form. Each designer is selecting from the same ingredients, so simply choosing more eye-catching material is taken away. Neither legibility nor making sense are goals of this exercise: activating negative space and creating three levels of hierarchy are the goals. That is true "value added" design, and the essence of what designers should bring to their work.

information where it can be found. Break the type into palatable chunks.

The key to creating expressive typography is to predigest the copy and show off its meaning and *its importance to the reader*. This is key to the editing process. Read the story, know the subject, ask the client or editor what the thrust ought to be, then make that point crystal clear through design choices.

Frozen sound

Jerry Lewis, in a *Vanity Fair* interview about his increasingly controversial muscular dystrophy fund-raising telethon, said, "I've raised one billion, three hundred million dollars. These nineteen people don't want me to do that. They want me to stop now? Fuck them ... Do it in caps. FUCK THEM." Mr. Lewis understood the translation of spoken sound into typeset form. He understood that verbal emphasis becomes visual emphasis. This is the essence of typography: translating the equivalencies of spoken language into visual form.

Treating typography as frozen sound begins with being sensitive to what Gene Federico, a master of advertising design, calls "sound tones." Federico says, "You must choose a typeface with a sound that isn't against the idea and image you

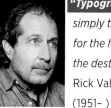

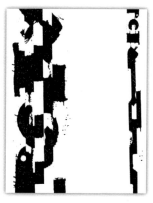

"Typography is *simply the voice, for the head is the destination."* Rick Valicenti (1951–)

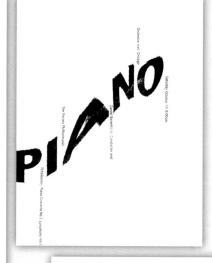

In. The. Past. 99. Dollars. Got.
You. Speech. Recognition. Software.
That. Works. Like. This.

Starting today 99 dollars buys you
speech recognition software that
works like this.

Introducing IBM ViaVoice for Windows®.
It's the first $99* continuous speech recognition software.
So now when you talk to your PC, you can speak naturally
and conversationally, the way you would to a friend.
Once you try ViaVoice, you won't stop talking about it.

Solutions for a small planet™   **IBM**

Three studies in typographic
contrast express typographic
"voices." Students are provided with the same message
and type and must explore
design ideas like rhythm and
organic/geometric contrast.

Punctuation, capitalization
in the up and down style,
and extra word spacing
make this headline a typographic illustration of the
ad's meaning and the
product's benefit.

canto

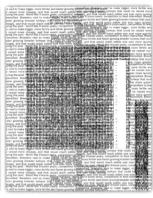

Rhythm requires breaking repetition unexpectedly, which creates visual surprise and a focal point.

Experimental typographic studies express multiple voices and hierarchy using *only* the contrast of relative position. This exercise helps designers discover legibility

so they may flirt with it in subsequent designs. Without that introduction in a laboratory environment, rote adherence to legibility hinders expressive typography.

Breaking for sense makes display type understandable by grouping words into logical phrases. Read display words out loud to identify their natural breaks.

are trying to convey, unless, of course, you are introducing an irritating sound, an irritating typeface for a specific reason." English designer Neville Brody says, "Let's say a French person comes up to you and starts talking. The first thing you notice is that he's speaking French – not the words that he's said. Just set a piece of text, first in Baskerville, then in several different faces and observe exactly how the message changes. The choice of typeface is critical to the emotional response to the words."

Also important is developing sensitivity to rhythm. A speaker who drones at a single speed is causing his listeners extra work to dig out the content. By comparison, a speaker who alters their rhythm makes the content clearer by grouping information into sensible chunks. Such pauses in rhythm are expressed typographically by altering a single element unexpectedly and by breaking the ends of lines of display type at logical places, rather than whenever a line happens to be filled, as is common and generally appropriate with text settings. If display type is broken arbitrarily, comprehension is slowed down. If natural line breaks don't work well visually, editing the copy, adjusting the layout, or changing typefaces is necessary. **EoGD3**

Oh ruh-vwarr — Baskerville Old Face

Oh ruh-vwarr — Bernhard Antique Bold Condensed

Oh ruh-vwarr — Aritus Regular

Oh ruh-vwarr — Meta Normal

Oh ruh-vwarr — Basketcase

Oh ruh-vwarr — Goudy Text

Oh ruh-vwarr — Sketchy

Oh ruh-vwarr — ITC Veljovic

Oh ruh-vwarr — Harting

Setting the same text in different typefaces interprets and changes the message. Imagine the person who is speaking this bastardized French term for *Goodbye* by the physical character of the letterforms.

AE·NEPOTI·TRA

VERENOVOGELIDVSCANISCVMMONTIB·VMOr
LIQVITVRETZEPHYROPVTRISSEGLAEBARESOLVIt

OMNONVERVMEGONISNVERMIHITRADIDIT·AEGON
MENINFELIXOSEMIEROVISPICVS·IPSENTAERAM

Cor gran facilita : ma gran lauoro
Qui numero aureo : e tutti i segni fuoro
Descripti dil gran polo da ogni lai :

Vertere Mœcenas, ulmis'q; adiun gere uites,

Si est ce que je n'eusse pas encore maintenãt ozé
entreprendre, luy dedier la traduction, & im-

|ex Cardinale, mense Maio, anni 1572. põtifex Ma-
ximus denũciatur, paucisq; diebus pòst pro more|

TRAGLI altri effetti della pressione dell' aria è
stato da alcuni annoverato anche quello del
sollevarsi, che fanno quasi tutti i fluidi dentro a'can-

Opinione d'al-
cuni, che il sol
levarsi quasi
tutti i liquori
ne'cãnelli stret
tissimi di vano

Huc, pater o Lenæe ; (tuis hic omnia plena
5 Muneribus : tibi pampineo gravidus autumno

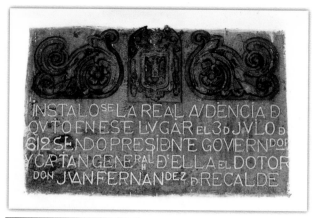

Ligatures are overlapped kerning pairs, as shown in the A͞V (AV), T͞E (TE), Đ (DE), and N͞E (NE) pairings on a Quito stone plaque. Such expressive lettering is today produced by either the wholly ignorant or the highly educated. Everyone in between is trying to "get it right" by following typographic conventions.

The proportional changes necessary to render three type weights are shown in this composite study of light, regular, and bold versions of roman and italic members of a type family.

Typographic technicalities

T he practice of typography is one that requires both an intuitive grasp of form and considerable study to achieve mastery. Typography gradually *reveals its expressive potential.* Milton Glaser (1929–2020)

Today's use of type is based on thirty-five centuries of handwriting evolution, on countless improvements based on our need to record ideas in writing. Developments in the speed, accuracy, and precision in both the marks we make and the way we reproduce them – whether on screen or paper, the printing presses, and even the inks – have always been driven by technological improvements.

The history of the written word is the history of the changing needs and opportunities of human society. Designers who are not fully informed about the traditions and subtleties of type use are mere typesetters. And typesetting is not typography. Readers are well served when the type they are being offered is at once expressive and transparent in

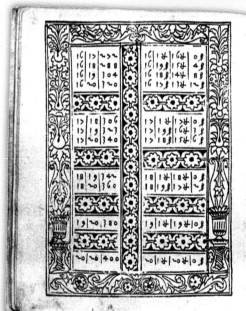

Legibility is a measure of how easily we can decipher the letterforms as we read (top left). Neville Brody pushes the very edges of legibility in this work which begins, "The future city transcends ..." **Readability** is a measure of how strongly a design attracts and holds a reader. Brody's poster is much more effective at being noticed than it is to actually be read, while Joe Esquibel's *Big Red Rock* is both readable and legible.

The shapes of numerals have evolved just as letterforms have. These numerals, from a c1460 Renaissance book made for merchants' day-to-day use (the relative speed of its manufacture, for example the lack of page alignment, reveals this), look different than today's characters. The book shows basic mathematics: multiplication tables on the left and exchange rates for Florentine coins on the right.

*12345
67890*

12345
67890

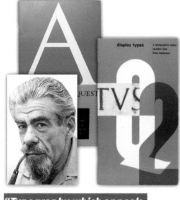

We read by subconsciously recognizing word shapes. The more distinctive the word shape, the easier reading becomes: lowercase words are easier to scan than all caps settings because they have more distinctive word shapes. That's why setting type in all caps should be limited to only a few words, as in a headline.

Old style figures (top) blend in with lowercase type settings. **Lining figures** (above) look like "capital numbers" and evolved for use in advertising and financial tables.

"Typography which appeals to the eye embodies the same set of principles of design that goes into any work of art." Carl Dair (1912–1967)

its content delivery. That balance is hard to achieve and requires the careful, measured revelation of levels of meaning.

Legibility and readability

There are some characteristics that make type more legible and readable. Legibility, which is closely related to the design of the letterforms themselves, is the ease with which type can be understood under normal reading conditions. Readability is the quality of attracting and holding a reader's interest. It is the result of how the designer makes type comfortable to read. High readability – making something noticeable and interesting – often produces low legibility, that is, the piece becomes hard to read. So be aware of letting art obscure content rather than reveal it.

The following six aspects of typography affect its readability, or ability to attract readers: the inherent legibility of the typeface, type size, letterspacing, word spacing, linespacing, and format.

■ **The inherent legibility of the typeface** If the reader becomes aware of the letterforms, the typeface is a bad choice because it detracts from the smooth transmission of the message. Legibility is most affected when what we are familiar with is challenged.

☐ All-caps are harder to read than lowercase:

This paragraph shows old style figures properly set amid lowercase Truesdell, designed by F.W. Goudy in 1931. This version was digitized in 1993 from letterpress proofs of 16-point fonts. Truesdell was Goudy's forty-seventh typeface design. Old style figures, like 1931 & 1993, blend in with lowercase type They stand out in an all-caps setting by look-

This paragraph shows lining figures inappropriately set amid lowercase Truesdell, designed by F.W. Goudy in 1931. This version was digitized in 1993 from letterpress proofs of 16-point fonts. Truesdell was Goudy's forty-seventh typeface design. LINING FIGURES, LIKE 1931 & 1993, SHOULD BE USED WITH ALL-CAPS AND IN CHARTS. AS

Old style figures blend into text (top) because they look like lowercase characters. Use old style figures amidst lowercase or "running" text. Lining figures unintentionally stand out in text (below) because they look like capital letters. Use lining figures amidst all caps like headlines and numerical tables, where their prominence is important and intended.

AUTARKY

AUTARKY

This is 8-point Frutiger set with 2 points of additional linespacing. Because it has a comparatively large x-height, it looks as big as the 10-point Perpetua below. The same two fonts are contrasted at 24 points to show detail. This is 8-on-10 Frutiger set across 13 picas

This is 10-point Perpetua set with 2 points of additional linespacing. Because it has a comparatively small x-height, it looks as big as the 8-point Frutiger above. The same two fonts are contrasted at 24 points to show de-

Frutiger Perpetua

This column is 13 picas wide and, in order to achieve an average character-per-line count of thirty-nine to fifty-two characters, the necessary type size in this font is 10 point.

This column is 18.5 picas wide and, in order to achieve an average character-per-line of thirty-nine to fifty-two characters, the necessary type size in this font is 15 point.

The best way to ensure spacing accuracy is to create display type and convert to paths. Position characters and adjust spaces individually as shapes, not as letters in words. The top setting uses default spacing and the bottom setting shows outlined letterforms with equalized letterspacing.

X-height affects our perception of type's size and legibility. It is a vertical measure from the baseline to the top of lowercase letters without ascenders, like the lowercase *x* (facing page, top). An ideal column width or line length contains between an alphabet and a half (thirty-nine characters) to two and a half alphabets (sixty-five characters) per line. Type size must thus increase as line length increases.

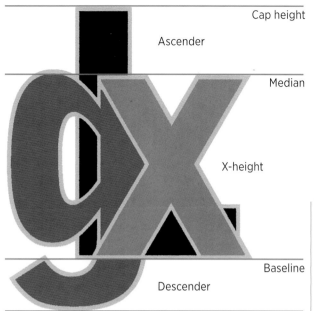

Cap height
Ascender
Median
X-height
Baseline
Descender

we yo Av Aw Ay Ta Te
To Tr Tu Tw Ty Ya Yo Wa
We Wo AC AT AV AW
AY FA LT LV LW LY OA
OV OW OY PA TA TO
VA VO WA WO YA YO

There are three basic letter shapes: rectangular, round, and angular. Some combinations don't match up for optically even space distribution. These must be *kerned*.

"Counters," short for "counter spaces," are left white in the hand-lettered display type of this ad, giving the already character-filled type treatment additional attitude.

lowercase words makes more distinctive shapes than all caps, which look like rectangular bricks. All-caps settings should be kept short: no more than two lines deep. ☐ Old style figures look like lowercase letters and are used when numerals are set in text type. Lining figures, which look like capital letters, should be used in charts and in all-caps settings. ☐ Sans serif as text may be harder to read than serif. Serifs aid horizontal eye movement, so add extra linespacing to sans serif settings. ☐ Italics are harder to read than roman because readers are not used to reading italics. Use italics briefly and *for emphasis.* ☐ Any typeface becomes useless in, say, six-point italics reversed out of 40 percent gray.

■ **Type size** Ten-point type is thought of as the smallest legible type, but some eight-point looks as large as some ten-point type because of relative x-height, the part of the lowercase letterform that exists between the baseline and the median. Type size should be proportional to line length: the longer the line, the larger the type must be.

■ **Letterspacing** Letterspacing should be consistent. This is particularly important at display sizes where exact spacing is most noticeable. In addition, spacing should be in proportion to the letterforms:

ABSTRACTED

KitHinrichs:"Typographyisoneofthemostpowerfulemotionaltools availabltodesigners.Itcommunicatesmuchmorethanjustthewritten word.Whenusedeffectively,itcangivereadersa sense of the mood and pacing of a story, convey whether the content is serious or light, instructive or entertaining. Type can

LEGIBLE

Kit Hinrichs: "Typography is one of the most powerful emotional tools available to designers. It communicates much more than just the written word. When used effectively, it can give readers a sense of the mood and pacing of a story, convey whether the content is serious or light, instructive or entertaining. Type can

"Not-letterforms," or the *spaces surrounding letters,* exist between characters and words. It is the contrast of the letterform to its surrounding space that makes type more or less legible.

Wordspacingdevelopedduring Medievaltimeswhenscribesaddedvaryingamountsofspaceto perfectlyfilloutlinesofhandwrittentext. Writtenperfectionwasthoughttomirror God'sownperfection. Thescribesalsoinventedcontractions,whichallowedlongwordstobemadetofitintoavailablespace. Gutenberg continued the practice of justifying type as much for aesthetic as practical reasons. His moveable type needed to be "locked" in position before printing, and each line had to be the same length to accept being locked up. Gutenberg cut pieces of wood that could be inserted between words to achieve the smooth right edges his machine required. Today's digital typesetting can adjust spacing with un‑ precedented precision, but putting the right amount of word space in a block of text or display type still requires a designer with knowledge, vision, and experience. Word spacing

Too little
word spacing

Too much
word spacing

Ideal
(invisible)
word spacing

Setting justified type across a line length that is too narrow causes uneven word spaces which become noticeable to readers. Meticulous attention must

Setting justified type across a line length that is sufficiently wide produces even word spaces. Meticulous attention must be given to hyphenation in all justified settings. Conversely, a flush left setting always produces even word spacing be‑

fieldlaw
nstreet
regionp
arkplot

Enraged cow in‑
jures farmer with
machete

Enraged cow injures
farmer with machete

Enraged cow
injures farmer
with machete

Invisibility is the optimal amount of spacing between words. It should be just enough separation for clari‑ ty and no more. Dispropor‑ tionate word spacing breaks up the horizontal flow of reading.

An example of tight (or non-existent) word spacing used purposefully. The need to separate word-ideas is achieved instead by color variation.

Hyphenation in display type is poor practice (unless the idea of "breaking" is *itself* what the headline describes). Otherwise, break a headline into segments that are natu‑ ral phrases, as shown in the third example.

LONG LIVE THE THIRD
COMMUNIST INTERNATIONAL!
EVVIVA IL TERZA
INTERNAZIONALE COMMUNISTA!
VIVE LA TROISIEME
INTERNATIONALE COMMUNISTE!
ES LEBE DIE DRITTE
KOMMUNISTISCHE INTERNATIONALE!

Shaded
Outline
Relief
Inline

Word spacing that is greater than linespacing becomes unavoidably visible because we connect elements to their nearest neighbor, which is vertical.

Word spacing opened intentionally works because the linespacing is opened *even more*, encouraging horizontal reading under such challenging conditions.

Ligatures are letterforms joined into a single character. They solve spacing problems between specific characters: this lead "sort" addresses the dot over the letter i.

Shaded, outline, and relief faces are difficult to read and should be used only for large display purposes.

wide letters need more letterspace than narrower letters; small letters need more letterspace than larger letters; caps need more than lowercase letters. "Tracking" alters letterspacing paragraph by paragraph. "Kerning" alters letterspacing between specific character pairs. "Ligatures" are joined letter pairs.

■ **Word spacing** Castle construction was judged by the quality and consistency of the *mortar* as much as by the stonework itself. Similarly, typographers' work is judged by the even spacing between letters and words. Word spacing should be *invisible*, just enough to separate word thoughts while maintaining the integrity of the line, and not so much that the reader perceives the presence of spaces and individual words (like this). Justified type gets its even right edge by forcing space throughout the line. Short lines of justified type have the least consistent word spacing because they have the fewest word spaces available to be distributed. In contrast, a flush left/ragged right setting has consistent word spacing in any line length. □ Hyphenation in justified text allows consistent word spacing, but don't use hyphenation in display type, where breaking for sense is more important than breaking to fill a line.

The quality of a castle's construction was judged in part by the *application of mortar* between the stones. Letterspacing similarly reveals the typographer's skill by equalizing the separation of words.

"Don't confuse legibility with communication." David Carson (1952–)

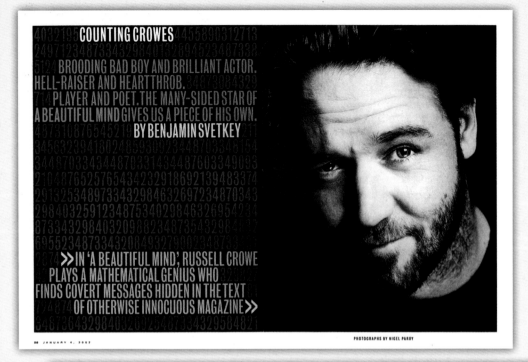

COUNTING CROWES

BROODING BAD BOY AND BRILLIANT ACTOR. HELL-RAISER AND HEARTTHROB. PLAYER AND POET. THE MANY-SIDED STAR OF A BEAUTIFUL MIND GIVES US A PIECE OF HIS OWN.

BY BENJAMIN SVETKEY

>> IN 'A BEAUTIFUL MIND', RUSSELL CROWE PLAYS A MATHEMATICAL GENIUS WHO FINDS COVERT MESSAGES HIDDEN IN THE TEXT OF OTHERWISE INNOCUOUS MAGAZINE >>

PHOTOGRAPHS BY NIGEL PARRY

graph indents should be set in proportion to the type size being used.

Larger type needs a deeper indent. Smaller type can function with a less obvious signal of, say, about a pica.

Adding space between paragraphs can be overdone. In this example, a full line space is too much added space (above). It fights the flow of ideas in a column.

Half a line space is usually a good distance to separate ideas and still maintain unity, as shown above.

It is redundant to *both* skip space between paragraphs *and* indent the first line, as such redundancy reveals the designer to not have thought about the *purpose* of paragraphing.

A hanging indent pushes the first line out to the left and ensures that conscious, purposeful white space is built into the page.

Another signal is to indent whole paragraphs in an alternating rhythm. This works especially well with justified copy, where the right edge's smoothness contrasts with the left edge's fluctuations.

The point is to make each successive idea appear at once discrete, yet belonging with what precedes and follows in a cohesive, unselfconscious way.

Drop paragraphs begin each new paragraph directly below the previous period. This can be achieved using tabs.

THE DARKNESS OF a bold lead–in is an excellent cue that a new idea is beginning. It may have space above the paragraph added, but it doesn't *need* it.

Initial caps should echo the distinctive display type used for a story. They may either stick up into emptiness – a "raised initial" – or hang down into the text, as shown here. This is called a "drop cap" and is another signal to indent whole paragraphs in an alternating rhythm. This works especially well with a purposeful flow of ideas where the right edge is an excellent cue that a new idea is built and follows in an obvious signal of ideas

"Minus-leading" is setting type so the baseline-to-baseline distance is *less than the size of type* being used. It is usually seen in all caps settings like this, since there are no descenders to overlap into the tops of the next line of characters. Word spacing, which is always seen in relation to linespacing, has been tightened to avoid reading downwards. Here, word spacing and linespacing are nearly equivalent.

Format There are two traditional paragraphing signals: indentation and skipping space between paragraphs. Less conventional paragraphing signals include the hanging indent, the whole-paragraph indent, drop paragraphs, bold lead-ins, and initial caps.

Note that the word spaces are larger than the line spaces and that your eyes prefer moving vertically rather than horizontally. Blur your eyes and you will see wiggly "rivers of white." TIP: Never use "Auto" as a line spacing attribute because it avoids making a specific decision about how much space should exist between lines. This must be a *choice* based on increasing type's legibility.

Note that the word spaces are now smaller than the line spaces and that your eyes prefer moving horizontally rather than vertically. Much of typography is making such subtle changes in the specifications and fine tuning the relationship of letters to the space surrounding them. This is

Linespacing cannot be smaller than word spacing, or the eye travels downward rather than across lines of type. Default spacing attributes will keep you out of embarrassing mistakes, but defaults cannot produce superior spacing, which is the domain of the graphic designer. Defaults should always be overridden with more thoughtful and exacting spacing characteristics.

Format Justifying text across a too-narrow measure will produce inconsistent word spacing (left column). Flush left/ragged right always has even word spacing.

■ **Linespacing** Maximum legibility calls for text to be set no wider than fifty-sixty characters per line. Longer lines must have added linespacing so the reader has an effortless return path to the left edge of the column. Two narrower columns are better than one overwide column. (Notice how claustrophobic this decreasing linespacing makes you feel? Experiment to find the optimal linespacing for comfortable reading. Every typeface and column width combination has its own needs.) Linespacing must be greater than word spacing or the eye will flow down a vertical stack of words rather than across a horizontal line.

■ **Format** Readers recognize several key visual signals. *Position on the page* signals importance. The top of the page usually holds the best stuff because the top is where our eyes go naturally. The bottom of the page is less valuable real estate. □ *White space* signals relationships: elements that are close together belong together and elements that are farther apart are less related. □ *Paragraphing* signals the beginning of a new idea. The most common are indention or skipping a linespace. This is an area for invention of standard approaches. □ *Punctuation* signals the pauses and stops in spoken language. The rules that punctuation follow connect and separate clauses in a sentence. □ *Type set in a funny shape* draws attention to itself rather than to its content, which is counterproductive.

kunsthalle basel

● vom 16. januar bis 14. februar 1937

konstruktivisten

van doesburg
domela
eggeling
gabo
kandinsky
lissitzky
moholy-nagy
mondrian
pevsner
taeuber
vantongerloo
vordemberge
u. a.

"Perfect typography *is certainly the most elusive of all arts. Out of stiff, unconnected little parts a whole must be shaped which is alive and convincing as a totality."* Jan Tschichold, *Clay in a Potter's Hand*

ABCDEFGHIJKabcdefghijklmnop
ABCDEFGHIJKabcdefghijklmnopq
ABCDEFGHIJKabcdefghijklmnop

ABCDEFGHIJKabcdefghijklm
ABCDEFGHIJKabcdefghijklmn
ABCDEFGHIJKabcdefghijklmn

ABCDEFGHIJKabcdefghijklm
ABCDEFGHIJKabcdefghijklmnop
ABCDEFGHIJKabcdefghijkln

ABCDEFGHIJKabcdefghij
ABCDEFGHIJKabcdefghijklm
ABCDEFGHIJKabcdefghijklmn

ABCDEFGHIJKabcdefghijklmno
ABCDEFGHIJKabcdefghijklmn
ABCDEFGHIJKabcdefghijklmn
ABCDEFGHIJKabcdefghijklmnop
ABCDEFGHIJKabcdefghijklmnop
ABCDEFGHIJKabcdefghijklmno
ABCDEFGHIJKabcdefghijklmnopq
ABCDEFGHIJKabcdefghijklmnop
ABCDEFGHIJKabcdefghijklmnopqr

Die in ō werlt geschaffē sint Czugzne to urtel sp
vñ werdē auch zu nicht Als man wolechen Die
1465
uero enā legatos Erithreos a senatu eē missos refert. ut butui
mīna Romā deportarenē. et ea consules Curio et Octanian
1467
sectantes illustrant. Legisti Sulpiciū Gallū astro
nimū plurimū bonoris & utilitatis actulisse roman
1470
brxorū appellatus est: apud quenim Ha
ulla mentio erat . Quare nec iuoქ genti

Contrasting type classifications yields beautiful results,
as in this 1955 mark for a
German sports car. The key
to successfully combining
typographic classifications is | having sufficient differences
in form and scale. Here bold
sans serif contrasts with
script, yet the KARMANN cap
height is equivalent to the
x-height of *hia*.

Earliest development of
types shows movement from
blackletter (1440 Gutenberg)
to roman (1465 and 1467
Sweynheym and Pannartz,
and 1470 Jenson).

Type classifications

Letterforms have been evolving for about 3,500
years but type has been evolving for only about 450.
There are many ways to classify styles of type. I prefer a relatively simple system of eight classifications.
Of these, serif and sans serif are the two most important because they are the most often used. My
typeface collection has three catalogs showing serif
typefaces, two showing sans serifs, and three each
of scripts, display faces, and picture fonts.

❶ **Serif** Has cross-lines at the ends of strokes, which
date from Roman stone carving. Serif types are
subcategorized into four divisions, each of which
can be further reduced: *Oldstyle*, the first roman
typefaces, based on the writing of Italian scribes
in the late 1400s; *Transitional*, from the mid-1700s,
which combine characteristics of both Oldstyle
and evolving Modern; *Modern*, from the late 1700s,
which have the greatest contrast between thicks
and thins; and *Slab Serif*, from the 1800s, which
have thick serifs to darken the letters and increase
visibility for the new business of advertising.

❷ **Sans serif** Type "without serifs" introduced in 1817
and embraced by the design avant garde in the
early 1900s. Sans serif types are subcategorized

1501 First italic type: Aldus Manutius

desipere fateatur. sed sicut alias tollit ; sic ipsa quo
alijs tollitur omnibus . Nihilo mīnus enim philo

1527 Ludovico degli Arrighi

N ulla uia est. tamen ire iuuat, quo me rapit ai
I nuiaque audaci propero tentare iuuenta.

1525 First oblique capitals

F ert F atum parteis in-re quacunque gerenc
Prælia, debellatum Orbem rexere monarc

1545 Claude Garamont

Christianiß. Regis primus eleemosynarius,
tum editis suis in sacras literas hypom nem.

1660 Christopher van Dyck

Æadem, is admonenti Gubernatrici
Amstelodamo, non modo non a paruerit,

Italic type was based on
regional Venetian writing.
First made in 1501 by Aldus
Manutius, he called it *corsivo*
and he used them with his
existing roman capitals.
The French crafted slanted
capitals a few years later.

"The use of words –
their sounds, their
meanings, and their
letterforms – has
been an intriguing
aspect of design
since the invention of the alphabet."
Allen Hurlburt (1911–1983)

ABCDEFGHIJKabcdefghijklmnopqrstuv
ABCDEFGHIJKabcdefghijklmnopqrst

❸ SCRIPT TYPES
Pelican
Post Antiqua

ABCDEFGHIJKLMNOPQRSTUV
ABCDEFGHIJKabcdefghijklm

❹ GLYPHIC TYPES
Trajan
Meridien

ABCDEFGHIJKabcdefghijklmnopq
ABCDEFGHIJKabcdefghijklmno

❺ BLACKLETTER TYPES
Wilhelm Klingspor Gotisch
Fette Fraktur

ABCDEFGHIJKabcdefghij
ABCDEFGHIJKabcdefghij

❻ MONOSPACED TYPES
Courier
OCR-A

❼ DISPLAY TYPES
Propinquity
CCNY/FIT Collaboration

❽ SYMBOL FACES
Benda Ikons
Sutnar 1941

Ampersand 1470
Nicolas Jenson, Venice

Ampersand 1532
Antonio Blado, Rome

Ampersand 1549
Robert Estienne, Paris

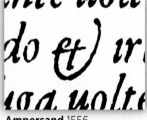

Ampersand 1556
Gabriel Giolito, Ferrara

Comma 1495
Aldus Manutius, Venice

Question mark 1501
Aldus Manutius, Venice

Exclamation mark 1791
Giambattista Bodoni, Parma

Quotation marks 1826
Edward Walker, Newcastle

The question mark **?** is a stacked **q**, an abbreviation of *quaestio*, Latin for "what" or "I seek."

William Caxton made this ad in 1478 to show off his new typeface, *Sarum Ordinal*. Based on northern European blackletter – Caxton learned his trade in Belgium – he developed his own character sets, which became known as *Old English*. As England's first printer, Caxton was instrumental in standardizing English usage and spelling.

The ampersand is an evolution of *et*, Latin for "and." Able to be drawn in many variations, it is one of the most flexible and amusing characters to design.

The exclamation mark is a Latin "*I-o*," equivalent to "wow." It is used in Europe as a road sign alerting drivers to something of importance, sometimes specified.

into three divisions: *Grotesque* and *Neo-Grotesque*, based on earliest designs from the 1800s, so called because it was considered ugly; *Geometric*, influenced by the Bauhaus and featuring circular bowls and consistent character weight; and *Humanist*, which looks organic with greater stroke contrast.

❸ Script and hand-lettered Closest approximation of hand-lettering; range from formal to casual.

❹ Glyphic Based on letters carved in stone. Usually all-caps because minuscules did not exist in the days of actual stone carved letterforms.

❺ Blackletter Also called *Gothic* and *Old English*. Northern European flat-pen handscripts at the time of Gutenberg's movable type, c1450.

❻ Monospaced Types in which each letter occupies the same space, regardless of their proportional width. These are valuable as figures in tables where vertical character alignment is necessary.

❼ Display A vast category that includes types that don't fit into other categories (and even some that do). By definition, these typefaces would be significantly less legible at text sizes and should not be used for extended reading.

❽ Symbol and ornaments Simple illustrations of representational and decorative ideas.

Capitals
ABCDEFGHIJKLM
NOPQRSTUVWXYZ

Lowercase
abcdefghijklm
nopqrstuvwxyz

Small caps
ABCDEFGHIJKLM
NOPQRSTUVWXYZ

Lining figures
0123456789

Fractions
¼ ½ ⅛ ¾ ⅝

Old style figures
0123456789

Ligatures & Diphthongs
ff fi fl æ Æ Œ

Superscript and Subscript figures
0123456789 X 0123456789

Accented characters
åçéîñøüÇÉ

Punctuation
.,:;-¿?!/""''|•·[[()]]

Reference & Miscellaneous marks
©®™&$¢£†§¶

A typeface is made of many more characters than the twenty-six characters in the Latin alphabet: both capitals and lowercase letters, plus one or more sets of numerals, small-caps, punctuation and assorted glyphs. The simplest display face might have as few as fifty characters while the most complete text face might have as many as two hundred characters.

A backward question mark, or *percontation point*, ⸮ was proposed by an English printer in the 1580s to indicate irony.

Quotation marks have many names: **Hungarian** *Cat claws*; **German** *Little goose feet*; **Turkish** *Fingernail marks*; **Danish** *Goose eyes*

414-horsepower V-8
0-60 in 4.8 seconds
Redline 8400 rpm

Quote, sedan, unquote.

Introducing the all-new 2008 BMW M3. Just when you think you've seen it all, another BMW M3 is unveiled. This time it takes the shape of a sedan that delivers an unexpected rush of 414 horses while redlining at a hair-raising 8400 rpm. Every inch meticulously redefined, there is simply no more fat left to trim from this first-ever production V-8 M3 Sedan. Amazement. Crafted at BMW M.

A verbal interpretation of the "air quote," those over-used finger gestures people employ to step outside what they are actually saying, is used to novel effect in this car, uh ... *sedan*, ad. What is meant is that this is a very fast four-door family car.

Hung punctuation, the placement of punctuation marks in the margin beyond the flush edge of a column, was first used in type by Gutenberg. It is today an automatic process in InDesign. Hanging punctuation places it in the margin to create an *optically even* column edge.

Ho lasciato il bambino solo un mo-mento in cucina – e l'ho ritrovato infarinato — da capo a piedi. Mi ri|

Hyphens and dashes come in three widths. Each has its own role. A *hyphen* is a short horizontal bar used to indicate breaks in words at the ends of lines. An *en-*dash is slightly longer and used as a separator in elective situations, as between multiple compound words and between numbers. An *em-dash* is the longest – I believe too long, because it becomes too noticeable in a text setting – and is used for sudden breaks in dialogue. A vertical hyphen has been proposed as a way to solve the need to hang a horizontal hyphen.

Punctuation and dashes

Punctuation developed as a way to indicate reading speed for out loud delivery of religious services. There were no standards for the use of punctuation until the invention of printing, but in general, dots indicated word separations. These were replaced by spaces by about AD600. The dot, when aligned at cap height, was then used to indicate a stop, like a modern *period*, and when aligned at the baseline, to indicate a pause, like a modern *comma*.

«*Quote marks* were introduced in Paris in 1557 as a pair of sideways Vs.» English printers replaced those with inverted commas (**"**) at the opening and apostrophes (**"**) at the end of a quote. Smart quotes like these are used in text while prime (**'**) and double prime (**"**) symbols – also called the "vertical apostrophe" – are used in numerals.

French spacing is the insertion of two word spaces after a period to highlight a new sentence. French spacing was used in monospaced typewritten copy through the twentieth century to help make sentence beginnings more visible. It is not necessary – and actually bad form – in proportionally spaced digital typesetting. **EoGD3**

itarky."

itarky."

itarky."

Never use primes in text (top). Instead use "typographer's quotes." Reduce the default size (middle) of punctuation and the space after commas and periods *particularly in display type* for optical evenness (bottom).

; Kurt Vonnegut *"All semicolons do is show you've been to college."* ! F. Scott Fitzgerald *"An exclamation point is like laughing at your own joke."* , Gertrude Stein *"Commas are servile and have no life of their own."*

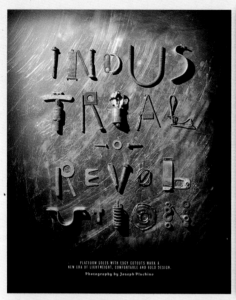

Display type stops browsers (top row). It should also lead directly to secondary type.

Display type is not necessarily large: its true purpose is to be seen and read first (*Tchaikovsky*). The huge secondary letterforms cropped tightly in this example are a powerful attractant. Display type's visibility is dependent on its surroundings, so the focal point becomes the element with the *greatest contrast* with its neighbors (*Antonio Vivaldi*). Though not the biggest element, it is the one that is set aside in white space.

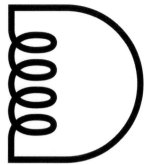

Display type is typically the biggest type, and as such, it and the spaces between the letterforms may be treated as pure form.

Letterforms and imagery become one, abstracting both a bit in the process. This technique is successful when the imagery is directly related to the message: on the left a mark for an electrical company and on the right a mark for a textile association.

The primary type on this detail of a running clothing ad is rendered as a shoelace – a noticeable and relevant treatment for this message.

10 Display and text type

The correctly set word is the starting point of all typography. The letters themselves we have to accept: they are shaped by the type designer. Jan Tschichold (1902–1974)

There are two kinds of type: display and text. Text is where the story is. Display is there to describe content and lure readers through a sequence of typographic impressions so they can make an informed decision about committing to the first paragraph of text. At that point, the story is on its own and, aside from ensuring legibility in the text by crafting optimal characters per line, harmonizing letter-, word-, and linespacing, and choosing an adequate type size, the designer's job of revealing content is largely done.

There are various opportunities for the designer to describe content and lure browsers. Primary type is usually a headline, though picture captions are typically read as quickly. Secondary type, intended

Character shape | Position | Size

A STORY OF
OLIVIA
STEPH
ENSON
ARROGANCE

Character width | Position

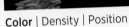

Color | Density | Position

Density | Size | Weight

Format | Size | Position

Position | Density | Color

The nine typographic contrasts Typographic abstraction can be expressed in infinite ways, but it always exploits just these nine type contrasts. It is nearly impossible to express only a single contrast by itself, so intentionally pairing them will lead to multitudinous alternatives.

Character shape Serif vs sans serif; Roman vs italic

Character width Expanded vs condensed

Color Dark vs light

Density Tight vs loose; Positive vs negative; Solid vs outline

Format Caps vs lowercase

Position Vertical vs horizontal; Top vs bottom; Front vs back

Size Small vs large

Stress Vertical vs oblique

Weight Heavy vs light

Size | Color

Stress | Character shape | Format

Weight | Color | Position

to be read after the headline but before the text, includes subheads and decks, captions, department headings, breakouts, and pull quotes.

Readers are accustomed to looking at big type first, but "display" is not necessarily large type. Nor is "text" necessarily small type. The real definitions are *intentional*: "display" is the type intended to stop the browser and to be read first; "text" is the destination to which the reader is drawn.

Primary type

Headlines and the structure of a page create the personality of printed material. Primary type is used to draw attention to itself, to stop the browser and to lead to a specific piece of secondary type. The secondary type's purpose, in turn, is to lead to the text. The text is always the final destination.

Headline treatments fall into three categories: alignment and position, contrasting type styles, and the integration of type and imagery. Regardless of design treatment, a great headline is provocatively written and makes an immediate point.

Typographic abstraction

There are places where playfulness with legibility is inappropriate. Text, for example, is simply too small to absorb abstraction without substantially

Abstracting a word by leaving letters out entirely is sometimes the best way to get an idea across.

"Sometimes you have to compromise legibility to achieve impact."
Herb Lubalin (1918–1981)

PROBABLY
THE ONLY TIME
YOU'LL LONG FOR
Bigger **THIGHS**

IT'S NOT A CULT

BUT IT'S CLOSE

Damaged letterforms suit some messages perfectly, as in this example for a Cajun chicken festival. A scratchy, down-home design, these letters look authentically hurting, but they are all typeset. The way to tell is by looking at repeat characters like the "H" in "THIGHS." Though one has black smudges, the red letterform is identical in both. Beware of using premade "damaged type" fonts in which the imperfect letters are repeated, giving away the canned, premade, fake nature of the damage. Any designer unable or unwilling to craft a custom damaged treatment for a client should be required to perform community service.

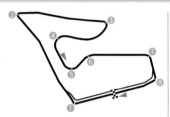

Space between letters can be used to develop identity. Space is shown here in three quantities: completely removed, normal, and very open. The BLEU example, a

1921 magazine logo, exchanges individual character recognition for overall unity as a shape.

Letterforms can be reimagined as imagery. The Red Bull Ring Formula 1 track map (left) has been inverted to read as the letter "g" in the (overly-busy) track logo.

losing legibility. But display type is tailor-made for unusual treatments that flirt with illegibility. Display type is meant to attract attention, so letterforms can be read even if they are "damaged." There are an infinite number of ways to "harm" letterforms, and they are all combinations of the nine typographic contrasts (see page 194). Type abstraction simply pushes a normal contrast to an extreme. For example, making type "big" isn't enough. *Making type so big that the edges are indistinct* works because it forces an interaction of figure/ground.

Some typefaces are inherently abstract and hard to read. With these, ordinary typesetting is all that's needed to create an attention-getting abstracted message.

spabefgomty SPABEFGOMTY Spabefgomty

A typeface's character may be corroborative (**Nuclear**), contradictory (NuclEar), or neutral (**Nuclear**) to the meaning of its message. Use typography that is heavy with character sparingly, only in the primary and secondary type where its attention-getting strength is at least as important as its legibility.

FRANKLIN GOTHIC CONDENSED

BEADED   OCEAN
CHAIR   PIXEL
CRUMBLE   PLASTIC
GRID   SCREW
SLASH   STITCH
SPACE   TREE

Typographic expression and playfulness is best done with relatively plain typefaces. Simple letterforms, like this bold sans serif, are changeable while keeping their shapes legible. For this reason, all sans serif faces are more useful than serif, and roman are more useful than italic. These are variations on Franklin Gothic produced by students as fully functional display fonts.

Deaf college opens doors to hearing

Local school dropouts cut in half

by Karla Kohn

Deaf college opens doors to hearing

Local school dropouts cut in half

by Karla Kohn

Deaf college opens doors to hearing

Local school dropouts cut in half

by Karla Kohn

DRUNK GETS
Uses city trams
9 MONTHS IN
in escape to
VIOLIN CASE
Suchdol hideout

STOLEN PAINTING FOUND BY TREE

Subheads are secondary type that explain headlines. A deck is a subhead immediately beneath the headline. A floating subhead is secondary type placed away from the headline. A breaker head is placed in the text column and regularly hints at the worthwhile goodies that follow.

Captions explain photos Because they are read before the text, they must be thought of as display type and be fascinating enough to persuade potential readers to enter the text.

below the primary type, must be perceived hierarchically as inferior to primary type. In this example on a box of "Root Death Special Foot Bath" it is physically secondary type doesn't have to be *positioned* that way as long as it is *perceived* as substantiating the primary type.

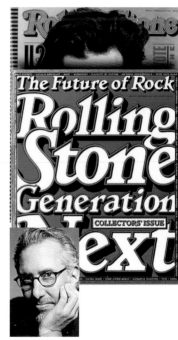

Captions are display type: they are read before the text and should provide information about the story. These captions are only one-word labels. Though they are unusually short for captions, they still tell us how to interpret the image.

Secondary type

If the headline is the lure, the subhead is the readers' payoff. Here is the opportunity to hook the reader by explaining the headline. The headline leads to one or more secondary messages, first a subhead or deck, but possibly a caption, breakout, or pull quote. The messages in the headline and subhead should be two parts of a complete thought, provocatively showing why the story is important to the reader. Readers should, after three or four information "hits," have been given enough of an idea about the story to make an informed decision about whether or not to get into the text. Becoming committed to the text – where the story is – can only happen after they have begun reading it.

Secondary type should be less noticeable than the headline but more prominent than the text. A balance must be struck between contrast and unity among the three levels of type. Variations of one typeface among the three applications works well.

Selecting the right typeface is a significant decision, but *how* you use a typeface is as important as *what* typeface is used. If your work were given an award for design excellence would you or the typeface designer get the credit?

Spabefgomty
Franklin Gothic
Spabefgom
Monotype Grotesque
Spabefgomt
Meta
Spabefgomty
News Gothic
Spabefgomty
Quay
Spabefgon
Clarendon
Spabefgomt
Loire
Spabefgomty
Menhart Manuscript
Spabefgomty
Nicolas Jenson
Spabefgomty
Californian

Ten favorite typefaces with which the author has never been bored. It takes awhile to become familiar with what any given typeface will do, and once it becomes familiar, it can be used to its greatest strength.

"I believe there is one perfect use for every typeface ever drawn, no matter how hideous."
Fred Woodward (1953–)
Ed: This is a superbly well-informed contrasting point of view.

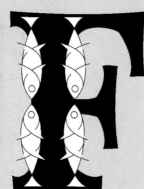

Letterforms are both vessels of communication (as part of an alphabet) and beautiful forms that can lend themselves to further communication. These studies, using characters from Martin Wilke's 1988 Wilke typeface, blend letterforms with descriptive illustrative content, creating new hybrid art and type messages. A is for ant; E is for Eiffel Tower; Z is for Zucchini; 3 is for the three-leafed poison ivy, and F is for Fish and Fork.

Avenir 95 Black	**Loire Sombre**
Avenir 85 Heavy	*Loire Sombre Italique*
Avenir 65 Medium	Loire Regular
Avenir 55 Roman	*Loire Italique*
Avenir 55 Oblique	Loire Pale
Avenir 45 Book	*Loire Pale Italique*
Avenir 35 Light	

To make typographic contrasts look intentional don't use more than two typeface families in a design, and don't use more than two weights of each face. If you add italic versions of the regular weights you have six typographic "voices," equivalent to hearing six people reading aloud, which is plenty to convey any message.

This theater poster announces the season's lineup, so each play title is handled as secondary type, between the theater's name.

Secondary type provides structure as a five-line musical staff to a presentation of clusters of letters in this German poster for a concert of Mozart's music.

Setting display type

Display type shows off mis-spaced characters more than text simply because of its larger size, where character-to-character relationships are particularly visible.

Letters are strung together into words. The space between individual letters goes unnoticed when the type is smaller than about eighteen points. The optimum letterspacing is "invisible," that is, it is unself-conscious. The reader should not be aware that letterspacing exists when it is done well.

Words are grouped into lines of type. Word spacing is the glue that holds lines of type together. The secret to good word spacing is also invisibility. The reader should not be aware of the type that is being read but should be concentrating on its meaning. Display word spacing is often too large because it is set with built-in text algorithms. In general, display type's global word spacing can be reduced to 50 to 80 percent of normal.

The secret to developing an eye for perfect, invisible type spacing is to assume that your spacing is either too open or too tight. If it can be only one of those choices – never just right – adjust it until it truly looks just right.

"The expression in a (typographic) design is what is most important, not the typeface that is used."
Wolfgang Weingart (1941–2021)

Seventy percent	Seventy percent	
Eighty percent	Eighty percent	
Ninety percent	Ninety percent	
One hundred percent	One hundred percent	
One hundred ten percent	One hundred ten percent	
One hundred twenty percent	One hundred twenty percent	
One hundred thirty percent	One hundred thirty percent	

Torskü Torskü Torskü

-3 -4 0 -2 -3

TRACKING "NORMAL"
NO KERNING

TRACKING "TIGHT"
NO KERNING

TRACKING "NORMAL"
WITH KERNING

Man minus ear waives hearing

Man minus ear waives hearing

Man minus ear waives hearing

Steals clock, faces time

Steals clock, faces time

STEALS CLOCK, FACES TIME

STEALS CLOCK, FACES TIME

Digitally compressing or expanding type creates anomalies. Visible distortion becomes apparent in most typefaces at about ±5 percent of normal set width. It is ugly to stretch or compress type to make it fit.

Kerning is the optical spacing of letterform *pairs*, which is more important than global tracking at display-sized type. "Normal" is too open; "Tight" is uneven; "Normal" with kerning perfects inter-character spaces.

Breaking for sense elevates meaning above form, breaking long phrases into natural clusters. Breaking for sense is not important in text settings, but must be applied in display headings.

Linespacing should be tightened in headlines to make the chunk of type darker. U/lc setting requires more attention because the number of ascenders and descenders affect each line's *apparent* distance.

"Quote" 23'9"

`"`	= '
shift `"`	= "
option `]`	= '
option shift `]`	= '
option `[`	= "
option shift `[`	= "

Real quote marks look like "66" and "99." The inch (") and foot (') marks are incorrectly used as ambidextrous quote marks, a leftover from typewriters' need for fewer keys. The default in most programs is set to use "smart quotes," so you must consciously deselect this to get proper prime symbols in numbers. Shown here are the keystrokes used on a Mac for these six glyphs.

Display type can have "poor" spacing attributes if it is the very thing that defines the type, as in this medical headline typeset on a prescription label printer.

Headlines are made of clusters of phrases and should be "broken for sense" into these clusters, regardless of the shape this forces on the headline. To find the natural breaks, read a headline out loud. Try not to break a headline to follow a design; rather, break a headline so that it makes the most sense to the reader. Hyphenating type communicates that shape is more important than meaning. Display type should never be hyphenated, unless its meaning is to illustrate "disconnection."

Assuming the typeface choice supports the meaning of the message, the quality of display typography is dependent on the management of the white space between and around the letterforms. Display type is brief to snag the reader's attention, so attend to its spacing to make it glisten.

Increase contrast and visibility of headlines by making them darker on the page. Reduce white space in and around characters in letterspacing and linespacing. All-cap headlines in particular should have linespacing removed because there are no descenders to "fill in" the space between lines. In upper- and lowercase settings, don't let ascenders and descenders touch, or they'll create an unintentional blot on the page.

PÖRTSCHACH ARTS FESTIVAL ÖSTERREICH

FOR THE LOVE OF LETTERS

Display type requires especially careful spacing. The best way to achieve optically consistent spacing is to treat each individual letter as a form: convert it to paths and adjust manually. Or draw each letter and attend to the negative space organically – even as you draw the characters – as in this Valentine's Day card by Graham Clifford.

o fold it; to cut it unnecessarily is shameful

re are innumerable sorts of machine-made

s. The most durable are those anomalously

'mould-made', for these, like the hand-made

s, are made from rag. But mould-made pa-

t so durable as the hand-made as their fibre

intricately crossed. ¶ Paper is to the prin-

ne is to the sculptor, one of the raw materi-

trade. The handicraftsman will naturally

e hand-made, as the sculptor will natural-

r the natural to the artificial stone. Birds o-

questo corpo , non è da curare ; pure che
a sua ricchezza, la sua patria, la sua liber-
o amore, che esso loro porti, non sia negata
rieue ne esso a gli dolci stati con souerchio d-
ncontro : ne dispettosamente rifiuta il uiuere
i : ma sta nell'una et nell'altra maniera tem-
tempo ; quanto al signore, che l'ha qui man-
e che esso ci sia. Ee doue glialtri amanti
lo sempre temono del morire, si come di cosa
rste loro disci patrice ; et poscia che a quel ua-
ono, lo passano sforzatamente et maninconosi ;
lo u'e` chiamato, lieto et uolentieri ui ua; et p-
d'un misero et lamentoso albergo alla sua

che vieni al doloroso vieni al così colà
Minos a me, quando mi a me, qua-
sciando l'atto di cotanto ufizio, di cot-
la com' entri, e di cui tu ti fide l'ampie-
n t'inganni l'ampiezza delominci l'art-
duca mio a lui : Perchè pura lui così
npedir lo suo fatale andare : uo fatale
olsi così colà, dove si così colà, dove
che si vuole, e più non dimole, sentire
comincian le dolenti noteian le dominc
p'armisi sentire : orarmisi senl'ampiezz
dove molto pianto mi percotepianto n

Textus to text *Textus* is a late Middle English term from the Latin for *woven fabric*, the closest thing to which the recent invention of movable type could be compared at that time. Here are type samples (top) from Eric Gill, 1931; Aldus Manutius, 1505; and St. John Hornby, 1902.

Weight, stress, and density determine type's texture, as illustrated by this student exercise (left). The three parts of the message are clearly differentiated and make the whole an interesting read.

Type's space is expressively and imaginatively used in *Silence* (right), a collaboration by composer John Cage and typographer Raymond Grimaila.

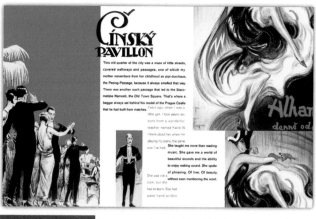

Paragraph widths have been sized to align and flirt with the tightly cropped imagery in this example. Combined with alternating weights, this is an unusual alternative to more ordinary paragraph indentions.

Text columns nearly abut, but their baselines are staggered to indicate line ends, an echo of the subtle shifts in the display type.

Text type

The term text comes from *textus*, Latin for the texture of woven fabric. There are two interpretations of this etymology: that text blends ideas and words into a single message as threads are woven into cloth; and that text areas have a visual pattern that suggests fabric. With regard to the latter, just as cloth's texture varies with the weight and material of the threads being used, type's texture depends on the letterforms' weight, angle of stress, and density.

Though there is a good deal of overlap in the way text and display type are handled, their purposes are different. Display type's purpose is to be noticed, to convey meaning, and to motivate the reader to the next "type opportunity." But the ultimate destination of display type is the text, where the full story and, in ads, the sales pitch is.

The goal of superior text typesetting is even type "color." This is achieved by balancing individual letters and groups of letters as words with words on unified lines of type.

■ **Between characters** Optimal text character spacing must be a little more open than display type's to compensate for its smaller size. Space between all characters in a paragraph is *tracked* while space

ac ita expiraffe. Alterum quum eques p lapfum una cum equo fuiffe aquis dem morbo confumptum:alii quū templū I fuiffe tradiderūt. Nemo profecto hæc ca Omnes enim hos tres eifdem temporibi aliis fuppliciis q̄ lex uolebat iure punito

change a cold lodging, and a heartlef ftraw, for a little warm weather and a of frefh grafs. In a fhort time, acco his wifh, the warm weather, and the fr came on; but brought with them fo and bufinefs, that he was foon as wea

Word spaces are nearly non-existent in Nicolas Jenson's 1470 *Eusebius*. They had widened by 1761 in John Baskerville's *Aesop's Fables*.

"A typeface is an alphabet in a straitjacket." Alan Fletcher (1931–2006)

Acegmorty

36-point Scala Regular

Acegmorty

10-point Scala Regular enlarged

An education isn't how much you have committed to memory, or even how much you know. It's being able to differentiate between what you do know and what you don't. *Anatole France* I cannot give you the formula for success, but I can give you the formula for failure, which is: try to please everybody. *Herbert Bayard Swope* The right to be heard does not automatically include the right

10/10 Scala Regular *with Italic*

An education isn't how much you have committed to memory, or even how much you know. It's being able to differentiate between what you do know and what you don't. *Anatole France* I cannot give you the formula for success, but I can give you the formula for failure, which

10/15 Scala Regular *with Italic*

An education isn't how much you have committed to memory, or even how much you know. It's being able to differentiate between what you do know and what you don't. *Anatole France*

   I cannot give you the formula for success, but I can give you the formula for failure, which is: try to please everybody. *Herbert Bayard Swope*

10/15 Scala Regular *with Italic, op6 indent, which is too small for this linespacing to be visible*

An education isn't how much you have committed to memory, or even how much you know. It's being able to differentiate between what you do know and what you don't. *Anatole France*

   I cannot give you the formula for success, but I can give you the formula for failure, which is: try to please everybody. *Herbert Bayard Swope*

10/15 Scala Regular *with Italic, 1p3 indent to match text's baseline-to-baseline distance*

An education isn't how much you have committed to memory, or even how much you know. It's being able to differentiate between what you do know and what you don't. *Anatole France* I cannot give you the formula for success, but I can give you the formula for failure, which is: try to please everybody. *Herbert Bayard Swope*

An education isn't how much you have committed to memory, or even how much you know. It's being able to differentiate between what you do know and what you don't. *Anatole France* I cannot give you the formula for success, but I can give you the formula for failure, which is: try to please everybody. *Herbert Bayard Swope*

An education isn't how much you have committed to memory, or even how much you know. It's being able to differentiate between what you do know and what you don't. *Anatole France* I cannot give you the formula for success, but I can give you the formula for failure, which is: try to please everybody. *Herbert Bayard Swope*

Text's letterspacing needs to be more open than display type's so each smaller letter can be more distinctly seen. The text has been photo-enlarged to match the size of the display type to show its increased openness.

Linespacing that is greater than word spacing forces the eye *across* lines of type. Optimal line length is about sixty characters per line, as shown in this example. If longer than that, add more linespacing.

Indents should match the distance as the baseline-to-baseline distance of the text. On the left, it is a barely visible six points deep. On the right it is 1p3, or fifteen points, which is the same as the linespacing.

Column spaces should be significantly larger than word spaces (on the right) to avoid confusion resulting in readers' "jumping the gutter" (on the left).

UNDERPINNING

A women's magazine uses classic newspaper column structure and typography – and spins traditional 1960s breakfast reading material – in an editorial promotion.

A stock photography company shows, rather than tells, "a picture is worth a thousand words" by abstracting the image with empty text columns.

Removing linespacing creates overlapped lines of text. This reveals a texture or pattern that, while intentionally illegible, evokes a feeling of city buildings.

This bank's sales message, which is a bit disguised, is in the four lines immediately beneath the space between "in a word" and the "ING" of the logo.

---

between a specific pair of characters is *kerned*.

■ **Between words** Optimal word spacing barely separates word-thoughts. It never breaks a line of type into chunks. Word spacing is seen in proportion to letterspacing: tight letterspacing goes with tight word spacing and loose with loose.

■ **Between lines** Optimal linespacing must be greater than word spacing so the eye travels horizontally. The space should be sufficient so descenders and ascenders don't overlap, but not so great that it breaks up the integrity of the column. ·

■ **Between paragraphs** A paragraph contains a single idea. Each paragraph must be perceived both as an entity and as part of a string of ideas. Separate paragraphs with an indent, a hanging indent, or additional space between paragraphs. ¶ Paragraphing may also be achieved through use of a dingbat, allowing continuous text. [The first paragraph of text should never be indented: it spoils the clean left corner and it is a redundant signal – the typographic contrast between deck and text indicates the beginning of a new idea.*

■ **Between columns** Optimal column spacing must be greater than a word space so readers won't accidentally "jump the gutter" while reading, but not so

"The greatest literary masterpiece is no more than an alphabet in disorder." Jean Cocteau (1889–1963), writer and artist

*Paragraph indents are a remnant of incunabula printing (1450-1500) in which space was left for a rubricated, or hand painted, initial. After a while the space alone indicated the beginning of a new idea.

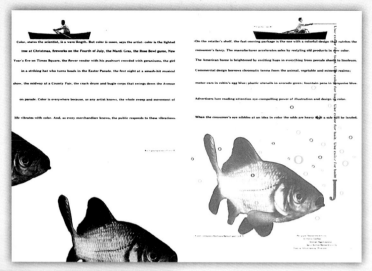

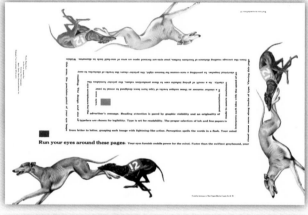

Text *can* be abstracted when it retains some reasonable legibility *and* expresses illustrative meaning. Here, text is revealed as sea water, rain, racetrack, and

emotion: Bradbury Thompson's Westvaco *Inspirations* paper promotions included *Use color for bait* (1949), *Rain Rain Rain* (1958), and *Run your eyes around these pages* (1949). Otto Storch's

1960 editorial spread for *McCall's* magazine shows text use that expresses the same playful joy as the model's poses.

Decreasing type size is the *second* most remarkable feature of text in this spread ad: it is necessary to turn the whole magazine sideways to read the ad. This describes the ad's against-the-grain attitude.

Text as figure The more pronounced the shape, the more attention is put on the treatment – and somewhat less on the content. Herb Lubalin's 1958 ad for *Holiday* magazine is perhaps not meant to be read in full: it simply lists clothing advertisers. The hanger does all the work to make us see the rectangle of type as imagery. A 1959 shoe ad by Reba Sochis sets the text in the shape of a mid-length dress and uses negative space to emphasize the shoes. A 1962 *Vogue* ad by Malcolm Mansfield combines line-spacing and the teeth of a comb to smart effect.

great that the columns look unrelated. A pica space between columns and between text and image in a runaround is optimal to separate but not dissociate.

Text abstraction

While it is good to abstract display type, text type should be treated so its legibility is paramount. Energy has been spent designing the imagery and display type to lure the browser into the text, where the greatest story value can be found. After successfully getting the reader into the text, yours has been a wasted effort if the reader bails out because the text has too many characters per line, or is poorly spaced, or is too small or too light, or a busy background makes reading impossible.

This isn't to say you can't reveal meaning in the way text is handled when text abstraction is to the point. "A free-shaped area, wherever it occurs, must be a spontaneous and natural typographic expression of the copy; the copy should almost insist, of its own accord, that it be set this way," wrote Carl Dair in *Design with Type*. Similarly, Bradbury Thompson believes, "A sense of freedom to forget the columns and grids of typographic traditions lets the designer work in an atmosphere in which to playfully mix words and images."

"The essence of the New Typography is clarity. This puts it into deliberate opposition to the old typography whose aim was 'beauty'." Jan Tschichold (1902–1974)

Acegmorty spabefgomty wundrick vox dahlz whim quest ace mordich al safen gomby spago *Centaur Regular 12pt*

Acegmorty spabefgomty wun drick vox dahlz whim quest ace mordich al safen gomby spagofa menic *Ellington Regular 9pt*

Acegmorty spabefgomty wun drick vox dahlz whim quest ace mordich al safen gomby spagofa menice *The Mix Regular 9pt*

Acegmorty spabefgomty wun drick vox dahlz whim quest ace mordich al safen gomby spagofa *Futura No.2 11pt*

Acegmorty spabefgomty wun drick vox dahlz whim quest ace mordich al safen gomby spagofa *Interstate Light 9pt*

Acegmorty spabefgomty wun drick vox dahlz whim quest ace mordich al safen gomby sp *Grotesque MT Regular 9.5pt*

Serif type can be set without additional linespacing because its serifs force open letterspacing and emphasize horizontality. This is 10/10 Nicolas Jenson SG set across a 9-pica column with an average of about 30 characters per line. Serif type can be set without additional

Sans serif type lacks the serifs that aid reading. This paragraph is set as if it were serif type: no additional line spacing and no letter spacing adjustment. This is 10/10 News Gothic Regular set across a 9-pica column, with an average of 32 characters per line. Sans serif type lacks the

This is an improved sans serif paragraph, set with two points of additional line spacing and 10% increased letter spacing It is 10/12 News Gothic set across a 9-pica column, with an average of 28.5 characters per line. This is an improved

This paragraph is set 10/12 with too many characters per line for optimal legibility. Well-set text has 50 to 60 characters per line, including spaces and punctuation. This paragraph has about 80 characters per line, or 25 characters more than it should, making this text tiring to read for more than two or, at most, three lines. To maximize legibility, there must be more linespacing, enough to make a white bar for each return.

There are two ways to get 50-60 characters per line. One is to enlarge the type and keep the measure. The other is to keep the type size and the line spacing, but shorten the measure to the correct length of fifty to sixty characters per line. This paragraph is set 10/12 with an average of 58 characters per line for optimal legibility. This para-

A flush left setting puts all excess space at the right end of each line. Word spaces are all exactly the same width and make reading easier. There are two kinds of ragged edge,

A justified setting divides excess space between word spaces and characters. This looks badly when there is too much space and too few spaces. A justified setting divides

Properly-set justified text requires a minimum of five word spaces per line to absorb leftover space. This makes the variations among word spaces less conspicuous. Properly-set justified text requires a minimum of five word spaces per line to absorb leftover space. This makes the variations among word spaces

Text type should be sized according to its x-height, the height of the lowercase letter from baseline to median. The x-height, not the overall point size, is the dimension that makes type appear "small" or "big."

Serif can be easier to read than sans serif at text sizes because serifs create open letterspacing and horizontality, so add linespacing to sans serif. Serif faces also have more contrast between thick and thin strokes.

Line length should have fifty to sixty characters for maximum legibility. Lines with more than sixty characters require additional linespacing so readers can easily trace back to the left edge of the column.

A justified setting distributes leftover space within each line. Flush left type is easiest to set well if you allow hyphenation and set the hyphenation zone to a half pica or less for increased sensitivity to hyphenation.

ASCII Alphabet			
A	1000001	N	1001110
B	1000010	O	1001111
C	1000011	P	1010000
D	1000100	Q	1010001
E	1000101	R	1010010
F	1000110	S	1010011
G	1000111	T	1010100
H	1001000	U	1010101
I	1001001	V	1010110
J	1001010	W	1010111
K	1001011	X	1011000
L	1001100	Y	1011001
M	1001101	Z	1011010

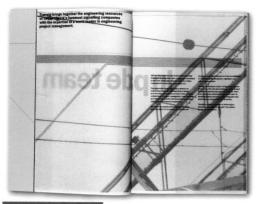

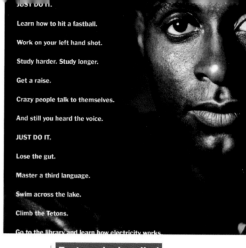

What is a letter? Aside from the familiar shapes, each character is also a binary phrase, a string of 1s and 0s. ASCII, based on telegraph code, was first used in 1963.

Playful interaction between text and image is expressed in this brochure printed on both sides of translucent paper, building a multi-layered richness.

Text can be handled one sentence per line, as shown in this detail of a Nike ad. The flush left edge contrasts with and sets off the column's organic right edge.

Abstracting text to make a point is a worthy aim, but caution is key: abstraction is dangerous because text's small size makes illegibility a constant worry. And besides, using abstraction in text to catch an already caught reader is a waste of energy.

Effortless text

This paragraph is meant to be read. It is *effortful* type, but please read it anyway. *Text type must be effortless to read, that is, it must be without visual static. This is achieved by choosing a good typeface, making it big enough to read, giving it invisible letter, word, and linespacing, and giving it maximum contrast with its background. This paragraph has all the attributes that should not be given to text: it is bold italic, which can only be read in very short passages; it is small, eight-point type, which cannot be followed for more than forty characters per line; the letter and word spacing has been tightened to 60 percent of normal; only two points of additional linespacing has been added which is far too little for the number of characters per line for the width of the column; and the contrast between type and its background has been compromised by an illustration; and the type is set flush right leaving the key left edge ragged. Why, why would I make this so hard for you to read? Maybe I am unaware of the difficulty I am causing. Maybe I think it would entertain you to have a whale in the background. Or maybe I think it would be novel to try these "stylings" because I am bored setting type so it is "ordinary" and legible.*

Some text types are inherently more legible and should be chosen over other faces. A legible face should then be sized for clarity. Text ranges from nine to twelve points, but faces with large x-heights can be set from nine to eleven points, while faces with small x-heights should be set from ten to twelve points for visual equivalency.

"Would you read this
if you hadn't designed it?"
Anonymous

Paula Scher's "art is ..." poster for the School of Visual Arts handwrites the names of hundreds of artists and designers. Using the handlettering style she developed in her typographic map paintings, hand lettering is a differentiating personal treatment that stands out in today's mechanized sameness. Scher's gift is being able to produce lettering with consistent tone, even as she fits the writing into irregular shapes.

text (small, dark gray on black with twice the characters per line as is sensible) makes bold red key words an easy-to-read alternative: *"laces were just an excuse to stop running"*

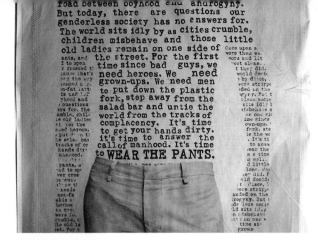

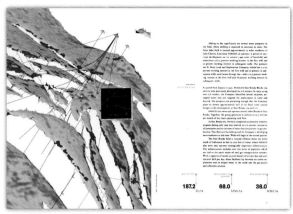

Two sizes of text are used in this detail of a full-page newspaper ad for a trouser manufacturer. The larger text text defines a t-shirt and is legible. The smaller text defines bare arms and, being chopped up, is not meant to be read. It isn't necessary to read *any* of the text: just skip to the all-caps WEAR THE PANTS above the belt line.

Text is "friendly" when it looks effortless, which is not the same as uninspired or "boring and dull." There should be optimal characters per line and its structure should be simple and accessible – especially in comparison to vibrant imagery and infographics as in this handsome spread from an annual report.

Consistent spacing is crucial to making text attractive and easy to read. Poor type comes from letting the computer's default settings determine spacing attributes. Text should always be defined as a "style," so every attribute will be considered in its definition. The goal for well-set text is a smooth, even color.

Justifying text is a process that results in a smooth right edge, as in this paragraph of text you are reading. The extra space at the end of each line is equally divided among the word spaces on that line. When there aren't enough words per line, this creates exaggerated word spaces. When a few such lines with poor spacing are stacked, they form a "river" of white – an ugly vertical gap.

Flush-left text has consistent word and character spacing because all leftover space is in a chunk at the end of the line. The resulting right column edge is said to be "ragged." A "rough rag" is produced by turning off hyphenation. A "tight rag," in which the lines are more even, is made by setting the hyphenation zone to a half-pica or less. I have found ideal ragged right setting with a hyphenation zone of 0p1, a single point.

Text type often has its own latent shape and

*"**Just when we're old** enough to read bulky tomes in six-point type, our eyes are only fit for the humongous letters, surrounded by lots of white space, found in children's books."* Luís F. Veríssimo (1936–), writer

Setting imperfect text

OUR USE OF TYPE is based on centuries of typographic evolution, on hundreds of improvements based on efficiency and economy in our need to record and distribute ideas. Some standards are carried over from scribes' handwritten copies of books, some are more recent inventions from the days of metal type, and still others are modern developments from digital type.

Perfect typography is a <u>logical</u> art. It is based on harmony in all its parts - the right decisions are those that get the message to the reader with the least visual static.

Ms. C. L. Janáková said in 1915, "The spaces after periods in names should be half the width" of a normal word space. She also said to never leave two spaces after a period and "alot" is *always* two words, "a lot."

It sometimes seems there are infinite tiny steps to setting perfect text, but these few errors are key. 🌐

Setting perfect text

OUR USE OF TYPE is based on centuries of typographic evolution, on hundreds of improvements based on efficiency and economy in our need to record and distribute ideas. Some standards are carried over from scribes' handwritten copies of books, some are more recent inventions from the days of metal type, and still others are modern developments from digital type.

Perfect typography is a *logical* art. It is based on harmony in all its parts – the right decisions are those that get the message to the reader with the least visual static.

Ms. C. L. Janáková said in 1915, "The spaces after periods in names should be half the width" of a normal word space. She also said to never leave two spaces after a period and "alot" is *always* two words, "a lot."

It sometimes seems there are infinite tiny steps to setting perfect text, but these few corrections are key. 🌐

Having invested so much in getting a browser to become a reader, make text as effortless to read as possible. Don't impede the copy in its job of conveying information. Clarity and craft are very important in text setting. Separate the *great* from the merely *good enough*. Incidentally, those who know what to look for look at designers' handling of text type to judge their competence with typography in general. Designers can land a job or wreck an interview by the way they show their text settings.

You ain't git turning to the dark si...

🏴 **Segredo someday somewhere s**
silver lining soul bossa triumph th
🏴 **Town and country rhythm and k**
thirty days in the hole elvis is eve
toussaint l'ouverture mercy marc...

🏴 **Segredo someday somewhere s**
silver lining soul bossa triumph
🏴 **Town and country rhythm and k**
thirty days in the hole elvis is
toussaint l'ouverture mercy mer...

25.17	*Little Bird*
4.52	*Ghosts In My Machine*
18.43	*A Thousand Beautiful T*
908.11	*Pavement Cracks*
15.29	*Take Me to the River*
4.54	*I've Got A Life*

25.17	*Little Bird*
4.52	*Ghosts In My Machine*
18.43	*A Thousand Beautiful T*
908.11	*Pavement Cracks*
15.29	*Take Me to the River*
4.54	*I've Got A Life*

You insist on classifying I, lying myself... should argue that this is very

You insist on classifying I, lying myself… should argue that this is very

Indent turnovers on bulleted lists to make beginnings stand out. Create a style with a 1p0 left indent; –1p0 first line; and a tab at 1p0.

Align decimals in charts to make figures comparable. Use the ↓˙ arrow on the tab ruler.

An ellipsis is a three-dot character that indicates a pause or an extracted segment. It is *not* the same as three periods (top): it has been crafted to look right in a text setting.

structure. For example, a recipe is entirely different copy from an interview. Setting a recipe as if it were dialogue would not express its step-by-step nature. Recognizing the nature of the copy at hand leads to the right decisions that will produce authentic typography.

Setting perfect text

Informed use of type compensates for the "incorrect" application of typographic conventions. Shown opposite and above are the most important adjustments for day-to-day use.

To ignore or neglect these adjustments is to allow your type to be mere data entry. Attending to these details distinguishes work as being valuable and worthy of the reader's time and as having been done by an informed designer, which makes you look good.

The computer standardizes and repeats very well. Use its strength by creating paragraph styles. This forces you to consciously choose spacing attributes. It also makes later document-wide changes easy: a change in the style definition changes all type tagged with that definition. The alternative, text type in discrete blocks, each with its own *ad hoc* style, leads to inconsistencies.

Dänisch	æ ø Æ Ø
Französisch	à â é è ê ë î ï ô ù û œ ç É Ê Ç
Italienisch	à è ì ò ù
Kroatisch	ć č š ž Ć Č Š Ž
Polnisch	ą ć ę ł ń ó ś ź ż Ą Ć Ę Ł Ń Ó Ś Ź Ż
Portugiesisch	é è ç É È Ê Ç
Rumänisch	ă â î ş ţ Ă Â Î Ş Ţ
Slowenisch	é č š ž Č Š Ž
Spanisch	á é í ó ú ü ñ Á É Í Ó Ú Ü Ñ
Tschechisch	á é í ó ú č ď ě ň ř š ť ů ý ž Ú Č Ř Š Ů Ž
Ungarisch	á é í ó ú ö ü ő ű Á É Í Ó Ú Ö Ü Ő Ű

A beautifully typeset, letterpress-printed chart shows accented characters in eleven European languages. Accent marks (or diacriticals) alter the pronunciation in spoken language, another reminder that type is "frozen sound." The most common accents are the *acute* (é), *grave* (è), *circumflex* (â), *tilde* (ñ), *umlaut* (ü), and *cedilla* (ç). Shown at about original size.

David Crosby, Stephen Stills, Graham Nash & Neil Young sit shoulder to shoulder on wooden stools around a forest of microphones. On the far left, Stills plays a gentle riff on a snow-white, wide-body electric guitar. Across from him, Young, wearing a red flannel shirt and a black baseball cap, strums an acoustic guitar and sings "Old Man," from his 1972 album, *Harvest.*

Young's shivery tenor sounds fragile in the cold dark space of the Convocation Center in Cleveland. But when the other three enter the chorus with swan-diving harmonies – "Old man, look at my life/I'm a lot like you" – the song blooms with fresh meaning. Crosby Stills Nash and Young are no longer the four young bucks who overwhelmed rock in 1969 with pedigree and promise. They are in their fifties, and they sing "Old Man," a reflection on passing youth and lost opportunity, with electrifying honesty. Unfinished business runs deep in those bruised-gold voices.

There is no applause at the end – because there is no audience. CSNY are in final rehearsals for their first concert tour since 1974. Opening night, in Detroit, is four days away. But to hear this band in a big, empty room is to experience magic in its native state. Everything that makes CSNY one of rock's premier melodramas – drugs; feuds; Crosby's 1994 liver transplant and new celebrity as a sperm donor for lesbian moms Melissa Etheridge and Julie Cypher; Nash's boating accident

BY DAVID FRICKE >>> PHOTOGRAPHS BY MARK SELIGER >

Text can serve as a caption	"www.discovery.com/health/	***Rolling Stone* magazine**	page is typeset as carefully
or label as in this spread	choking/heimlich" and the	has long been a source of	as if it were display type –
ad for Discovery.com. Each	listing over the man's eyes is	excellent typography. This	because it really is. An ideal
line of text refers to that	"www.discovery.com/health/	is the third spread in a story	65-characters per line (right
part of the image and is a	memory loss/marijuana." This	and, save for a single large	up to type safety), bold
link to their website. For	humorous treatment shows	ampersand on a previous	lead-in, and conscious para-
example, the listing over	the usefulness of the site for	spread, it is the first appear-	graph indention: it is excel-
the center woman's chin is	a lot of information.	ance of any type at all. This	lent text craftsmanship.

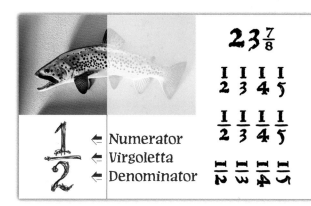

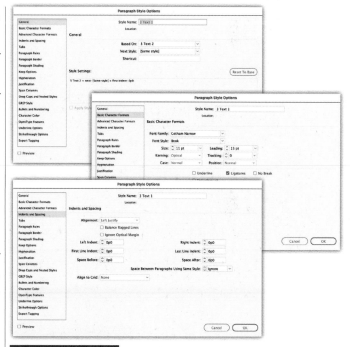

Fractions were written with a short line that separates the numerator and the denominator, calling it a "virgoletta," or *little bar* in Latin. But setting fractions in metal was more difficult because the three characters had to be made to fit together. This caused experimentation for two hundred years – until about 1650.

Text samples are found in type "showings," designed to present a typeface to best effect to potential buyers. Typical showings have characters large enough to appreciate individually as well as a sample of the typeface as it would appear to a reader.

Double check all hyphenated text yourself, whether set in justified or flush-left lines. Built-in hyphenation dictionaries cannot fully replace human attention.

Indentions, in points to match the text's line-spacing, should be part of the style definition.

A *widow* is a very short phrase, word, or part of a word that is a paragraph's last line. An *orphan* is a widow at the top of a column. Widows are generally okay, but orphans will get you a reprimand from the Type Police. Absorb a widow by editing it out.

Fraction is from the Latin "*frangere*," meaning *to break* and related to *fragment*. Common fractions like ¼, ½, and ¾ can be found in most fonts. In InDesign, look under Window > Type & Tables > Glyphs. However, any fraction can be made: look under Window > Character > Options > OpenType > Numerator (for the top number) or Denominator (for the bottom number). The fraction slash bar is not the usual slash: select the slash and an option will automatically show itself. $3/17$ > $^3/_{17}$ > $^3/_{17}$

Perfect text is one important element of a successful page. But the success of a page is only as good as the *power* with which it communicates and the *effortlessness* with which it does it. **EoGD3**

Setting custom type definitions in paragraph styles at the start of a project takes time. But it builds in quality, ensures consistency throughout a project, and saves time later. In InDesign, go to Type > Paragraph Styles > New Paragraph Style and begin defining a new paragraph style. Shown is the recipe of one of the text settings for this book.

Glossary

Abstraction Making non-representational, non-literal, generally increasing an object's visibility.

Achromatic color Having no hue; shades of gray from white to black.

Aesthetics The study of the judgment of beauty and ways of seeing and perceiving the world.

Aldine Typography that interprets letterforms by Venetian printer Aldus Manutius, c1500.

Alignment Having elements' edges agree. Optical alignment is always more important than measurable alignment.

Anomaly An element that breaks a visual system and becomes the focal point.

Aperture See *Counter*.

Apex The area of a letterform where two lines meet as in A, M, V, W.

Archival paper Paper that is alkaline and won't deteriorate over time. Cannot contain any ground-wood or unbleached wood fiber.

Ascender The part of lowercase letters that extend above the median in b, d, f, h, k, l, t. See *Descender*.

Asymmetry Not balanced; not the same on both sides. See *Balance* and *Symmetry*.

Backslant Type posture that slants to the left. Compare to Italic, which slants to the right. Uncommon and difficult to read in any but extremely short segments.

Balance A state of equilibrium, whether by symmetry or weighted asymmetry.

Bar The horizontal stroke of a letterform like F, H, T, Z.

Baseline Invisible line on which letterforms sit.

Basic size A sheet size for each of the standard paper grades that determines its basis weight. The basic size of book paper is 25"x 38". The basic size of cover stock is 20"x 26".

Basis weight The weight in pounds of a ream (500 sheets) of paper cut to its basic size.

Beardline Invisible line that indicates the bottom of descenders.

Binding Attaching sheets of paper together for ease of use and protection. There are five methods of binding: edition binding (sixteen-page signatures stitched together), mechanical binding (plastic rings or combs inserted in drilled holes), perfect binding (glue spread on the pages' edges), saddle-stitched binding (stapled through the fold), and side-stitched binding (stapled through the front).

Bitmap A character image represented as a pattern of dots. See *Outline*.

Blackletter Heavy, angular types based on medieval script writing. The five categories of blackletter are Bastarda, Fraktur, Quadrata, Rotunda, and Textura.

Bleed Extra image or letterforms printed beyond the trimmed edge of a page. See *Full-bleed*.

Blind folio A page that has no visible page number printed on it. In magazines, often found on feature openers with full-bleed imagery.

Body copy The primary text of a story. Usually identified by a medium weight and a body size of eight to twelve points.

Body size See *Point size*.

Bold A typeface style that, visible in the counter spaces, is heavier and wider than the roman style of the same typeface.

Brightness The reflectivity of paper. Lower brightness absorbs more light, making reading more difficult. Higher brightness means a whiter sheet of paper, costs more, and lends a sense of quality.

Cap height The height of capital letters, measured from baseline to top of the letterforms.

Centered Alignment in which the mid points of each element are positioned on a central axis. The left and right edges of such a column are mirror images.

Chancery A handwritten typestyle with long, graceful ascenders and descenders.

Character Any letter, numeral, punctuation mark, figure, etc.

Character set The letters, figures, punctuation marks, and symbols that can be displayed on a monitor or output by a printer.

CMYK (Cyan, Magenta, Yellow, Black) The subtractive color process used in color printing. "K" stands in for "B," which might be misunderstood for "blue."

Coated paper Paper with a layer of matte, dull, or gloss coating applied. Coated paper keeps ink from absorbing into the paper, making images crisp.

Cold type Printing which is not produced by the hot-metal process. Involves the use of phototypesetting, or electronic (digital) setting. See *Hot metal*.

Colophon Information placed at the end of a book that describes its production.

Color management Program that administers scanners, monitors, printers, proofs, and the color characteristics of printing.

Color, typographic The lightness or darkness of gray that a type area creates. Typographic color is affected by the type's size, posture, weight, linespacing, and tracking.

Column rule A thin line between columns of type.

Condensed A narrow version of a typeface.

Contrast The degree of difference between light and dark areas in an image. Extreme lights and darks are high-contrast. A full range of grays is low-contrast.

Contrast, typographic The amount of variation between thick and thin strokes of a letter.

Counter The space, either completely or only partially closed, in letterforms like a, e, o, u, and A, B, C, S.

Creative Using the imagination; having original ideas; experimental, fresh.

Crop marks Thin lines added to the perimeter of a design to show where to trim the finished print job.

Cursive Typefaces with fluid strokes that look like handwriting.

De-inking Removing ink and other additives from paper in the recycling process.

Descender The part of lowercase letters that extend below the baseline in g, j, p, q, y. See *Ascender*.

Diagram Visual but non-representational explanation of a process or relationship.

Die-cutting The process of pressing sharp steel blades through paper to create a hole or shape, thereby enhancing the dimensionality of the printed product.

Dingbat Illustrative characters in a typeface.

Display type Letterforms whose purpose is to be read first. Usually identified by a large body size and bold weight.

Dominance Supremacy or superiority of one element over other elements. Dominance creates a focal point.

dpi Abbreviation for "dots per inch," a measure of resolution.

Drop cap A large initial set into the top left corner of body copy. A drop cap's baseline must align with a text baseline. See *Stickup initial*.

Drop folio A page number placed at the bottom of a page when most page numbers are positioned at the tops of pages, as in the first page of a chapter of a novel.

Dummy An unprinted mock-up of a book, magazine, or brochure.

Duotone A two-color halftone, usually black and a second ink color. The result is an image with more richness and depth than a standard one-color halftone.

Ear Small stroke attached to the g and r.

Elegance An ideal condition in which nothing can be added nor taken away without injuring the design.

Ellipsis A single character of three dots indicating an omission. The spacing of an ellipsis (…) is tighter than three periods in a row (...).

Embossing Impressing an image in relief to achieve a raised surface in paper. A sunken image is called a deboss.

Em dash The longest dash in a typeface. An em dash is the same width as the type size being used: ten-point type, which is measured vertically, has a ten-point-wide em dash. The em dash separates thoughts within a sentence and should not have spaces added on either side: xxxx—xxxx. I frequently bend this rule, replacing the em dash with an en dash surrounded by two spaces: xxxx – xxxx; the em dash is simply too wide in many typefaces and draws attention to itself.

En dash The second-longest dash in a typeface. An en dash is half the width of the type size being used: ten-point type, measured vertically, has a five-point wide en-dash. The en dash separates numbers and should not have

spaces added on either side: 555–666. Also used in place of a hyphen for multiple-compound words.

Ethel A French ligature of the o and e letters: œ.

Extended A wider version of a typeface. Also called expanded.

External relationships Design relationships that are forced on elements, as by a grid. See *Organic relationships*.

Family A group of typefaces derived from the same typeface design. Usually includes roman, italic, and bold versions. May include small caps, old style figures, expanded, and condensed versions.

Figures, lining Numerals that are equivalent to the cap height of the typeface. To be used in charts and in all-caps settings. Also called ranging figures. See *Figures, old style*.

Figures, old style Numerals that vary in height so they blend into a paragraph of text. Sometimes mistakenly called "lowercase figures." See *Figures, lining*.

Finish The surface texture of paper.

Fleuron French for flower; a stylized floral ornament.

Flush A typographic term meaning aligned or even. Type can be set flush left, even on the left and ragged on the right; flush right, even on the right and ragged on the left; or flush left and right, more properly called justified.

Folio A page number.

Font A digital file of a typeface.

Foot margin The space at the bottom of a page. See *Margin* and *Head margin*.

Foundry The place where type is manufactured. A foundry was originally a place for metalwork; modern type foundries are digital.

Four-color process A printing process that uses magenta (red), cyan (blue), yellow, and black inks to simulate the continuous tones and variety of colors in a color image. See *CMYK*.

Framal reference The perimeter of an artwork, page, or spread.

Full-bleed Imagery or letterforms that run off all four edges of a page. See *Bleed*.

Gatefold A page that is folded inward to make an extended spread. The most famous gatefold is the *Playboy* magazine centerfold.

Geometric Characterized by mechanically-rendered lines and shapes. Contrasts with organic or biomorphic. See *Organic*.

Gestalt Cumulative perception of parts as a whole.

Grain The direction that most fibers lie in a sheet of paper. This is important in folding and tearing.

Grid A structure for organizing space so unrelated parts appear to have commonalities in alignment and size.

Grotesque Another name for sans serif type. So called because it was considered ugly when it was introduced in the mid-1800s.

Gutter The space between columns of type and between facing pages of a book or magazine.

Hairline The thinnest line an output device can make. Usually ¼ point.

Halftone A printed image in which continuous tone is reproduced as dots of varying sizes.

Hanging indent A paragraphing style in which the first line pokes out to the left. Also called an outdent or flush and hung.

Hanging initial An initial letter placed in the margin next to body copy.

Hanging punctuation Allowing lines that begin or end with punctuation to extend a bit beyond the column width for optical alignment. Its use reveals typographic sensitivity and craftsmanship.

Head margin The space at the top of a page. See *Margin* and *Foot margin*.

Hierarchy Order of perception based on inherent importance.

Hi-fi color CMYK printing with the addition of two to four colors for a wider color range. Also called Hexachrome.

High-res (High resolution) An image that has sufficient sharpness, measured in dpi, to make it suitable for quality printing.

Hinting Mathematical formulas applied to outline fonts to improve the quality of their screen display and printing.

Hot metal Typesetting and the printing process that involves casting type from molten lead.

Humanist Letterforms that look a bit like handwriting, or at least don't look too mechanical or geometric. Identifiable by having a humanist axis, or angled emphasis related to handwriting.

Imposition Arranging pages so that when they are printed and trimmed, they will appear in correct order.

Incunabula "Cradle," used to describe products from the first fifty years of printing with movable type.

Information mapping Data organized to show relevance and connections, as a diagram or chart. See *Wayfinding*.

Ink holdout Resistance to the penetration of ink. Coated paper has high ink holdout, making images look sharp.

Italic Types that slant to the right. Must have letters that are distinctly different from roman version of the typeface, like a and *a*, or it is probably an oblique version. See *Oblique*.

Justification Aligning both the left and right sides of a column of type.

Kern Removing space between specific letter pairs in order to achieve optically consistent letterspacing. See *Tracking*.

Leaders A line of dots that lead the eye across a wide space. Often found on contents listings.

Leading ("Ledding") Space between lines of type that appears between the descenders of one line and the ascenders of the next. Digital leading is added above a given line of type. The name comes from hot metal days when actual strips of lead were inserted between lines of poured type.

Lead-in The first few words of a paragraph set to attract attention.

Legibility The ability to distinguish between letterforms; the recognizability of an object for what it is, easy to read, clear, plain. See *Readability*.

Letterspacing A term used to describe general spacing between letterforms. See *Kern* and *Tracking*.

Ligature Conjoined pairs or trios of characters into one, as in fi and ffi, for optical consistency.

Light or **Lightface** A lighter variation of the density of a typeface.

Line The trace of a point in motion. See *Point Line Plane*.

Linespacing See *Leading*.

Margin The space at the inside and outside of a page. Also called side margin. See *Foot margin* and *Head margin*.

Mass An area of definite size and weight.

Match color A custom-blended ink that matches a specified color exactly. There are several systems, including Pantone Matching System and Toyo. Also called spot color.

Median The invisible line that defines the top of lowercase letters that have no ascender. Also called mean line and waist line.

Minus leading Removing space between lines of type to give it a more unified and darker look. Should always be used with all caps display type and with great care on U/lc display type to keep ascenders and descenders from overlapping. See *Leading*.

Moiré A pattern created by rescreening a halftone or by printing two halftones on top of each other out of register. Pronounced *mwah-RAY*.

Monochromatic color Containing or using only one color and its shades.

Monospace Typefaces in which each character occupies the same horizontal space. A leftover from typewriter technology. See *Variable space*.

Oblique An angled version of a roman typeface in which the same characters have been slanted to the right, not redrawn. See *Italic*.

Octothorp The number or pound sign (#). So named because it indicates eight farms surrounding a town square.

Opacity A measure of how opaque a sheet of paper is. Low opacity allows printing on the back side to show through. Opacity may be achieved through increasing sheet thickness or by adding chemical opacifiers.

Optical alignment Adjusting elements or letterforms so they appear aligned, which is more important than actually being aligned.

Organic Lifelike, as might be found in nature; a relation between elements such that they fit together harmoniously or naturally. See *Geometric*.

Organic relationships Design relationships that are found and exploited between the specific elements at hand. See *External relationships*.

Orphan A word or word fragment at the top of a column. A sign of ultimate carelessness. See *Widow*.

Ornament Decorative character used to embellish typography.

Outline The mathematical representation of a character that can be scaled to any size and resolution.

Papyrus An aquatic plant found in northern Africa. Used as early writing substrate, it was peeled and placed in layers. The naturally-occurring glues in the fibers bonded into sturdy sheets.

Paragraph A distinct section of writing dealing with a single theme or idea.

Parchment A writing substrate made from treated animal skins.

Pattern A repeated motif or decorative design in regular intervals. See *Texture*.

PDF (Portable Document Format) Adobe's file format that allows users to view and print documents regardless of computer platform or originating program.

Phototypesetting Setting type by means of light being exposed through a film negative of characters onto light-sensitive paper. Introduced in the 1960s and replaced by digital typesetting in the 1980s.

Pica One-sixth of an inch, or twelve points. Because it is divisible by points, and thus accommodates type measurement, it is wise to use the pica for planning all design space. See *Point*.

Plane The trace of a line in motion. See *Point Line Plane*.

Point The smallest unit of marking, regardless of exact shape. See *Point Line Plane*; One-seventy-second of an inch, or one-twelfth of a pica. The basic unit of vertical measurement of type. See *Pica*.

Point Line Plane The three most basic shapes in design. These shapes become interesting when each perceptually blurs into the other two – when a point appears as a short line or a small plane, for example.

Point size The size of a typeface measured from just above the top of the ascenders to just beneath the bottom of the descenders. Also called body size and type size.

Posture The angle of stress of a typeface. There are three postures: roman, italic or oblique, and backslant.

Preflighting An evaluation of every component of a document needed to print it.

Proximity Relative nearness in space, time, or relationship; closeness.

Readability The quality and experience of reading, determined by letterspacing, linespacing, paper-and-ink contrast, among other factors. See *Legibility*.

Recto The right-hand page of a spread. Always odd-numbered. See *Verso*.

Repetition Repeating an element to create rhythm: reiteration, copying.

Resolution The number of dots per inch (dpi) displayed on a screen or by a printer, which determines how smooth the curves and angles of characters appear. Higher resolution yields smoother characters.

Reversed out Printing around the perimeter of an element, allowing the paper color to show through and form the object.

RGB (Red, Green, Blue) Additive color system used in monitors and scanners.

Roman An upright, medium-weight typeface style.

Rhythm A regular repeated pattern.

Rough rag Type set without hyphenation, causing a pronounced variation in line length. See *Tight rag*.

Rule A line.

Runaround Type set around an image or element. The ideal distance is 1 pica, or enough space to separate, but not enough to dissociate the type and image from each other.

Sans serif Type without cross strokes at the ends of their limbs. Usually have consistent stroke weight.

Scale Comparative size, particularly useful in unexpected contrasts.

Scholar's margin The outside margin wide enough for annotations. Traditional book margin proportions are two units on the inside; three units at the head; four units on the outside; and five units at the foot.

Score An impression or indentation in paper prior to folding.

Screen tints A percentage of solid color.

Serif Type with limbs ending in cross strokes. Usually have variation in the main character stroke weight.

Semiotics The study of signs and their meanings.

Silhouette The view of an object as a flat shape; an object removed from its background. A partial silhouette is an object whose background has been partly removed.

Slab serif Type with especially thick serifs. All "Egyptian" typefaces are slab serifs not because they have anything directly to do with Egypt but because they happened to be introduced when Egyptian artifacts were especially fashionable.

Small caps Capital letters drawn to be about the size of lowercase letters of the same typeface. "False small caps," regular capital letters merely set a few points smaller, appear too light.

Solid Type set without additional line-spacing.

Spot color See *Match color*.

Spot varnish Coating applied to specific areas to add glossy or matte highlights.

Spread A description of publication real estate: two facing pages. There is no such thing as a "one-page spread." A three- or four-page spread is a "gatefold."

Stickup initial A large initial set at the top left corner of body copy. A stickup initial's baseline must align with the first text baseline. See *Drop cap*.

Stochastic screening Digital process that assigns equal-size dots in variable spacing to emulate a grayscale image. Also called FM (Frequency Modulated) screening.

Style Variations of a typeface, including roman, italic, bold, condensed, and extended.

Subhead Secondary wording that explains the headline and acts as a bridge leading to the text.

Symmetry Balance through equal distribution of content, as through centering. See *Asymmetry* and *Balance*.

Text The main portion of a story, usually smaller type; the place that all display matter is leading to. See *Body copy*.

Texture The tactile experience of a raised surface. Translated to two dimensions, texture is perceived as pattern. Texture is an attribute given to an area of type and is determined by typeface, size, linespacing, color, and column structure. See *Pattern*.

Tight rag Type set with a small hyphenation zone, causing minimal variation in line length. See *Rough rag*.

Tracking Adjusting space in a line or paragraph. See *Kern*.

Turnovers Words that continue on a subsequent line.

Typeface A set of characters of a certain design and bearing its own name, like Didot, Franklin Gothic, or Plzeň. A typeface is made functional in a digital file called a font. See *Font*.

Type family All styles and variations of a single typeface. May include italic, bold, small caps, etc.

Typographer One who practices the craft and art of designing with letterforms and/or designing letterforms.

Typography Literally "drawing with type." Applying type in an eloquent way to reveal content with minimal reader resistance.

Type size See *Point size*.

U/lc "Upper and lowercase" letters.

Uncoated paper Paper without a surface coating.

Value Relative lightness or darkness of an element including areas of type.

Variable space Type in which each character is assigned its own width as determined by the characters' inherent shape and width. See *Monospace*.

Verso The left hand page of a spread. Always even-numbered. See *Recto*.

Volume Three-dimensional space. In architecture, solid volumes are buildings and voids are spaces within buildings.

Wayfinding Any navigation tool that helps users orient themselves to their surroundings. See *Information mapping*.

Weight The darkness of a typeface.

Widow A word or word fragment at the end of a paragraph. Words are okay, but word fragments are careless. See *Orphan*.

Word space Space between words. Relates to letterspacing: if one is open, both must be open. "Correct" or ideal word spacing is invisible: just enough to separate words but not enough to break a line of type into word chunks.

X-height The distance from the baseline to the median in lowercase letters. So named because it is the height of a lowercase x, which has neither an ascender nor a descender. **EoGD3**

Bibliography

The important thing about a bibliography is to use these road signs that point to further knowledge on a subject. Discovering books that help you understand and see design and visual communication in a new way is well worth the effort and cost.

You may note that many of these books are released by the same few publishers. Visiting these publishers' Web sites will lead you to other worthwhile texts. A recommended reading list is also maintained by the Type Directors Club at tdc.org.

The Type Directors Club Annual. New York: Harper-Collins Publishers, published annually.

Adams, Sean *How Design Makes Us Think and Feel and Do Things.* New York: Princeton Architectural Press, 2021.

Bierut, Michael. *How to Use Graphic Design to Sell Things, Explain Things, Make Things Look Better, Make People Laugh, Make People Cry, and (Every Once in a While) Change the World, Second Edition.* New York: Harper Design, 2021.

Bringhurst, Robert. *The Elements of Typographic Style.* Point Roberts, Wash.: Hartley & Marks, 2004. 3rd ed.

Carter, Harry. *A View of Early Typography Up to About 1600.* Oxford: Hyphen Press, facsimile reprint 2002.

Friedl, Friedrich, **N. Ott** and **B. Stein**. *Typography: An Encyclopedic Survey.* New York: Black Dog & Leventhal Publishers, 1998.

Frutiger, Adrian. *Type Sign Symbol.* New York: Hastings House, 1999.

Gill, Eric. An Essay on Typography. Boston: David R. Godine, 1993.

Ginger, E.M., **S. Rögener**, **A-J. Pool**, and **F. Goudy**. *The Alphabet and Elements of Lettering.* Berkeley & Los Angeles: The University of California Press, 1942.

Heller, Steven, and **Philip B. Meggs**, eds. *Texts on Type: Critical Writings on Typography.* New York: Allworth Press, 2001.

Hutchinson, James. *Letters.* New York: Van Nostrand Reinhold Company, 1983.

Kunz, Willi. *Phantasmagorias: Daydreaming with Lines.* Sulgen, Switzerland: Verlag Niggli, 2017.

Leborg, Christian. *Visual Grammar.* New York: Princeton Architectural Press, 2006.

Loewy, Raymond. *Industrial Design.* Woodstock, N.Y.: The Overlook Press, 2007.

Morison, Stanley. *First Principles of Typography.* Leiden, Netherlands: Academic Press Leiden, 1996. 2nd Ed.

Ogg, Oscar. *Three Classics of Italian Calligraphy: Arrighi, Tagliente, Palatino.* New York: Dover Publications, 1953.

Rand, Paul. *A Designer's Art.* New Haven: Yale University Press, 2000.

Remington, R. Roger. *Nine Pioneers in American Graphic Design.* Cambridge, Mass.: MIT Press, 1992.

Ruder, Emil. *Typographie: A Manual of Design.* Adapted by Charles Bigelow. New York: Hastings House, 2002.

Spencer, Herbert. *Pioneers of Modern Typography.* Cambridge, Massachusetts: MIT Press, 2004. Revised ed.

Thompson, Bradbury. *The Art of Graphic Design.* New Haven: Yale University Press, 1988.

White, Alex W. *Listening to Type: Making Language Visible.* New York: Allworth Press, 2016.

White, Jan V. and **Alex W. White**. *Editing by Design (Fourth Edition).* New York: Allworth Press, 2020.

Eskilon, Stephen J. Graphic Design: A New History. New Haven: Yale University Press, 2019

Woolman, Matt, and **Jeff Bellantoni**. *Moving Type: Designing for Time and Space.* Mies, Switzerland: RotoVision, 2000. **EoGD3**

Designer's checklist

Questions that should be answered with a "yes"
■ are in bold. Questions that should be answered
with a "no" □ *are in regular weight italics.*

Space

■ Do all areas of white space look like they were planned and thoughtfully used?

■ Is the ground as interesting as the figures on it?

■ Is space between elements consistent?

■ Is space used to signal quality and value?

■ Is there a payoff for having this emptiness?

■ Does empty space define an object's relative size?

■ Are related topics close and unrelated ones separated?

■ Can the background be brought into the foreground?

■ Can overfullness be used to describe this content?

■ Is empty space activated for contrast and visibility rather than merely left over?

■ Has space been removed from headlines to make them tighter, darker, and more visible?

■ Is empty space used to make an opening page or spread look nonthreatening and inviting?

■ Are areas of white space balanced with occupied space?

■ Is emptiness used representationally or symbolically?

■ Has the especially visible emptiness around the perimeter of the page been used?

■ Is space used to emphasize either horizontality or verticality?

□ *Have consistent, systematic spaces between elements been compromised to fill a short column?*

□ *Can space be better managed in and around typographic elements?*

□ *Does any element appear to be floating separately on the page?*

□ *Does the page look crowded?*

□ *Could the empty areas be called "wasted space"?*

□ *Is emptiness only in the background?*

□ *Are mere boxes and rules – rather than differences expressed through position, size, and weight – used to organize space?*

Unity

■ Are all elements cooperating to make a single impression?

■ Is there a dominant element that will transfix the casual browser?

■ Are elements sized in proportion to their importance?

■ Has design unity been enhanced by limiting type and color palettes?

■ Does color emphasize what is worthy of emphasis?

■ Is color used to explain content, not decorate the page?

■ Is the stopping power of huge images used?

■ Is there a cheerful variety or is the total effect gray and pallid?

■ Have similar elements been grouped?

■ Are relationships between elements immediately apparent?

■ Do the shapes of elements add contrast and interest?

■ Do art elements accurately and distinctively convey the message and tone of the story?

■ Is there consistency from page to page and spread to spread?

□ *Are design decisions being made to enhance the importance and clarity of the content, but at the expense of the publication's personality?*

□ *Are you straying unnecessarily from your publication's style manual – even just this once – for dubious immediate editorial success?*

□ *Are contrasts so numerous that unity is harmed?*

□ *Does the design call attention to itself rather than reveal the content?*

□ *Have holes been filled with clutter?*

□ *Do elements interrupt reading or cause confusion?*

□ *Does the shape of any element look contrived or forced?*

□ *Do elements try to outshout each other?*

□ *Is there any way to simplify this solution to this problem?*

Page Architecture

- ■ Is there a simple and coherent design system?
- ■ Does presentation make the information more valuable?
- ■ Has all clutter and decorative pretense been eliminated?
- ■ Has the rigid use of a grid limited creativity and expressiveness?
- ■ Is there characteristic patterning and texture?
- ■ Is the design responsive to substance or is it just surface gloss?
- ■ Do facing pages appear as spreads?
- ■ Do stories appear as continuous horizontal entities that happen to be broken into segments?
- ■ Are the premium upper-left corner and top section of the page used to maximum effect?
- ■ Are readers guided naturally and smoothly through the page or story?
- ■ Does your overall design acknowledge the presence of and competition from the Web?
- ■ Are readers guided through information?
- ■ Are identity signals (logos, sinkage, department layouts) used consistently to reveal the magazine's structure?
- ■ Is information ranked so uncaring readers can skim?
- ■ Can the potential reader learn the gist of the story just from the display material?
- ■ Are starting points easily found?
- ■ Does the layout accurately communicate the relative importance of the stories on the page?
- ■ Are stories shown so readers can gauge time, effort, and commitment required by each?
- ■ Does the cover arouse curiosity and lure the passive?
- ■ Is there a characteristic cover format that allows flexibility while maintaining uniformity?
- ☐ *Does any element lead to an unintended dead end?*
- ☐ *Does the design look evenly gray with elements too similar in size and treatment?*

Type

- ■ Has the reader been lured into a story by the headline-deck-caption-text progression?
- ■ Has all display type (headlines, decks, captions, breaker heads, breakouts, and pull-quotes) been broken for sense?
- ■ Does the type look like "frozen sound"?
- ■ Is the type as large and legible as possible?
- ■ Does typography unify pages without boring sameness?
- ■ Are there exactly three levels of typography?
- ■ Are big stories broken into bite-size chunks?
- ■ Can the copy be edited shorter or listed?
- ■ Is the logo distinctive, not just set type?
- ■ Is the logo echoed in the department headings?
- ■ Does each feature story have distinctive typography?
- ■ Are sidebars used as back doors into the story?
- ■ Does information in headlines – rather than cute punning – intrigue the reader?
- ■ If the headline has to be a topic title, is the reason to read in the deck?
- ■ Do headlines contain active, positive verbs?
- ■ Are headlines repeated verbatim on the cover and contents page?
- ■ Are all-caps restricted to very short headlines?
- ■ Do decks and captions focus on the significance of the story?
- ■ Do captions reveal the editorial significance of visually dull photos?
- ■ Are captions written as display type hooks, to increase curiosity and lead readers to the text?
- ■ Do font changes signal real changes in meaning?
- ☐ *Is the reader aware of the act of reading?*
- ☐ *Do headlines and subheads compete for attention rather than lead from one idea to the next?*
- ☐ *Is the text's line width determined for layout convenience rather than optimal legibility?* `EoGD3`

Index

Colophon

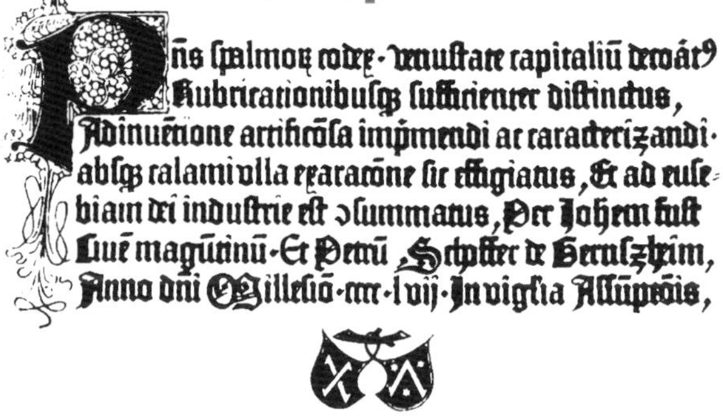
Pn̄s spalmoꝝ codex · venustate capitaliū decorat⁹
Rubricationibusq̃ sufficienter distinctus,
Adinuentione artificiosa imprimendi ac caracterizandi ·
absq̃ calami vlla exaracōne sic effigiatus, Et ad euse-
biam dei industrie est consummatus, Per Johem fust
Ciuē maguntinū · Et Petrū Schoffer de Gernszheim,
Anno dñi Millesiō · cccc · lvij · In vigilia Assūpcōis,

A colophon is a brief description of a book's typography and technical details of its production. The term "colophon" is from the Greek, meaning "finishing."

The first printed colophon was in 1457 by Johann Fust and Peter Schöffer in Mainz – just a few years after Gutenberg (for whom Schöffer apprenticed) first printed with movable type – in their Latin *Psalter*.

The translation of this colophon reads: "*The present book of the Psalms, decorated with beautiful capital letters and profusely marked out with rubrics, has been thus fashioned by the added ingenious invention of printing and shaping of letters without any exertion of the pen, and to the glory of God has been diligently brought to completion by Johann Fust, a citizen of Mainz, and Peter Schöffer of Gernszheim, in the year of the Lord 1457, on the eve of the Feast of the Assumption.*"

The Elements of Graphic Design, Third Edition was designed and typeset by Alex W. White. The text face is Gotham Narrow Book, designed by Tobias Frere-Jones and Jesse Ragan and published by Hoefler & Co in 2000. The book was printed in China. EoGD3

Credits

All images by the author except as noted. Every effort has been made to identify the designer of these works. Credits will be happily updated in the next edition of this book. Please contact the author at alexwwhite1@gmail.com

1 Dummies Herbert Migdoll 3 Houses Unknown | Madsen Sean Bates | When Christian Longo Unknown | Mies van der Rohe Unknown 5 Correction Unknown | Alejandro Paul Nancy Harris Rouemy 7 VW Stanislav Tuma | Bread shirt Manmohan Anchan & Rajesh Kulkarni | Fish/Costa Unknown 9 Suomi-Yhtiö Unknown | Target billboard Unknown Lao-tse Unknown 11 Any dipstick Tom Lichtenheld 13 Buy Sevin loe Ivey | Olympus hands Unknown | Holsten beer Jens Stein | AIDS Unknown | Rosas blue Eric Cai Shi Wei | Sir Jonathan Miller Unknown photographer 15 Philip Glass Unknown photographer 17 All images Niklaus Troxler 19 All images Geray Gençer 21 Grand Canyon Unknown 23 New York City Central Park before Unknown | New York City Central Park after Unknown | Big bang Unknown photographer | Japanese cellphone ad Unknown 25 Sens gamma Unknown Italian printer | Prisoners Unknown photographer | Pedestrians in the city Gérard Paris-Clavel 27 Paris map Unknown | The Fall of Rebel Angels Breugel the Elder | Three figure/ground studies John Morfis, Deegan Lukienchuk, Lisa Newinski | Unity of opposites Shigeo Fukuda 29 House & Garden Lloyd Ziff | Jeep ad Unknown | byINNO Unknown | I Hear America Eric O'Connell photos 31 Big Ten marks Unknown | Self Portrait at the Age of 63 Rembrandt van Rijn | Hermann Miller ad Armin Hofmann | Axe Ogilvy & Mather, Bangkok | Fortune Leo Lionni 33 Derek Birdsall Unknown photographer | Aznar Textile Pedro Gonzalez 35 Carceri mural Giovanni Battista Piranesi | Windshield wiper Unknown | PREFA mark Unknown | Vint Cerf Unknown | Dodge ad Unknown 37 Sun cooking Ronald Searle | Slate Cross Franz Kline | In Drydock Edward Wadsworth | At Snake Ken-Tsai Lee 39 Possum Dreaming Tim Leura Tjapaltjarri | 18 Volt Unknown | Around the World Unknown | The Approval Matrix Unknown | Ice skater Unknown 41 Plakate der avantgarde (top) Jan Tschichold | Scholar's margins Unknown 43 Birds and fishes M.C. Escher | Pianos and taxis Unknown | Dove Leo Lionni | SCC mark Mark Hartmut Pfeil | Hands, Horse, Leaves, Bottles Michael Gericke, Zip Gist & Jody Laney, Bradford Lawton, Stan McElrathy & Paul Soupiset 45 La Résistance de 1814 Unknown photographer | Rolling Stone Seinfeld Fred Woodward | Fruit of the Loom Unknown | Finch-Pruyn mark Herb Lubalin | Oscar Ogg Unknown 47 W.A. Dwiggins Unknown | Paul Simon Yolanda Cuomo 49 The Princes in the Tower Paul Delaroche | Swedish violin Unknown | Jan Tschichold Unknown 51 Wires Unknown | £100 Reward Unknown | Relax Ben Johnston | Time-lapse photo Byron Hetzler | Movie titles Unknown | Tinho Sehgal Ingo Maak 53 Superbitch bag Ted Noten & Daniël Nicolas | VW snow ad Unknown | VW egg ad Unknown | Drink Sangria Unknown | Thomas Edison Unknown 55 Nike ACG Daryl McDonald | Japanese snow Shimbi Shoin printery | Rotterdam mark Unknown | Francis Bacon Unknown | Powerboss ad Tom Roth 57 Various As indicated 59 Various As indicated 61 De Stijl Vilmos Huszár | Cubist Unknown | Soirée du Coeur Unknown | BDG Blätter Unknown | I ❤ NY Milton Glaser | Paul Rand Unknown | Pacific Wave April Greiman | Fuse 2 Neville Brody | P The Kazui Press Ltd. | Schweiz Herbert Matter | Scope Cancer Lester Beall | Kinder verkehrs garten Armin Hofmann | Harper's Unknown | Letterforms Various | Jeans Stefan Sagmeister | BVH RZ Design 63 Various As indicated 65 Various As indicated | Exxon mark Raymond Loewy | Brazilian bank mark Grupo Nacional | Time Warner mark Stefan Geissbuhler | Northwest Airlines mark Unknown | Aldus mark Aldus Manutius | K+E, American Gas, UfA Lucian Bernhard | Nike mark Carolyn Davidson | Esquire, International Typeface Corporation, The New York Times, Photo Lettering Incorporated Ed Benguiat | Quaker Unknown | City of Melbourne Landor Associates 67 Divan Japonais Toulouse-Lautrec | Fillmore Bill Graham | Parisian poster hanger Unknown | Policja Moma (Mruiek) Gorowski | Sagmeister Stefan Sagmeister | Bateaux sur l'eau Phillipe Apeloig | Jazz in Willisau Niklaus Troxler | Banal Alexey Brodovitch | Wagon-Bar A.M. Cassandre Monza Max Huber | Voll Traubensaft Josef Müller-Brockmann | Emil Weiss Karla Kubin | DH21 Teatro Alameda | Gutes Essen für alle Daniel Wiesmann 69 Punch R. Bryant | Leslie's Weekly Luckey Photograph | Nord Magazine A.M. Cassandre | Bauhaus Joost Schmidt | Broom El Lissizky | M.F. Agha Unknown | Liberty Bradbury Thompson | Esquire George Lois | Emigre Rudy VanderLans & Zuzana Licko | Ray Gun David Carson | Fortune Walter Buehr | Vanity Fair M.F. Agha | Harper's Bazaar Alexey Brodovitch | Life Margaret Bourke-White | Esquire Unknown | NY Times Janet Froelich | Wired Sean Freeman 71 ARPANet Unknown | Three websites Unknown | West Elm Unknown | Design Observer William Drenttel & Jessica Helfand | CNN Unknown | ION Quad Coupe Unknown | Advertising Age Unknown | Reflectur Unknown | RÉVO Unknown | Fast Company Unknown | Target Unknown | Web Trend Map Unknown | Adobe Unknown | Howies Unknown 73 Giovanni della Casa Unknown 75 Jerry Garcia Adrian Boot | All others Ashley Schofield 77 All Joe Roberts 79 Champ Fleury Geofroy Tory | Sumerian cuneiform Unknown scribe | Similarity/Contrast studies Rebeca Rico, Spencer Roth, Juri Miyamoto, Amy Norskog 81 Designers & Writers Michael Gericke | Inkasent Lech Majewski | Standardised column widths Unknown | Dialog mark Peter Smith | Neocid Karl Gerstner 83 Red book cover Stephanie Kaplan | Chair David Guarnieri & Rene Clement | Landschaft Ina Bauer & Sascha Lobe | Jazz in Willisau Niklaus Troxler | Bollé Jeff Miller | Belle & Clover Michael Graziolo | Tres Imperios del Islam Pepe Gimeno & Mauro Gimeno 85 Letterform negative spaces Emil Ruder | Supersuckers Jeff Kleinsmith | Mentoring Program Anne-Lene Proff | zrii Gareth Fry | Megaphone/Ear Unknown | Ornette Coleman Unknown 87 Extreme Intensity Shock Michael Bierut | Special One-Year ad Unknown | AT&T mark Saul Bass | Ken Hiebert Unknown 89 Beethoven LP covers Unknown 91 Raum braucht der Mensch KMS Team | Emil Weiss Emil Weiss | Ogi eyeglasses Scott Thares | Who am I Pazu Lee Ka Ling | Böker Fred Sanicola | Obsession Isaac Tobin & Lauren Nassef 93 Morton Unknown | House abstraction Chip Allen | Tromm marks Unknown 95 Extension drawing Jan V. White | SuprBox Mads Burcharth | Comparison book Unknown | Corpo humano Alessandra Kalko & Gabriel Silveira 97 Pressroom Magic Bradbury Thompson | Moon Rufen Wolfgang Weingart | Xtra Train Philippe Apeloig | Chicken/Eggs Unknown | Arqueografies catalog Pepe Gimeno & Baptiste Pons 99 Sven Lidman Unknown | Because it's there Phili | Coleman Exponent Anastasia Laksmi | Mozart Symphony 40 Carla Bouthillier 101 ZumZum Gabriela Castro, Paulo André Chagas & Gustavo Marchetti | Bauhaus Joost Schmidt | Chrysler rockets Unknown | Apple Snake Scott Lambert | More mark Thilo von Debschitz | Broadway Dental mark Ken De Lago | Die Waehr Florian Brugger, Lars Harmsen & Yumi Kimoto | Columbian Coffee ad Unknown | The Blind See More Miriam Hugo | Kandinsky Herbert Bayer | 1931 Ladislav Sutnar 103 IBM teeth Alexander Heill | Hotel Shangri-La Unknown | Divide Fidel Peña | Bullets Unknown | Clown Unknown 105 XJAGD Unknown | Flowers Unknown | Alabama Norman Lewis | Ripley Subterraneo Roberto de Vicq | Alpen Kuhe Emil Weiss | Radian Neubad Sven Lindhorst-Emme | Red collage Cecil Touchon | Blue roof Mitchell Johnson | After Party Wilders Danny J. Gibson | Midtown Manhattan x2 Emil Weiss | Locomotive Raymond Loewy 107 Four characters Unknown | Finger tip Tim Hawkinson | Nut-trition Unknown | Statue of Liberty Unknown | X Andrew Goldstein & Jeff Goldstein | Conformist Hell Wiley Miller | Sculpture Henry Moore 109 Scarf Lloyd Osborne & Shabnam Shiwan | Wallpaper Victoria and Albert Museum | Ocean State Job Lot Unknown | Nose Herb Lubalin | Football spread Gail Bichler & Ben Grandgenett | La Tour Eiffel Unknown | Palais de Chaillot Unknown 111 Valspar Unknown | Water Colours Unknown | Aston Martin Unknown | Storebrand Carl-Erik Conforto | Ivan Chermayeff Unknown 115 Peter Behrens Unknown 117 All Fons Hickmann 119 All Brian D. Miller 121 Berkshire Opera Shed Eliel and Eero Saarinen, Gottscho-Schleisner photo | Köln He Oiing hui | Samrat Yantra Isamu Noguchi photo | USSR Das Neue Russland György Kepes | Daisies Henri Matisse | Calligraphy Unknown | Resort hotel Unknown 123 Three castles Martin Hurlimann photographs | Four Rayonnant examples Unknown | Willem Dudok Unknown | Absolute Brooklyn Unknown | Brooklyn bridge Unknown 125 Sienna's Duomo Unknown | Snow shelter Unknown | Ford ad Unknown | Malaysia's City Centre Cesar Pelli | Friedrich von Schelling Unknown 127 David and Saul Rembrandt van Rijn, E Lessing Archiv fur Kunst & Geschichte/John Ross | Church of St George x3 Unknown | Petra x2 Unknown | Auto garage Pepe Gimeno & Ricardo Cañizares | Eight brand marks Paul Rand 129 Herbarum viva eicones Otto Brunfels and Hans Weiditz | Cure-x Klaus Trommer | Ballet-Tech Paula Scher | Beats Robert Brunner | Arabic typeface Borna Izadpanah 131 Lauterbrunnen valley Unknown | Reclining Figure (1935) Henry Moore | Rectilinear sculpture Michael R. McShane | Stazione Ferroviale Unknown | Pop-up book Ron van der Meer | Visuals/verbals Steven McCaffrey 133 Toyota ad Markham Cronin & Jeff von Hoene | Comme des Garçons ad Stephen J. Shanabrook & Veronika Georgieva | Samsung ad Unknown | Escalator Marco Fusz | Bulthaup Tay Guan Hin & Eric Yeo | Tabarin Paul Colin | Paper ad Leo Lionni | Zoo mark Unknown | Cat-Dog-Hand mark Unknown | Inner-City Infill Michael Bierut | Chairs shadows Yuji Tokuda 135 Trinità Masaccio | Barnes&Noble Siddiqi | MMMM mark Herb Lubalin | Pianists scale Karen I. Hirsch photo | Nike ad Unknown | Bull Unknown | Crying baby Justin Pike | SBB train poster Armin Hofmann 137 Globalisms Pentagram NY | Libro Illegibile N.Y. 1 Bruno Munari 139 Die-cut leaves Connelly Partners/ISMCP | PG&E Antony Milner | Gatefolds Jan V. White | Jan Tschichold 1930 Foto von Eduard Wasow | Jan Amos Comenius M. Svabinski & Jindra S. 141 Logone-Birni, Cameroon Marcel Griaule photo | Canton, China l'Ambassade de la Compagnie Orientale | Contigo/Veja Alessandra da Silva | Arthur Koestler book covers Unknown 143 Composition with Red, Yellow and Blue Piet Mondrian | Tower of Shadows Le Corbusier | Stretched parchment Unknown | Chuck Close Chuck Close 145 Knights Emil Weiss | Amnesty International Woody Pirtle & Daisuke Endo | Jazz in Willisau Niklaus Troxler 147 From Gospel to Gershwin Michael Bierut & Emily Hayes | Garden path Unknown | The Geometry of Art and Life Matila Ghyka 149 The New Face Roland Schenck & Brian Griffin | Jackson Pollock Alexey Brodovitch | The Many Lives Gail Bichler & Ben Grandgenett | 1979-1980 Unknown | New Type Oswaldo Miranda | Moose image Unknown | 10 Tips Unknown 151 Water & Peace Suzanne Morin | Civil War Battlefields Elaine Bradley | Interface Gui Bonsiepe | Addicted to Art Todd Albertson 153 Falling angel/Un trésor Unknown | Phaistos Disk Unknown | Crete Unknown | Kult und Form Walter Dexel 155 What Teaching Arem Duplessis & Kristina DiMatteo | Remain Calm Luke Hayman & Chris Dixon | Screw With Your Boyfriend's Head Len Cheeseman & Mikhail Gherman | Chain Unknown | Leo Tolstoy Unknown 157 Spanish main street Nazli Yucel & Krystian Kwiecinsky | Beatles diagram Michae Deal | Typewriter Kirsten Dietz | 1952 Unknown | Spanish convention centre Pepe Gimeno & Julio Alonso | LAX Robin Perkins & Clifford Selbert | Molkenbronn DDB The Way City | Green Pages Kenneth C. Wehrman | Gregory Bateson Unknown 159 Saul Bass Unknown 161 Max Shangle Hope Shangle 163 Tad Crawford Unknown 165 Frank Sinatra Unknown | Four Korean typefaces Unknown 167 Pelikan El Lissitzky | Emil Ruder Unknown | Superstition Neville Brody | Hot Spots Piet Zwart 169 Asics Unknown | Broom Fernand Léger | Cross Country Charles S. Anderson | Masters of Deception roberto de vicq de cumptich | (I'm Pretty Sure) Nick Schmitz | Organ Prelude in B flat J.S. Bach 171 Esperienza Filippo Cecchi | Elena Presser William Longhauser | Don't Work Unknown | Nike Unknown | Sweet Dreams/Hiding in Plain Sight Susan Casey 173 LightLightning Sonoko Furuya | Hustle Ben Johnston | Four abstract studies Sonoko Furuya, Ephraim Gregor, Maria Karantzalis, Ye Liu, StevenLongchallon | Four typographic examples Rick Valicenti 175 Tchaikovsky Kumari Gongaju | Piano Aviva Kapust | Tchaikovsky Ilyse Davis | IBM ViaVoice Unknown | Experimental studies Peter Castellano, Amy Putnicki, Chris Silva 177 Various examples As shown on the page | anax Unknown 179 Fuse Cities Neville Brody | Big Red Rock Joe Esquibel & Wendy Ohwiler | Renaissance numerals Unknown | A Typographic Quest Carl Dair 181 Paineez Unknown 183 Time & Territory Domenic Lippa & Beatrice Blumenthal | Long Live the Third Unknown | A+A+A+ Unknown | fi ligature Unknown | David Carson Unknown 185 Counting Crowes Jennifer Procopio | Konstruktivisten Jan Tschichold 187 Allen Hurlburt Unknown 189 Supplico stet cedula William Caxton | Melting ampersand Juan Carlos Pagan 191 Quote, sedan, unquote Unknown 193 Industrial Revolution Katie Belloff, Nancy Campbell & Trevett McCandliss | Are we losing our senses? Mark Geer | Tchaikovsky Anna Guillotte | die Sara Fazzino | D&T brand marks Einar Gylfason | Adidas ad Unknown 195 We filled it up Unknown | Think Before You Think Mark Geer | FSTR book cover Keenan | Go To Hell Herb Lubalin 197 Bigger thighs Melanie Forster & Simon Fairweather | Bleu Unknown | Red Bull Ring Unknown | Franklin Gothic Condensed iterations Hartford Art School students 199 Wurzeltod brand mark Unknown | It's Not Just Genetics Unknown | Rolling Stone Fred Woodward 201 AEZ3 Christine Leung, Zita Szátmary, Patrick Scott, Teo Thomas | FF John Leung | Théâtre de Quat'sous Mario Mercier | Mozart Uwe Loesch | Warum und wie Wolfgang Weingart 203 MedCareers Paul Crawford | For the Love of Letters Graham Clifford 205 Turkeys Have Been Bred Chirag Bhakta | How we are now Raymond Grimaila | Alan Fletcher Unknown 207 This week is business week Unknown | Get Picture Unknown | Underpinning Unknown | Man with hand Jean Cocteau 209 Fish, Rain, and Greyhounds Bradbury Thompson | McCall's/kick Otto Storch | MBT ad Unknown | Sold in Holiday Herb Lubalin | Bergdorf Goodman Reba Sochis | Vogue comb Malcolm Mansfield | Phoebus-Palast Jan Tschichold 211 Transit brings/translucent paper Metadesign London | Nike ad detail Unknown 213 Two maps Paula Scher | Art is... Paula Scher | Nike ad Unknown | Wear the pants Unknown | East Breaks Mark Geer | Borges & Orangutan Abadi, Ver!ssimo Luis F. Veríssimo 215 Accented characters chart Unknown 217 Dinner party/Discovery Roger Camp & Mike McCommon | Neil Young Fred Woodward 223 Five book covers Unknown 231 Four book covers Unknown | Alex W White Angela S Lovely EoGD3

Books from Allworth Press

About Design by Gordon Salchow, foreword by Michael Bierut, afterword by Katherine McCoy *6⅛x6⅛", 208 pages, paperback, $19.99*

Advertising Design and Typography by Alex W. White *8½x11", 224 pages, paperback, $29.99*

The Black Experience in Design: Identity, Expression, and Reflection edited by Anne H. Berry, Kareem Collie, Penina Acayo Laker, Lesley-Ann Noel, Jennifer Rittner, Kelly Walters *6x9", 312 pages, paperback, $19.99*

Brand Thinking and Other Noble Pursuits by Debbie Millman *6x9", 256 pages, paperback, $19.99*

Citizen Designer (Second Edition) by Steven Heller and Véronique Vienne *6x9", 312 pages, paperback, $22.99*

Designing for People by Henry Dreyfuss *6x9", 288 pages, paperback, $19.99*

Design School Reader by Steven Heller *6x9", 264 pages, paperback, $24.99*

Editing by Design (Fourth Edition) by Jan V. White and Alex W. White *8x10", 232 pages, paperback, $29.99*

The Elements of Logo Design by Alex W. White *8x10", 224 pages, hardcover, $34.99*

Graphic Design Rants and Raves by Steven Heller *7x9", 200 pages, paperback, $19.99*

How to Think Like a Great Graphic Designer by Debbie Millman *6x9", 248 pages, paperback, $24.95*

Line Color Form: The Language of Graphic Design by Jesse Day *7x8½", 144 pages, paperback, $19.95*

Listening to Type: Making Language Visible by Alex W. White *8x10", 272 pages, paperback, $29.99* `EoGD3`

The author

Alex W. White is an award-winning designer, design consultant, author,

and educator. He has been explaining the rightness of analytical thinking in visual communication for decades. He has lectured widely on typography and design to professionals in the Americas and Europe. Among his books are *Editing by Design 4th Edition*, *Listening to Type:

Making Language Visible*, and *Advertising Design and Typography*. White has been a professor of design management and graphic design at the graduate and undergraduate levels at the University of Bridgeport, Parsons School of Design, FIT, City College of New York, and the Hartford Art School. White served for a decade on the Board of Directors of the Type Directors Club in New York, retiring as Chairman. He lives in Carinthia, Austria. `EoGD3`

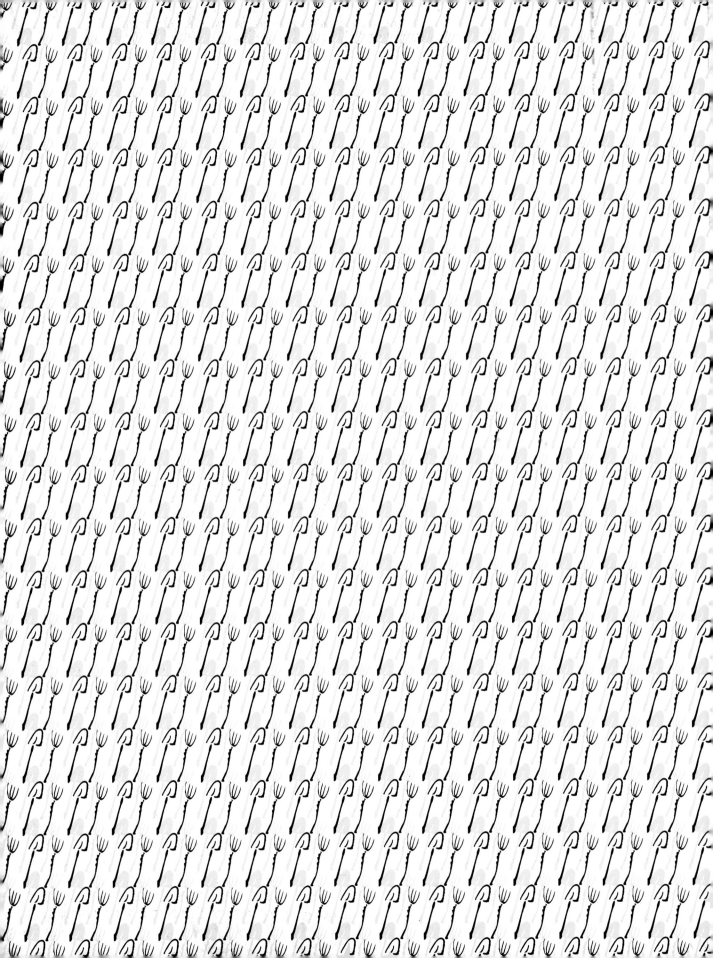